Vladimir Megré
The Ringing Cedars Series

English translation by John Woodsworth

- Book 1 **Anastasia**
  (ISBN: 978-0-9763333-0-2)

- Book 2 **The Ringing Cedars of Russia**
  (ISBN: 978-0-9763333-1-9)

- Book 3 **The Space of Love**
  (ISBN: 978-0-9763333-2-6)

- Book 4 **Co-creation**
  (ISBN: 978-0-9763333-3-3)

- Book 5 **Who Are We?**
  (ISBN: 978-0-9763333-4-0)

- Book 6 **The Book of Kin**
  (ISBN: 978-0-9763333-6-4)

- Book 7 **The Energy of Life**
  (ISBN: 978-0-9763333-7-1)

- Book 8, Part 1 **The New Civilisation**
  (ISBN: 978-0-9763333-8-8)

- Book 8, Part 2 **Rites of Love**
  (ISBN: 978-0-9763333-9-5)

Published by **Ringing Cedars Press**
www.RingingCedars.com

Anastasia herself has stated that this book consists of words and phrases in combinations *which have a beneficial effect on the reader.* This has been attested by the letters received to date from thousands of readers all over the world.

If you wish to gain as full an appreciation as possible of the ideas, thoughts and images set forth here, as well as experience the benefits that come with this appreciation, we recommend you find a quiet place for your reading where there is the least possible interference from artificial noises (motor traffic, radio, TV, household appliances etc.). *Natural sounds,* on the other hand — the singing of birds, for example, or the patter of rain, or the rustle of leaves on nearby trees — may be a welcome accompaniment to the reading process.

Ringing Cedars Press is an independent publisher dedicated to making **Vladimir Megré**'s books available in the beautiful English translation by **John Woodsworth**. Word of mouth is our best advertisement and we appreciate your help in spreading the word about the Ringing Cedars Series.

Order on-line	**www.RingingCedars.com**	ordering
call / fax toll-free	**1-888-DOLMENS**	details
or call / fax	**1-646-429-1986**	see last page

Generous discounts are available on volume orders. To help spread the word as an independent distributor, or to place the books in your bookstore, or to be kept up to date about future book releases and events, please email us at:

info@ringingcedars.com

or write to the Publisher, Ringing Cedars Press, 120 Hana Hwy #9-230, Paia, HI 96779, USA. We also welcome reviews, poetry and artwork inspired by the Series.

Vladimir Megré

THE RINGING CEDARS OF RUSSIA

The Ringing Cedars Series
Book 2

Translated from the Russian by
John Woodsworth

Edited by
Leonid Sharashkin

Ringing Cedars Press
Paia, Hawaii, USA

The Ringing Cedars of Russia by
Vladimir Megré

Translation, Translator's Preface and footnotes by
John Woodsworth

Editing, Editor's Afterword, footnotes, design and layout by
Leonid Sharashkin

Cover art by
Alexander Razboinikov

Library of Congress Control Number: 2005901794

ISBN: 978-0-9763333-1-9

Published by
Ringing Cedars Press

www.RingingCedars.com

Contents

Translator's Preface

Most readers of this present volume will have already marvelled at the euphoric and mind-boggling revelations contained in Megré's first book, *Anastasia* (published in English translation by Ringing Cedars Press in February 2005).

In addition to offering the reader fascinating glimpses into the story of the publication of the first book, this second volume, *The Ringing Cedars of Russia*, delves deeply into the ethical and metaphysical concepts behind Anastasia's sayings presented so dramatically in the 'series opener'. The chapter-titles associated with these concepts range from the mystical ("The Space of Love") to the mysterious ("Illusory people") to the theological ("Why nobody can see God") to the downright practical ("How to produce healing cedar oil"). They all ring a chord of response in the reader's heart and soul and at the same time call upon the thinker in each reader. And out of concepts such as these pop up at least as many questions as answers — questions that may well cause the reader either to re-examine or re-affirm his or her basic concepts of life.

My own involvement with *The Ringing Cedars of Russia* did not pass without a personal effect on me (independently of the actual translation process, in which I take special care to be guided by objective professional standards). In no small measure the opportunity to work closely with the book not only *reconfirmed* much of what I already believed, but also helped me *rediscover* my own faith, allowing me a fresh look at a number of concepts I had been brought up on from childhood (like moving around a three-dimensional object and seeing it from a different angle). It also caused me to *re-examine the reasons* for believing in what I had long believed (including the practical understanding and application of a spiritual approach to healing), and for this I am grateful.

Indeed, it is hard for me now to believe that at this time last year I had never even heard of a Siberian recluse named Anastasia, or a Russian writer named Vladimir Megré, or a Russian-American forester named Leonid Sharashkin, or the mysterious 'Ringing Cedars'. Yet these are names that, since entering my field of awareness in September 2004, have not only become a significant focus of my professional activity as a translator but also figured prominently in my daily thought, conversation and life experiences.

Within four months I had not only read the first three books of Megré's Ringing Cedars Series but also completed the translation of Book 1, *Anastasia*. And now, less than four months after that, the translation of Book 2 is ready to go to press and I have already started work on Book 3.

Translating the 'cherry-tree' chapter brought back a particular memory of my initial read of the three books. This had taken place back in September and October, when our Ottawa weather still allowed a pleasant outdoor afternoon sit on our front porch. With its south-west exposure and view of nothing but the fields and trees across the road, the porch made an ideal spot in which to absorb this brand new literary adventure into the delights of a summer glade in the far-off Siberian taiga. The afternoon sun was bright and warm enough to permit me to dispense not only with heavy outer clothing (which had already sprouted on the backs of many pedestrians on downtown sidewalks here) but also with my eyeglasses, which I am accustomed to make use of during any indoor reading.

During the same period I was especially struck by the following incident. On the porch, right in front of where I was sitting, stood a clay pot containing several red geraniums my wife had planted earlier in the year. My reading prompted me to look at them — and one flower in particular (the one closest to me) — through new eyes. I began to regard it with warmth and affection (I would even say *love*) every time I saw it.

Of course I had known from news reports about the effect of people's thoughts and attitudes on growing things, but it was not until my reading of Vladimir Megré that I had really seen anything like this in practice. My newfound feelings for the geraniums remained strong throughout the month of October, and as the days gradually grew colder, most of the flowers in our garden (as well as other geraniums on the same porch) faded and expired for the season. But the geraniums in this pot, especially the one closest to me, refused to fade or even droop with the cooling of the air. Even toward the end of October, when I finished my reading of Book 3, it was still standing proud and just as bright red as when my attention was first drawn to it. And even when I saw it months later, all bent to the ground by winter snows, its vivid red hue had scarcely faded.

Two other extraordinary coincidences occurred in our home during this period. In mid-November, just after I had finished translating the "Concert in the taiga" chapter in *Anastasia* and was working on the description of Anastasia's dance routine in the morning mist in the following chapter ("Who lights a new star?"), my wife Susan, who had not read any of the text at this point, presented me with a poem she had recently written. The poem was entitled *Gracefully, the dancer...* and described a dance of a young girl "where all movement conforms to poetry" and whose "life itself had become a never-ending dance" — rather close indeed to Megré's own expression.

Three months later, shortly before the first print-run of *Anastasia* rolled off the presses in February 2005, Susan, an amateur artist as well as a poet, showed me a coloured-pencil drawing she had just been working on of a nude figure in her twenties with blonde hair, her hands upstretched to the heavens, the parts of her body drawn with colours of Nature instead of the flesh, and with a face very similar to the illustration of Anastasia on the cover of the Russian edition. The remarkable thing is that at that point my wife had not read any of the text about Anastasia, nor even seen a portrait of her, and did not have her consciously in mind as she was doing the drawing.

In his Afterword, editor Leonid Sharashkin will be sharing with you similar 'coincidences' from his own experience connected with the publication of the English translation of *Anastasia* in America. These and the hearty welcome of the book in the English-speaking world are indeed reminiscent of the surprising reaction of thousands of readers to the book's initial appearance in Russia in 1996.

Hearing the impressions shared with me by the first readers of *Anastasia* in English — by people from quite different walks of life — I have come to appreciate just how far-reaching and universal Anastasia's message is in its scope. For one thing, it does not limit itself to any formulated creed. It is not a new religion with a new set of doctrines for which we must necessarily abandon whatever we believed in previously in order to follow. It speaks to the hearts and minds of people of many different religions as well as, equally, to those who profess no religion at all. It speaks to the hearts and minds of many scholars and students of the physical sciences — especially those who are reaching out to explore the more holistic dimensions of their fields and to find answers that lift them beyond the confines of their specialist training and into an understanding of how their investigations relate to the universal aspects of Man, Nature, the Cosmos and even God.

In addition to a deeper exploration of these universal concepts, Book 2 offers an in-depth, behind-the-scenes look at how Book 1 finally came to be written and published. Like all great mind-stirring works of history, the birth-throes attending its emergence into light came at a considerable price to the author. Just how high the price was — indeed, the whole chain of extraordinary circumstances that led from the wilds of Siberia to the book's appearance on Moscow street-corners and its eventual inclusion in national best-seller lists — is part of the fascinating adventure you will now share with the author as you journey from the mental heights of a taiga glade to the urban depths of Russia's capital city, passing indeed "through the valley of the shadow of death"[1] en route, along with a surprising encounter in a completely different tree-lined setting and a final stop in the foothills of the Caucasus mountains for yet another amazing discovery.

While the book's message is indeed universal in its scope and applicable to individuals the world over, there is no escaping the fact that its original expression, in terms of not only words but concepts, draws in significant measure upon the *Russian* tradition, and this fact, as with its predecessor in the series, presented its share of challenges to the English translator. Two of these deserve particular mention here.

First, the Russian word *sviatyni* (derived from *sviatoi* = *holy* or *sacred*) has no direct equivalent in English. It refers not only to holy places such as sanctuaries, tabernacles, shrines and crypts, but also to sacred objects (including icons, statues and relics), sacred texts (e.g., the Bible or the Koran) and even trees. Having the same root as the Russian word for 'light' (*svet*), *sviatyni* may also be used to designate sacred concepts such as *spirit* or *grace*. None of these alternatives by

---

[1]Psalm 23: 4 *(Authorised King James Version).*

itself would be sufficient to compass the range of the original Russian term. Since most of its occurrences relate to what we call 'locations', it was eventually decided to use the awkward but more or less accurate combination *sacred sites* as a general equivalent and employ alternative translations where the context required.

Another Russian word whose translation engendered considerable discussion was *pervoistoki* — derived from two basic roots: *perv-* (*first, primary, primal*) and *istok-* (*origin, source, spring* — as in describing the headwaters of a river, for example). The compound term, especially as used in this book, unmistakably conveys the sense of a *pure, uncontaminated* source, and this eventually led to the selection of the particular combination *pristine origins*. Other specific translation challenges are documented, where appropriate, in the footnotes.

Again, as in Book 1, the footnotes are also used to give background information on specific people, places and events unfamiliar to most English-speakers.

And now, dear readers, I need only invite you once again to find yourselves a comfortable reading-place — preferably one shielded from the possible intrusion of artificial sounds (a quiet outdoor setting would be ideal!) — and join with me in exploring the second instalment of the author's adventure through both the geographical space of Russia's vast distances and the mental space of the spiritual essence of the Universe, as revealed by *The Ringing Cedars of Russia*.

Ottawa, Canada
April 2005   John Woodsworth

CHAPTER ONE

Alien or Man?

Before telling about further happenings connected with Anastasia, I should like to thank all the leaders of religious denominations, scholars and journalists, along with ordinary readers, who sent in letters, religious literature and comments regarding the events recounted in my first book. Anastasia has been called many things. The press has referred to her as Mistress of the taiga,[1] a Siberian wizard-girl, a fortune-teller, a divine manifestation, the girl from outer space. And so when one Moscow journalist asked me: "Do you now love Anastasia?", I replied to her: "I can't really tell what my feelings are." And all at once the rumour started flying around that I was incapable of grasping anything at all because of my immaturity in spiritual matters.

But how *can* one love when it's not yet clear just who is there to be loved? After all, no one has yet been able to come up with a single definitive description of Anastasia. On the basis of her assertion: "I am Man, a human being — I am a woman!"[2] I've been trying to come up with some sort of explanation for her extraordinary abilities. Initially everything seemed to be falling into place.

---

[1] *taiga* — the Russian name given to the boreal forest that stretches across much of Siberia and northern Canada.

[2] The word *Man* (with a capital *M*) is used throughout the Ringing Cedars Series to refer to a human being of any gender. For details on the word's usage and the important distinction between *Man* and *human being* please see the Translator's Preface to Book 1.

Who is Anastasia?

A young woman, born and living as a recluse in the remote Siberian taiga, brought up after the death of her parents by her grandfather and great-grandfather, who have also been living the life of a recluse.

Can one consider the loyalty of wild animals to her something unusual?

Even this is nothing out of the ordinary. Many animals in peasant farmyards get along peacefully with each other and treat their human masters with respect.

A much more difficult task is determining the mechanism whereby she is able to see things at a distance and can know details of various events, even those that occurred thousands of years ago, and to be completely conversant with our contemporary way of life. How does this ray of hers work when it heals people far away, when it penetrates the depths of the past or peers into the future?

Philosophy professor Kim Ivanovich Shilin,[3] who is also a Corresponding Member of the International Academy of Informatisation (MAI), has written a number of articles analysing Anastasia's sayings. In one of them he wrote:

> Anastasia's creative potential is a gift of God, a gift of Nature, which is universal, not merely a personal gift to her. All of us collectively, and each one of us in particular, are connected with the Cosmos.

---

[3]*Kim Ivanovich Shilin* — Doctor of Social Sciences, senior researcher at Moscow State University's Institute for Asian and African Studies, known for his interdisciplinary research in philosophy, ecology, sociology, cultural and Asian studies, aimed at a synthesis of Eastern and Western cultural principles. He has authored numerous articles and several books on *ecosophy* (the interpretation of cultural and social phenomena on the basis of a culture's relationship to and perception of Nature).

The means of escaping an approaching catastrophe lie in a harmonious synthesis of our cultural principles. The development of this type of harmoniously pure childhood culture results in a "feminine" cultural type. This cultural type has been expressed most fully and clearly in Buddhism, but also in our Anastasia. It may be formulated in the following identification chain:

Anastasia = Tara = Buddha = Maitreya.[4]

Anastasia is in the fullest sense Man in the likeness of God.

Whether this is true or not is not for me to decide. Only I can't understand why, then, she hasn't written down any teachings, like all other enlightened people in the likeness of God, and instead has concentrated, all during her two decades of conscious awareness, on *dachniks.*[5]

Nevertheless, in reading what various scholars have to say, I have been able to conclude that she is not some kind of crazy person, inasmuch as there are at least *hypotheses* in the scientific world about what she has talked about, and experiments are being conducted on certain aspects of her sayings.

So, for example, to the question: "Anastasia, by what means do you discern and depict all the different situations of thousands of years ago and even decipher the thoughts of the great thinkers of the past?" she replied:

---

[4]*Tara* — a female Buddha, a deity capable of removing interferences and putting things in perfect order. *Maitreya* (literally, 'the loving one') is described as the future Buddha, associated with friendliness, success and prosperity.

[5]*dachniks* — people who spend time (their days off, especially summer holidays) at their *dacha,* or cottage in the country. Unlike most cottages in the West, a dacha is invariably accompanied by a garden where fruits and vegetables are grown to feed the family all year long (for further details, please see the Translator's Preface to Book 1 in the Ringing Cedars Series).

"The first thought, the first word was the Creator's. His thoughts still live today, surrounding us unseen and filling universal space, reflected in material, living creations produced for the number one creation, Man! Man is the child of the Creator. And, like any parent, He could wish for His child no less than what He has Himself. He has given him all. And even more — freedom of choice! Man can create things and perfect the world by the power of his thinking. No thought produced by Man disappears into oblivion. If it is a thought of radiant brightness, it will fill the space of light and rise on the side of the forces of light. A dark thought, however, will fall on the opposite side. And today any Man may make use of any thought produced at any time either by people or by the Creator."

"Then why doesn't everybody use them?"

"Everybody does, but in varying degrees. To use them, one is obliged to think, and not everybody succeeds in doing this because of the vanity of daily life."

"So, all you have to do is think, and the ability comes to you? And you can even discern the thoughts of the Creator?"

"In order to discern the thoughts of the Creator, one must attain a purity of thought appropriate to Him, as well as the pace of His thinking. To discern the thoughts of enlightened people, one must possess their purity of thought and the ability to think at the same rate. If a given Man has insufficient purity of thought to communicate with the dimension of the forces of light — the dimension in which radiant thoughts dwell, — then Man will draw his thoughts from their dark counterparts, and will end up suffering himself and causing others to suffer."

I'm not sure whether this is directly or only indirectly explained by Academician Anatoly Akimov,[6] Director of the International Institute of Theoretical and Applied Physics at the Russian Academy of Natural Sciences, in his article in the magazine *Chudesa i prikliuchenia (Wonders and Adventures)* entitled "Physics recognises a Supermind". He writes as follows:

> There have existed, and there exist now, two schools of thought, two models of perceiving Nature. One model is associated with Western scholarship — i.e., knowledge gained on the methodological basis prevalent in the West: evidence, experiments, etc. The other is the Eastern approach, wherein knowledge is received from an external source through esoteric means in a state of meditation. Esoteric knowledge is not something acquired, it is considered a gift to Man.
>
> As it turns out, at some point this esoteric approach was lost and a different route was embarked upon — one extremely slow and complex. Following this route, it has taken us over a thousand years to arrive at a level of knowledge which was common in the East three millennia ago.

---

[6] *Anatoly Evgenevich Akimov* — first introduced in Book 1, Chapter 7: "Anastasia's ray". Though it is not commonly known, the USSR maintained an extensive research programme on psychic phenomena (for details please see the well-researched book *Psychic discoveries behind the Iron Curtain* by Sheila Ostrander and Lynn Schroeder). Anatoly Akimov headed one of the many groups of scientists charged by the KGB and the Soviet Defence Ministry to find a scientific explanation for paranormal phenomena and some people's extraordinary abilities in clairvoyance, telepathy and telekinesis (moving solid objects by mental power alone) with a view to their applications to intelligence and military purposes. Akimov's and other teams' experimental observations of these phenomena — in particular the direct control of human mind over physical objects — indicated that on a deeper level *consciousness* and *matter* have essentially the same nature, and led to the study of torsion fields. Many "traditional" scientists, jealous of the generous funding his group was receiving, were quick to label Akimov as a 'pseudo-scientist' and 'charlatan', and charge him with "fraud and falsification of scientific research", even though they themselves still cannot explain such phenomena, let alone answer even more basic questions such as *What is matter?* and *What is energy?*

I have the intuitive feeling that those are right who say that the matter filling the whole Universe on a field level[7] is some kind of interrelated structure. In his book *The sum of technologies,* in a chapter entitled "The Universe as super-computer", Stanislav Lem[8] proposed the existence of a gigantic computer-like Universal brain. Imagine a computer the size of the observable Universe (with a radius somewhere in the order of 15 billion kilometres), filled with elements taking up a volume of between 10 and 33 cubic centimetres each.

And here this brain which fills the whole Universe is naturally endowed with powers which we are incapable of imagining or even fantasising. But if you take into account that in reality this brain functions not according to any computer principle but on the basis of torsion fields,[9] then it all becomes clear: the manifestations of the Absolute

[7] *field level* (Russian: *polevoy uroven*) — the level of a number of 'fields' (such as electromagnetic and gravitational fields) filling the Universe but not directly observable by the material senses.

[8] *Stanislav Lem* — Russian science-fiction writer best known for his novel *Solaris,* first made into a film by Soviet director Andrei Tarkovsky in 1972 and thirty years later in a Hollywood version by Steven Soderbergh. Incidentally, Lem's *Solaris* appears to be the inspiration behind the plot of Gene Roddenberry's first *Star Trek* feature-length film (1979).

[9] *torsion fields* — the term first introduced in 1913 by a prominent French mathematician, Élie Cartan (1869–1951), to refer to a hypothetical field generated by a rotating object. This term later became used to signify the 'original' field permeating the whole Universe, a spinning field considered to have formed the physical vacuum and given birth to all matter. If matter can be thought of as 'frozen energy', then energy can be equated to 'frozen torsion fields'. While modern physics still lacks the appropriate technology to detect torsion fields, the notion that everything in the Universe is born from a spinning void is one of the oldest concepts in virtually all traditional cultures (note its ages-old symbolic manifestation in the rotating cross (or swastika) — a symbol found in all cultures on all continents).

proposed by Schelling[10] or the Shuniat[11] of ancient Vedic literature — these in essence constitute a computer. And there is nothing in the world apart from this computer. Everything else is some form or other of the Absolute.

This is what Academician Vlail Kaznacheev,[12] Active Member of the Russian Academy of Medical Sciences, wrote about the Ray in his article "Living rays and a living field"[13] in *Chudesa i prikliuchenia (Wonders and adventures)* of 3 May 1996:

[10]Friedrich Wilhelm von Schelling (1775–1854) — German philosopher, who developed a dialectic of Nature as a living organism and an unconscious, spiritual, creative principle.

[11]*Shuniat* — the Buddhist concept of the 'void', or the space in which all exists.

[12]*Vlail Petrovich Kaznacheev* (1924–) — a prominent member of the Russian Academy of Medical Sciences from Novosibirsk, specialising in the inter-relationship between Man and Nature, including bio-systems and information processes. A decorated World War II veteran, Dr Kaznacheev has received numerous awards for his research and publications.

[13]In America pioneer research on the fields surrounding living organisms was carried out by Dr Harold Saxton Burr (1889–1973), Professor of Anatomy at the Yale University School of Medicine. Dr Burr discovered "that man — and, in fact, all forms — are ordered and controlled by electrodynamic fields which can be measured and mapped with precision... the 'fields of life' are of the same nature as the simpler fields known to modern physics and obedient to the same laws. Like the fields of physics, they are part of the organisation of the Universe and are influenced by the vast forces of space. Like the fields of physics, too, they have organising and directing qualities which have been revealed by many thousands of experiments. Organisation and direction, the direct opposite of chance, imply purpose. So the fields of life offer purely electronic, instrumental evidence that man is no accident. On the contrary, he is an integral part of the Cosmos, embedded in its all-powerful fields, subject to its inflexible laws and a participant in the destiny and purpose of the Universe" — quoted from E.F. Schumacher's *A guide for the perplexed* (New York: Harper & Row, 1977), pp. 116–17, and used by permission of the Random House Group Ltd. For more information see Burr's *Blueprint for immortality: The electric patterns of life* (London: N. Spearman, 1972).

Vernadsky[14] was probably right in asking the question: how does the ideal, which is mental, translate the planet Earth into its new evolutionary phase? How? If you say: only through labour, only through explosions or only through technogenic activity, such a primitive answer will not do.

There is factual evidence showing that Man is capable of exerting a remote influence on many electronic equipment readings. He can throw the measuring device out of whack, and that from far away. Here in Novosibirsk experiments are taking place on telepathic communication with Norilsk, Dikson, Simferopol and Tiumen,[15] as well as an American centre in Florida, and the remote links between Man and Man as well as between the measuring device and the operator register accurately and reliably.

We are confronted with an unknown phenomenon — the interaction of living substance over huge distances.

These articles, unfortunately, contain many unfamiliar terms, along with references to works of other scholars. It would be quite a task just to read them all, let alone make sense of them.

---

[14] *Vladimir Ivanovich Vernadsky* (1863–1945) — a Russian scientist compared to Charles Darwin for his scope of contribution to the biological sciences. Vernadsky's prime interest was researching how the human mind influences the development of life on the planet. He viewed human intelligence as a powerful evolutionary force capable of transforming the whole biosphere onto a new level. Vernadsky introduced the term *noosphere* (literally, 'sphere of Intelligence') to refer to the incipient state of biosphere controlled by human intelligence — the new evolutionary stage transcending the conflict between technology and Nature.

[15] *Norilsk* — one of the most northerly cities in the world, close to the Yenisei River, and a major mining centre. *Dikson* — a port in Russia's Far North, on the Kara Sea. *Simferopol* — capital of the Crimea (now part of Ukraine). *Tiumen* — the oldest Russian city in Siberia, founded in 1581, which long served as a centre for the Russian colonisation of Siberia.

Still, I have found out that scientists are aware of Man's capability to make contact at a distance. They are aware, too, of the universal data bank used by Anastasia. She calls it *the dimension of the forces of light*, home to all thoughts ever produced by mankind. Modern science also speaks about this phenomenon, which it refers to as a *supercomputer.*

I then had to figure out how I, who had never practised any literary art, having never been trained for it, managed to write a book which continues to excite so many people.

When I was in the taiga, Anastasia told me: "I shall make you a writer. You will write a book, and many people will read it. It will have a beneficial influence on the readers."

Now the book has been written. And one might suppose that it was all due to her involvement. But then one would have to figure out how she influences other people's creative abilities. However, nobody has yet managed to figure this out.

It might make things easier, of course, to pretend that I myself possessed at least a little talent and was simply setting forth the interesting information I had learnt from her. Then, it seems, everything would fall into place. Everything would be explained. There would be no need to waste any further time on reading scientific or religious literature or badgering specialists with questions. And here Anastasia presented a new phenomenon for which neither I nor any of the people who have been helping me can find an explanation to date.

You may remember me writing in Book 1 what she said two years earlier: "Artists will paint pictures, poets will write verse and they will make a movie about me. You will see all this and think of me...."

To my question "What do you mean, can she predict the future?" Anastasia's grandfather replied: "Vladimir, Anastasia does not predict the future, she visualises it and turns it into reality."

Words, just words. Words come cheap. And to be honest, I didn't pay too much attention to these words, dismissing them as mere metaphor, since I had absolutely no way of even imagining how accurately everything Anastasia said would turn out to be true in real life. But the incredible does happen!

Anastasia's words are starting to come true in reality.

First there was the flood of poems. A few of these poems I published at the end of Book 1. Next, Anastasia clubs started springing up in various cities. The first of these was in the city of Gelendzhik, where they held an exhibit of paintings by the Moscow artist Alexandra Saenko, all dedicated to Anastasia and Nature.

I visited the clubhouse and looked at the walls hung with large pictures. The surrounding space seemed to change in appearance before my gaze.

From the many pictures Anastasia looked out at me with her kindly eyes. And the scenes! I couldn't get over it — some of the pictures showed scenes from this second book, which hadn't been published yet. And there was this glowing sphere, sometimes appearing right next to Anastasia. Later I learnt that the artist painted not with a brush but with her fingertips. Most of the pictures had already been sold, but left hanging for the duration of the exhibit, since more and more people were coming to see them. The artist presented one of them to me as a gift, depicting Anastasia's mother and father. I couldn't take my eyes off her mother's face.

Offers started coming in from various film studios about making an Anastasia movie. And this was now something I was already accepting as a matter of course.

As I touched the paintings and sheets of poetry with my hands, as I listened to the songs and looked at stills from a film which had already been made, I tried to make some sense of what was going on.

And now there is a Moscow Research Centre devoted to investigating Anastasia phenomena, which has concluded:

The greatest spiritual teachers known to mankind for their religious teachings and philosophical and scientific investigations, cannot match the fantastic pace of Anastasia's influence on the human potential. Their teachings have had a noticeable manifestation in real life only centuries and millennia after their first appearance.

In some inexplicable way, over a matter of days and months Anastasia has managed, without the aid of written doctrines and religious teachings, to directly influence people's feelings, provoking emotional outbursts and causing a surge of creativity manifest in artistic creations on the part of a whole lot of people who have been mentally touched by her. We are able to perceive them in the form of works of art and inspired impulses toward goodness and light.

How is it possible that this lonely recluse, all alone in the remote Siberian taiga, has at the same time managed to soar over our lives in real time and space?

How does she bring artistic creations into being through other people's hands? They are all about light, about goodness, about Russia, about Nature, about love.

"She will cover the world with her great poetry of love. Poems and songs will shower the whole planet like a spring rain and wash away its accumulated filth," Anastasia's grandfather told me.

"But how does she do it?" I asked.

And the answer:

"She gives off inspiration and illumination by the energy of the impulse of her own aspirations, by the strength of her dreams."

"What kind of power is hidden in her dreams?"

"The power of Man as a Creator."

"But Man should receive some sort of compensation for his creations — honours, money, titles. And here she is giving them away and asking nothing in return. Why?" I asked.

"She is self-sufficient. Her highest rewards are her own satisfaction and the sincere love of at least one person," replied Anastasia's grandfather.

But so far these answers are not something I've been able to make complete sense of. In attempting to grasp who Anastasia really is and my own relationship to her in particular, I have continued to seek out various opinions about her, and read as much as I can in the way of religious literature.

In fact, I've read more over the past year and a half than in all the previous years of my life taken together. But what has come of it? I have managed to come to only one indisputable conclusion: a number of 'learned' books claiming to be historically accurate, religious and sincere, are nothing but a pack of lies. This conclusion arose out of a situation connected with the historical figure of Gregory Rasputin.

In Book 1 I cited a passage from Valentin Pikul's[16] historical epic novel *U poslednei cherty* (At the last frontier).

---

[16] *Valentin Savvich Pikul* (1928–1990) — one of the most popular Soviet prose writers of the 1970s and 1980s. His famous novel, *At the last frontier* — published in 1979 in the major literary magazine *Nash sovremennik* as an abridged version of the novel *Nechistaya sila* (The demonic forces) — significantly strengthened the popular image of Rasputin as a corrupted immoral debaucher. Pikul's extensive use of documents of the period, including journalistic accounts, to give his works an authentic 'historical' feel, contributed to the popular perception of his novels as 'historical chronicles' (although this is not generally supported by historians and literary critics, who tend to dismiss them simply as adventure novels with an historical context). In 1981 *At the last frontier* was made into the 'historical drama' movie *Agonia* (Agony), directed by Elem Klimov (1933–2003), which won the prestigious International Federation of Film Critics award at the 1982 Venice Film Festival and became a must-see cinematic experience throughout the USSR. The passage below is quoted from Pikul's *At the last frontier.*

Pikul's narrative tells about a semi-literate peasant named Gregory Rasputin from the remote wilds of Siberia where the Siberian cedar grows. In 1907 he came to St. Petersburg, then the capital of the Russian empire. He not only endeared himself to the imperial family, impressing them with his predictions of the future, but ended up sleeping with a good many of the most prominent women in the capital. When a group of officers tried to kill him, they were amazed to find that even after swallowing the cyanide poison slipped into his drink, he was still able to get up from the table and make his way outdoors, where Prince Yusupov fired shots at him point-blank from his pistol. Even after being riddled with bullets, Rasputin would not die. His wounded body was thrown off a bridge into the river, then fished out and burnt.

The mysterious and enigmatic Gregory Rasputin, who impressed everyone with his stamina, grew up amidst the cedars of the Siberian taiga.

This is how a contemporary journalist described his staying power:

"At age fifty he could begin an orgy at noon and go on carousing until four o'clock in the morning. From his fornication and drunkenness he would go directly to the church for morning prayers and stand praying until eight, before heading home for a cup of tea. Then, as if nothing had happened, he would carry on receiving visitors until two in the afternoon. Next he would collect a group of ladies and accompany them to the baths. From the baths he would be off to a restaurant in the country, where he would begin repeating the previous night's activities. No normal person could ever keep up a régime like that."

As with many other people, such descriptions also shaped my impression of Rasputin as a hopeless debaucher. But fate threw my way a different concept, as though trying to induce me to reconsider.

This is what the Pope of Rome, John Paul II, had to say about Rasputin:

"Today from the river comes unscathed the body (never found) of a holy monk. And his secret offspring will enter into the ark with prayer."

What's going on here? On the one hand he's referred to as a debaucher, on the other — a holy monk. Where is the truth? Where is the lie?

There's more. The text of some of Rasputin's notes, written during a trip to the Holy Land, happened to fall into my hands (they were brought to Paris by a refugee from the USSR named Lobachevsky). This is what Rasputin himself wrote:

The sea effortlessly comforts. When you awake in the morning and the waves 'speak' — they dance and make glad. And the sunlight glistens on the sea, it seems to rise ever so quietly, and at that moment Man's soul forgets all about mankind and fixes its gaze on the glow of the sun; and a happiness kindles in Man, and he feels in his heart the book of life and the higher wisdom of life — indescribable beauty! The sea awakens him from the dream of earthly vanities, and many thoughts arise all by themselves, quite effortlessly.

The sea is a vast space, but the mind is even more spacious. There is no end to Man's higher wisdom, no philosophy can possibly contain it. Another moment of stupendous beauty comes when the sun sets over the sea and its rays fill the western sky.

Who can estimate the beauty of the sun's twilight rays? They warm and caress the soul and offer healing comfort. The sun disappears behind the mountains minute by minute, and Man's heart grieves a little at its amazing twilight rays. And then it grows dark.

And oh, what silence falls! Not even the sound of a bird is heard. Lost in thought, Man begins to pace the deck of the ship, involuntarily recalls his childhood and all of life's kerfuffle, and begins to compare the silence around him with the bustle of the world, and quietly talks with himself, desiring company to stave off the tedium inflicted upon him by his enemies...

So, who were you, you *Sibiriak?*[17] A Russian named Gregory Rasputin? Where is the truth written about you, and where the lie? How to make sense of it all? What can one rely upon in trying to fathom the essence of one's being, one's destiny? What great works can help one discern between truth and falsehood? Where is the spiritual and sincere, as opposed to a mere pretence of omniscience? Perhaps one should try probing one's own heart? I have never written poetry before, but I want to dedicate my very first poem to you, Gregory Rasputin.

People read *Anastasia* and come up with sincere, original poetry. I have tried, too. And this is the result — for you. My apologies if the rhyme doesn't always work out.

Dedicated to
Gregory Rasputin

"So you're semi-literate?" "Why yes, semi-literate.
From the cedar forests — well, those are my roots!"
"And barefoot?!" "Walking all the way from Siberia,
You're bound to wear out more than one pair of boots!

"I am going to the Tsar, to help our dear Batiushka[18]
Hold on just a little bit longer out there.

---

[17] *Sibiriak* — the Russian word denoting a resident of Siberia.

[18] *Batiushka* (pronounced *BAH-tioosh-ka,* lit., 'Father') — an affectionate name used (especially by Russian peasants) in reference to the Tsar.

I am going to our Russia, our dear Russia-Matushka[19]
To give her a taste of our pine-forest air!

"What about it, hussars? You dashing rogues, freely
Debauching the ladies, making bold in a brawl?
Just look at *me*, look, and see how one really
Debauches — you scum, thinking you know it all!"

Peter's city in fine Paris garb is assembling.
But watch, lest your corsets too tight squeeze your hearts!
The Sibiriak enters, and ladies are trembling
At the sight of this peasant from far eastern parts.

But as he went off to the morning-prayer service,
For others' redemption from error to pray,
He heard his land calling — She spoke in a whisper,
The only one telling him this: "Go away!

"The flesh-eating age of the beast is upon us,
All drunken and growling, it leads men astray.
While your fiery soul has been keeping it from us,
It can no longer do so. You must go away.

"You can't hold the savagery back for much longer.
Just a moment, that's all you will last — it's too strong.
I am Russia! You cannot imagine my sorrow!
I know now: you never will finish your song.

"Go back to your cedars. My rebounding is certain!
And then you may ask whatsoever you will..."

---

[19]*Russia-Matushka* (pronounced in Russian: *Ras-SI-ya MA-toosh-ka*) — an
endearing term signifying 'Mother Russia'.

"Oh how I'd love us to go to the *banya!*[20]
I'd beat you with besoms of birch, even pine,
My profligate Russia — for you I am longing!
I shall stay with you, Russia, for ever — you're mine!"

The age of dark madness with fury came howling:
Grishka[21] stumbled, his breast full of bullets that day.
While the blackness stood mocking, its dark visage scowling,
Saying "Crawl, you Sibiriak! Go on, crawl away!

"You can hold me back only a half-second longer,
And then from the depths of my pit you'll be shown
A punishment frightful, more painful and stronger
Than ever the world in its history has known!

"A hero you are, but you'll be called a blasphemer.
From bottles of poison[22] your image will peek.
And the scions you save will curse you as a schemer
And spit on your soul, you Siberian *muzhik.*[23]

"Crawl away. It is I who now have all the power!
Fly away, if you like, to your heaven on high!
But a moment is left, see? Not a day, not an hour.
So give me my moment! You're still going to die."

---

[20]*banya* — Russian baths or a bath-house, similar to a Finnish sauna, where boiling water is poured over hot stones to increase the temperature and bathers beat each other with birch besoms (brooms made of twigs tied around a stick) to stimulate blood circulation. Braver participants sometimes prefer besoms made of sharp-needled conifers (e.g., pine) instead of birch.

[21]*Grishka* — a diminutive form of the Russian name *Grigory* (Gregory).

[22]*bottles of poison* — referring to the *Rasputin* brand of vodka, popular all over Russia, with a picture of Rasputin's face on the label.

[23]*muzhik* (pronounced *moo-ZHIK*) — a Russian word for a peasant, especially one who lacks the refinement of an urban dweller.

"Bring on the Madeira, let's head for the *banya!*
And there I shall show you what's real and what's crass.
A Sibiriak, you say? I'm a down-to-earth peasant!
So what's all the babble and gab about, ass?"

His body was shot through and drowned in the river,
Then burnt in a courtyard midst rubble and sand.
Today as spring winds blow their way over Russia,
They carry his ashes across the whole land.

"Well, *muzhik,*" said the blackness, still standing there mocking,
"Where on earth is your tombstone, and where are your eyes?
You can never bring back now the days of your living,
And your scions will see but an image despised.

"Show them the debt they owe! I give you power!
Show them the bills for your service unpaid,
Or is it your wish just to weep and to cower?"

Grishka spit a lead bullet: "You, Satan, are foolish!
As if I could care about either weeping or loans?
Come now, my *muzhiks* — how's the banya, dear fellows?
Time for more boiling water to be poured on the stones?!"

    Gregory Rasputin from the cedar forests of Siberia stepped
into the life of pre-revolutionary Russia in an attempt to head
off the storm of revolution, and perished.
    Anastasia also lives amongst the cedars and is also trying to
do good for people, also trying to head off something before
it happens. But what fate has our society prepared for her?

CHAPTER TWO

A money-making machine

During my first days of talking with Anastasia I saw her as a recluse with her own unique way of looking at the world. Now, after all that I have heard and read about her, after all her subsequent penetrations into our lives, she has become a kind of an anomaly. My head has started to swirl in confusion. It is with great effort that I am trying to let go of the incoming tide of information and conclusions and get back to the simplicity of my first impressions. And to answer the oft-repeated question: "Why didn't you bring Anastasia out of the taiga?"

I wanted very much to bring Anastasia out of the taiga. But I realised it couldn't be done by force. I needed to try and show her how useful and appropriate her stay in our society would be. I reflected on which of her abilities could be used by people — and my business in particular — with benefit accruing to her as well. And suddenly I realised something: this Anastasia standing before me would be a real *money-making machine!*

For one thing she is easily capable of healing people from any disease. And she does this without making any kind of diagnosis, but simply chasing out of the body any pains and sores that have invaded it. And she doesn't even have to touch the body. I experienced this for myself. She becomes utterly concentrated, looking out with her kind, unblinking bluish-grey eyes. And the body seems to warm up from her look, and even one's feet begin to perspire. All sorts of toxins escape through the perspiration.

People pay big money for medicines and operations. If one doctor can't help, they go to another, or go to psychics, or bio-energy therapists, just to get cured of a single disease, some-times spending weeks or months or even years in their search for a cure, while Anastasia's method takes but a few minutes. I calculated that if she spends even fifteen minutes on one patient and charges just two hundred fifty thousand roubles for that (although many healers charge a good deal more), that would make one million roubles an hour. But that's by no means the limit. Operations, for example, can cost up to thirty million roubles.[1]

It seemed as though a sound business plan was taking shape in my head. I decided to work out some details and asked Anastasia:

"So, that means you can rid a person's body of any and all ills?"

"Yes," replied Anastasia. "I think I could eliminate any and all."

"How much time do you need to spend on a single patient?"

"Sometimes quite a lot."

"A lot — that's how long?"

"Once it took me more than ten minutes."

"Ten minutes — that's nothing. Some people take years to get better."

"Ten minutes is a long time, considering the fact that I have to concentrate, as it were, and decrease my sense of conscious awareness."

"That's not a problem, conscious awareness can wait. You know so much as it is. I've thought of something, Anastasia."

---

[1] *two hundred fifty thousand, one million, thirty million roubles* — equivalent to approx. US$50, 200 and 6,000 respectively at the June 1995 exchange rate. With an average Russian's monthly income of under $100 at the time, those figures were truly astronomical.

"What have you thought of?"

"I'll take you with me. In a big city we'll hire a decent office for you, I'll advertise and you can treat people. You'll be of a great help to all sorts of people, and we'll have a right good income."

"But I sometimes treat people right now as it is. When I visualise various situations with the dachniks, to help them understand the world of plants around them, my Ray also eliminates their diseases, only I try not to eliminate *all* diseases..."

"But they don't even know that *you're* the one that's doing it, they don't pay you any money for it, or even say 'thank you'! You don't get anything for your labours?!"

"I do."

"What?"

"I feel happy."

"Well, that's fine then. You can be happy, and delighted, and the business will have an income as well."

"But what if somebody does not have any money to pay for treatment?" she enquired.

"Now why are you jumping into trifling matters like that? You don't have to think about that. You'll have secretaries, and an administrator. All you need think about is treating people, perfecting yourself and attending seminars to share your experience and exchange ideas with other healers. Do you know yourself how your method works, your Ray, and what the underlying principle is?"

"Yes, I know. And this method is known in your world too. Doctors and career scientists know about it. Or at least they feel its beneficial effect. In hospitals they try to talk with their patients cheerfully, so as to uplift their spirits. Doctors have long noticed that if someone is in a state of depression, it is difficult to cure their disease, and medicines do not help, while if you treat a patient with love, the disease will go away more quickly."

"So why has nobody tried learning this method and developing it to the degree you have?"

"Many scientists are trying to learn it. And many people you call folk healers also use this method, and they are having some success. This is the same method Christ Jesus healed by, as well as the saints. Much is said about love in the Bible, because this feeling has a beneficial influence on Man. It is the strongest feeling of all."

"Why do healers and doctors have so little success, and you have so much?"

"Because they live in your world, and they, just like everyone else in that world, have taken in harmful feelings."

"What kind of harmful feelings, and what do *they* have to do with it?"

"Harmful feelings, Vladimir, are anger, hatred, irritation, jealousy, envy... and others. They and other similar feelings make Man weaker."

"You mean to say, Anastasia, that you hardly ever get angry?"

"I never get angry."

"All right, Anastasia. It's not important how this effect comes about, it's the final result that's important, and what benefit can be derived from it. Tell me, would you agree to go with me and get involved in treating people?"

"Vladimir, you see, my home is here — this is my motherland, the place where I belong. It is only by staying here that I can fulfil my purpose. Nothing gives Man greater strength than his motherland, the Space of Love created by his parents. Treating people, delivering them from physical ailments — I can do that right here from a distance, with the help of my Ray."

"Well, all right. If you don't want to travel, you can do your treating from a distance. You and I can set up an arrangement as to where those wishing treatment can come. They will pay their money, and you will heal them at a specific time. We'll draw up a schedule. Would you agree to that?"

"Vladimir, I know you want to make a lot of money. You shall have it. I shall help you. Only that is not the way to do it. In your world people charge for treatment — there is no other way in your world. But I would rather do that without any question of money. Besides, I cannot treat everybody indiscriminately, since I have not fully realised in which cases healing will be helpful, and in which ones harmful. But I shall try to become aware of this and understand. And as soon as I can decipher —"

"What drivel is that?" I broke in. "How can healing or treating a person be harmful? Or do you mean harmful to yourself?"

"Healing of physical ailments can often bring harm to the one healed."

"It seems, Anastasia, your sophistications have given you a somewhat inverted concept of good and evil. Doctors have always been held in high regard by society, even though they have not performed their services free of charge. And, since you cite the Bible so much, you'll find that is not forbidden even there. So cast those doubts out of your head. Curing someone is always a good thing!"

"You see, Vladimir, I know this from experience. My grandfather showed me an example of the harm that healing can bring when it is not thought through, when the patient himself does not participate in the healing."

"What kind of strange philosophy you have here! I offer you a joint business venture. What have such examples got to do with it?"

Chapter Three

Healing for hell

"One day I saw with my Ray a lonely old woman working on her garden plot," Anastasia began. "She was spritely, slim and always cheerful. She caught my interest right away. She had a very small plot, and a lot of different things growing in it, and they grew very well, because she tended them with love.

"Then I learnt that the old woman would put everything she grew into a basket and take it into town and sell it. She tried not to eat the early fruits of her labours, but sell them when they would still fetch a high price. She needed the money to help her son. She had given birth to him late in life, and soon afterward she was left without a husband. Her relatives never communicated with her. Her son liked to draw as a child, and she had dreams that he would become an artist.

"Several times he tried to get in some place where he could pursue his studies. Finally he made it. And once or twice a year he would come to visit his elderly mother. These visits were the highlight of her life, and each time she would save up her money and prepare a whole supply of food for him. As the time for his visit approached, she would pack vegetables into glass jars, put their lids on tight and give the whole supply to him when he arrived.

"She loved him very much, and kept dreaming about her son becoming a top-notch artist. She lived on that dream. The woman was kind and cheerful.

"Then for a while I did not watch her. The next time I saw her she was very ill. She had a hard time bending over to work on her plantings — each time she bent over, a sharp pain ran right through her body.

"But she proved to be very resourceful. She made her beds long and narrow. Each time she went out to her plot she would take with her the seat from an old stool (minus the legs) and use it to sit on while she did her weeding, and that way she was able to move around the whole plot without having to bend over. She dragged the basket along on a string. And she was looking forward to a good harvest.

"It really looked as though the harvest that year would be quite plentiful, since the plants felt her state of mind and reacted accordingly. The woman sensed that she would soon pass on, and to make things easier for her son, before she died she bought a coffin and a wreath and made all the funeral preparations.

"But she still wanted to bring in one last harvest, and prepare the winter's food supply for her son before she died. I did not pay much attention then to why she was still sick even after such close contact with the plants. I thought perhaps it was because she herself ate almost nothing from her plot. She sold what she grew and then used the money to buy things she needed on the cheap.

"I decided to help her, and one night when she lay down to sleep I began warming her with my Ray, removing the pains from her body. I could feel some kind of resistance to the Ray, but I still kept on trying. I did this for about ten minutes until I succeeded in healing her flesh.

"Then, when Grandfather came, I told him about the old woman. And I asked him why the Ray had met some resistance. He thought about it, and then told me I had done the wrong thing. It made me very distraught.

"I began asking Grandfather to explain why. At first he did not say a word. Then he said, 'You healed the body.'"

I was amazed. "What harm could you have possibly brought to the woman's soul?" I asked.

Anastasia sighed and went on:

"The woman's health got better and she did not die. Her son came to see her earlier than usual. This time he came only for two days and told his mother he had quit his studies and did not want to be an artist any more. He was now involved in some other work that brought in more money. He had got married. Now he would have a lot of money. And he no longer wanted her to prepare 'those insipid food jars' for him, since transporting them would now cost more.

"'You can eat better yourself, now, Mother,' he said.

"He left without taking anything. That morning the woman sat on her porch, looked at her plot, and her eyes were filled with such emptiness and depression — they looked as though she did not want to live. You see, her body was healthy, but it was as if there were no life left in it. I saw, or rather felt, the terrible emptiness and hopelessness in her heart.

"If I had not cured her body, the woman would have died at the right time, she would have died peacefully with her beautiful dream and hope intact. Now here she was, still alive, but in great despair, and this was many times more frightening than physical death.

"Two weeks later she passed on."

Chapter Four

A confidential conversation

"I realised," Anastasia continued, "that physical disease is nothing compared with mental torments, but at the time I was not yet able to treat the soul. I wanted to know how I could do this or even if I could do it at all. Now I know — it is possible!

"And I found out something else — that physical diseases appear in Man not just as a result of his self-withdrawal from Nature around him, and not just as a result of the dark feelings which he allows himself to take in. They (the diseases) can also be a means of warding off or even deliverance from considerably greater torments. Diseases are one of the devices or means of communication between the Supreme Intelligence (God) and Man. Man's pain is His pain, too. But it could not be otherwise. How else could you get the message, for example: 'Do not keep throwing into your stomach all sorts of harmful stuff.' You tend not to listen to words of reason, after all. That's why the message comes through pain. But instead you swallow pain-killers and go back to stubbornly doing your own thing."

"So," I countered, "it follows then, in your opinion, that there's no need to treat people at all? No need to help them with their ailments?"

"Help there should be, but first of all to gain a proper understanding of the origins of the disease.

"Man needs help in discerning what the Supreme Intelligence, God, desires to say to him. But that is a most difficult task. One can make mistakes. Pain, after all, is a confidential conversation between two beings who know about each other. Interference from a third party often harms Man instead of helping him."

"Well, why then did you rid me of *my* diseases?" I asked Anastasia. "Does that mean you've harmed me in some way?"

"All your diseases will come back to you if you do not change your lifestyle, your attitude to things around you and to yourself. If you do not change some of your habits. They are the causes of your diseases. I have done no harm to your soul."

It became clear to me that it would be impossible to persuade Anastasia to make money out of using her healing abilities until she had sorted things out for herself. My business plan had fallen apart. Anastasia must have noticed my irritation, for she said:

"Do not be upset, Vladimir. I shall try to grasp everything as quickly as possible. And now, if you really want to help others and yourself and not just make money, I shall tell you about the means by which Man can cure himself from many diseases without undesirable side-effects, as might happen when outsiders try to interfere in his destiny. If indeed you want to listen to this..."

"What choice do I have? I'm not going to change your mind, in any case. Tell me."

"There are several main causes underlying the diseases of the human flesh, namely: harmful feelings, emotions, an artificial dietary régime — an unnatural meal schedule and food composition, the lack of short-term and long-term goals, and a misapprehension of one's essence and purpose in life. Positive emotions, a variety of plants and a reappraisal of one's essence and purpose in life — all these are capable not only of counteracting diseases but also of significantly enhancing one's physical and mental or emotional state.

"As far as bringing back — under the conditions of your world — Man's lost connection with plants, I have already told you about that. After Man has established a direct personal contact with these plants, it is much easier to make sense of everything else.

"The Ray of Love, too, is capable of curing many diseases of one's fellow-Man and even prolonging his life by creating around him a *Space of Love.*

"But Man himself, once he has managed to arouse positive emotions in himself, can use them to extinguish pain and cure the diseases of the flesh — even the effects of poison."

"What does that mean — 'arousing positive emotions'?" I queried. "How can one think good thoughts if one has a toothache or a stomach-ache?"

"Pure, clear moments of life, positive emotions, like guardian angels, will overcome pain and disease."

"But what if someone doesn't have enough pure and clear moments to arouse the positive healing emotions — what should he do then?"

"He should create at once something to make them appear. They appear when people around you treat you with genuine Love. So you must create a situation along those lines, create it by your actions in respect to those around you, otherwise your guardian angel will not be able to help you."

"I wonder whether I have ever had them myself, and if so, how strong they were. How does one call them forth?"

"This can be done through reminiscing. For example, let us recall something good, something pleasant from your past. With the help of that image try to feel the soft and pleasing state of mind you experienced back then. Do you want to try it now? I shall help you. Try it."

"All right, let's give it a try."

"Please, lie down on the grass and relax. You can remember starting from this point in your life right now going back into the past. Or you can start with your childhood and proceed up to the present day. Or you can jump at once to the most pleasant moments and feel the sensations connected with them."

I lay down on the grass. Anastasia lay down beside me and pressed her fingers against mine. I thought her proximity might prevent me from concentrating on my reminiscences, and I said:

"Perhaps I'd better be alone."

"I shall be very quiet. When you start remembering, you will forget about me. And you will not feel the touch of my hand. But I can help you remember everything more quickly and vividly."

Chapter Five

Where are you,
my guardian angel?

The chronicle of my life-story took me back to my childhood. My reminiscences continued up to the point where I was playing in the sand with the country kids, and then broke off. At that moment my soul was overwhelmed with an inexplicable sense of alarm. Not a single event in my whole life aroused positive emotions or feelings comparable to those I experienced that morning after spending the night with Anastasia. Or with those that arose in me after she brought the rhythms of surrounding Nature in tune with the beating of my heart (I described this experience in the chapter "Touching Paradise"). But I considered these marvellous feelings to be something created in me by Anastasia — they weren't my own. They were artificial, a gift from Anastasia. Involuntarily, I compared them with those of my previous life, and found no analogy whatsoever.

Again and again I hunted down recollections of my life, as though running a movie reel, backward and forward. Everything I saw was related to my efforts to get or achieve something. Sure, I got what I wanted, one thing after another, but there was no great feeling of satisfaction. Instead, some new desire merely appeared. And the most recent years of my life, when those around me thought how splendidly everything was turning out for me, aroused an even greater feeling of confusion and chaos. The cars I had acquired, the women, the banquets, the gifts and congratulations I had received — all seemed empty and pointless.

I quickly got to my feet and said, with some irritation, either to myself or to Anastasia:

"There are none of these healing sensations in Man's life! At least, not in mine. And I would say there are many lives where they can't be found."

Anastasia also rose to her feet and calmly observed:

"Then you should create them as quickly as possible."

"*What* do I need to create? Tell me, what?"

"First you must understand what holds the greatest meaning, or significance, for you. You have just been looking over your past life. But even with the opportunity to analyse it, to look at it objectively, as it were, you still were not able to notice what was really significant. You kept latching on to the usual values, as you saw them. Tell me the situations where you felt you came closest to a sense of happiness."

"There were two situations, but each time something prevented me from feeling truly happy in them."

"What kind of situations?"

"Back in the early days of *perestroika*[1] I managed to acquire a long-term lease on a steamship. This was the best passenger ship in the Western Siberian river fleet — the *Mikhail Kalinin*.

"After the lease agreement was drawn up, I went to the harbour and there she stood. What a beauty! I remember the first time I stood on the deck of my very own ship."

"And did your feelings of happiness greatly increase when you stood on the deck?"

"You know, Anastasia, our lives are filled with all sorts of problems. As soon as I had climbed aboard, I was met by the

---

[1]*perestroika* — the policy of restructuring the economic and political system of the Soviet Union, initiated by Gorbachev in 1985, which eventually led to the collapse of communism and the break-up of the USSR in the early 1990s.

captain. We went to his cabin and had a bottle of champagne together. During our conversation the captain advised that all the water pipes needed cleaning at once, or the health authorities would not allow us to set sail. And there were other things he told me..."

"And so, Vladimir, you immersed yourself in all the problems and cares involved in the running of the ship."

"Yes, that's right. There were a lot of them."

"It is inherent in the nature of artificially created matter and various mechanical devices, Vladimir, that they bring more problems than pleasures. Their benefit to Man is quite illusory."

"Well, I don't happen to agree. Maybe in themselves these mechanical devices have problems — they need constant repair and maintenance. Still, they help us get a lot of things."

"What, for example?"

"Even love."

"Genuine Love, Vladimir, could not possibly be under the control of artificially created objects. Even if you owned all the objects in the world, you would not be able, just with their help, to gain access to the true Love of even one woman."

"Well, you simply don't know our women. You're spinning theories, that's all. I managed to get it."

"What did you manage to get?"

"Love. I quite simply succeeded. There was one woman I loved a great deal. I loved her for many years. But she didn't really want to go off with me anywhere alone. When I got my ship, however, I invited her aboard, and she accepted. Can you imagine how great that was?! Here we were sitting alone at the ship's bar. There was champagne, first-class wine, candlelight, music — and nobody else around. Here we were alone in the empty bar on my ship. She was the only one there with me.

"I had the ship set sail without taking on any other passengers, just so we could be alone. The ship proceeded down the river. There was music playing in the bar. I invited her to dance. Her figure was fantastic, especially her breasts. I hugged her tight, my heart was pounding for joy, and I kissed her on the lips!

"She didn't run away, she even hugged me back. Do you see? There she was right beside me, and I could touch her, and kiss her. All this was because of the ship, and you say it can only bring problems."

"And then, Vladimir, what happened?"

"Nothing much."

"Please try to remember, anyway."

"I tell you, it was nothing important."

"Can *I* tell *you* what happened there, on the ship, between you and that young woman?"

"You can try."

"You had a lot to drink. You made a deliberate effort to drink as much as possible. Then you put the keys to your cabin — your luxury apartment — on the table in front of her, and you yourself went down to the lower decks. You slept almost twenty-four hours in the cramped crew's quarters. And do you know why?"

"Why?"

"The moment came when you noticed a strange expression on the face of that beloved young woman of yours — a preoccupied smile. Intuitively, even subconsciously, you realised that she, your beloved, was thinking how happy she would be if only it were her own beloved that was sitting across from her in this bar, instead of Megré. Your precious girl was dreaming of someone else, someone she really liked. She fantasised that it was he, and not you, who was master of the ship. You were at the mercy of inert matter, to which you had tied your living feelings and aspirations, and were choking them to death."

"Don't go on, Anastasia!" I pleaded. "These recollections aren't happy ones for me. In any case, the ship did play its role. It was thanks to the ship that you and I met."

"The happenings of the present are the result of previous feelings and impulses of the soul, and it is only *they* that determine the future. And it is only *their* momentum, only the beating of *their* wings, that is clearly reflected in the heavenly mirrors. And only *their* impulses and aspirations will be reflected in happenings here on the Earth."

"What do you mean by that?" I asked in some bewilderment.

"Our meeting may well be the culmination of many aspirations of the soul on both your part and mine — perhaps on the part of our immediate or even more distant forebears. Perhaps it came from a single impulse of the cherry tree growing in the garden of your country home. Only not the ship."

"What has the cherry tree in my garden got to do with it?"

"In all your many glances back at your life, you failed to pay any attention to this cherry tree and your feelings connected with it, yet those feelings have played a leading role in your life in recent years. The Universe did not react to your ship. Just think, what could a primitive, run-down material device, incapable of either thinking or restoring itself, possibly mean to the Universe?

"But the cherry tree... a little Siberian cherry tree, which you could not even make room for in your recollections, excited the cosmic expanses and changed the course of time and history — and not only yours and mine. Because it is a living being, and, like all living beings, has an inseparable connection with creation as a whole."

Chapter Six

The cherry tree

"Remember, Vladimir, everything within you associated with this little tree. Remember, starting right from the moment you first made contact with it."

"I shall try to remember, if you think it's important."

"Yes, it *is* important."

"I was riding in my car, I don't remember where I was going. We stopped near the Central Market. I asked my driver to get out and buy some fruit. I stayed in the car and watched people leaving the market carrying all sorts of saplings."

"You watched them and were surprised. Why?"

"You see, their faces were happy and contented. Even though it was cold and rainy out, here they were hauling away some kind of saplings with their roots all bound in cloth. These saplings were heavy to carry, but the people's faces were content, and here I was sitting in my warm car and I was sad.

"When the driver returned, I got out and went over to the market myself. I kept walking up and down past the merchants' stalls and bought three cherry saplings. As I was tossing them into the baggage compartment, the driver said that one of the saplings wouldn't survive, since its roots had been cut too short, and I'd better throw it out right off, but I decided to keep it. It was the most graceful of the three. Then I went and planted the saplings in the garden of my country home.

"I threw in extra topsoil around the tree with the short roots, and a sprinkling of peat moss, along with a bit of fertiliser."

"In trying to help it, you burnt two more little roots of the sapling with the fertiliser," Anastasia added.

"But it survived! In the spring, when the buds started coming out on the trees, its branches came to life, too. Little leaves began to appear. Then I set out on my commercial expedition."

"But before that," Anastasia observed, "every day for a period of more than two months you would drive out to your country house and the first thing you did was go and see how the little tree was getting on. Sometimes you stroked its branches. You were so happy to see the leaves, and kept watering the tree. You drove a stake into the ground and fastened the trunk to it with twine all around so the wind wouldn't break it.

"Tell me, Vladimir, do you think that plants react to people's attitude toward them? Do you think they feel good and bad thoughts?"

"I've heard, or read, somewhere that house-plants and flowers do react that way. They can even become all withered when their care-giver goes away. I've heard about scientific experiments where they attached sensors to various plants, and the needles jumped one way when the plants were approached aggressively, and the other way when someone approached them with thoughts of gentleness and kindness."

"So, Vladimir, you know about plants reacting to the expression of human feelings. And, according to the Grand Creator's design, they strive to do all within their power, all that they can, to meet Man's needs — they bring forth fruit, and try to arouse positive emotions in Man with their flowers beautiful and fair — indeed, they put oxygen into the air so that we can breathe.

"But plants have been granted yet another function which is no less important. Plants which come into direct contact with an individual Man create for him a *Space of true Love*. The kind of Love without which life for the human race would be impossible.

"Many dachniks are in a hurry to get out to their plots because it is there that such a Space has been created for them. And this little Siberian cherry tree you thought to plant, the one you cared for yourself, it tried to do the same as all other plants and perform its assigned function.

"If there are a lot of them, plants can create for Man a significant Space of Love — if they are of different varieties and Man communicates with them, and approaches them with Love. All together plants can create for Man a significant Space of Love which enhances the soul and makes the body whole.

"You see, Vladimir — all together, when there are a lot of them. But you looked after just one sapling. And so this one little Siberian cherry tree began aspiring to do what only a number of plants acting together can do.

"Its aspiration was aroused by your special relation to it. It was something you yourself realised only intuitively — in all your surroundings only this one little tree was not asking anything of you, it was not being hypocritical, it only aspired to give of itself — and then you came along. You were tired after a busy day. You went over to the tree, stood and pondered. You looked at it, and it responded.

"Before the first ray of dawn appeared in its perfection, the leaves of the tree tried to catch that ray's reflection in the brightening sky. And when the Sun went down afar, it tried using the light of a bright star. And as it persisted, something transpired by and by, just a wee bit of something transpired.

"Its roots, twisting themselves around the burning fertiliser, were able to take in what they required from the Earth. And the Earth's juices began turning and running through the veins of the tree a little more quickly than usual. And then one day, in an early morning hour, you came and saw the little flowers to which the tree's delicate branches had given birth. The other saplings were devoid of flowers, but this one, thanks to your gift of caring, had already blossomed. You were overjoyed. Your spirits were uplifted and then... do you remember what you did, Vladimir, after seeing the flowers?"

"I really was overjoyed. For some reason my mood was on a high, I felt a lightness in my head. I went and stroked its branches with my hands."

"You *gently* stroked its branches. And you said, 'Well now, my beauty, you've blossomed!'

"You see the trees, Vladimir, and you see the leaves, and the fruit borne thereof. But more than that, the trees create a Space of Love. The little cherry tree very much wanted you to have this Space. But where was the place for the tree to find the strength to give back to Man what it had received from him? It had tried and tried and had already given everything that was in its power, but it had received something extraordinary besides — a showing of tenderness toward itself and the flowers it bore. And then it had the desire to do more! All by itself!

"You went off on your very long expedition. And then, completing your journey and returning, the first thing you did was go to the garden plot to see your little cherry tree. But along the way you were eating cherries you had bought at the market. As you approached it, you noticed that there were three red cherries growing on your tree. You stood there beside it, all tired out, eating the bought cherries and spitting out the stones. Then you tore one of the cherries off your tree and tried it. Indeed, it was just a little bit more sour, a little less sweet than the market cherries you had decided to eat, and you did not touch the other two."

"I had had my fill of the other cherries. And this one was indeed more sour."

"Oh, if only you had known, Vladimir, how much power those little cherries contained on their own that was so beneficial to you! How much energy and Love! From the depths of the Earth and the expanses of the Universe and more, the tree had gathered everything helpful for you and poured it into these three cherries. It had even let one of its branches wither in order to make these three cherries ripen. One of them you tried, but you left the other two on the tree to die."

"I had no idea. But still, I was happy that it was capable of bearing fruit."

"Yes, you were happy. And then... do you remember what you did this time?"

"Me? Well, I stroked the tree's branches some more."

"And you not only stroked them. You even bent over and kissed the leaves on the branch which was resting on the palm of your hand."

"Yes, I did. Because I was in such a good mood."

"And something incredible happened with the tree. What more could it do for you, since you had not taken the fruit thereof that had been grown with so much Love? What could it do?

"It trembled from the kiss of Man, and the thought and feelings inherent only in Man but produced by this little Siberian cherry tree took flight into the Universe's space of light — to give back to Man what it had received from him. To give back to Man its kiss of Love, to warm him with this — the bright feelings, the Space of Love. And against all laws that thought swept across the Universe but could not find a resting-place, a means of manifesting the breath — the life — of itself.

"Knowing that one cannot find a resting-place means *death*.

"Then the forces of light returned to the cherry tree the bright thought it had produced, so that it might destroy the thought within itself and not perish. But the tree did not pick it up!

"The little Siberian cherry tree's burning desire endured unchanged, extraordinarily pure and trembling.

"The forces of light did not know what to do. The Grand Creator was not about to change the established laws of harmony for you. But the cherry tree did not perish. It managed to endure because the thought, aspiration and feelings thereof were extraordinarily pure, and by the laws that constitute creation as a whole nothing can destroy pure Love. And it circled over your soul and dreamt of finding a resting-place, a place to thrive. Alone in the Universe, it was striving, aspiring to create for you a Space of Love.

"I came to your ship to at least try to be of some help and fulfil the cherry tree's desire to find this resting-place, to manifest its love. Even though I did not know to whom it was addressed."

Anastasia paused.

"You mean to say," I queried, "that your relationship to me arose out of your desire to help the tree?"

"My relationship to you, Vladimir, is simply that: my relationship. It is difficult to say who was helping whom here — the cherry tree me or I the tree. Everything in the Universe is interrelated. To perceive what is really going on in the Universe one need only look into one's self. But now, by your leave, I am giving an embodiment to this, to what the cherry tree desired. May I give you a kiss from the tree?"

"Of course you may. Since it's the right thing to do. And when I get home, I shall eat all of its fruit."

Anastasia closed her eyes. She pressed her hands to her breast and quietly whispered:

"*Feel* this, little cherry tree. I know you can feel it. I shall now do what you wished. This will really be your kiss, little cherry tree."

Then Anastasia quickly placed her hands on my shoulders and, without opening her eyes, drew near, touched her lips to my cheek and held them there.

It was a strange kiss, just the touch of her lips. But it was not like any I had ever received before. It aroused an extraordinarily pleasing sensation, one I had never felt up to now. The technique of moving the lips or tongue or body probably had nothing to do with it. What counted, most probably, was what was hidden in the inner Man that was manifesting itself in the kiss.

But what was hidden inside this taiga recluse? Where did she get so much knowledge from, so many unusual abilities and feelings? Or maybe everything she said was simply the product of her imagination? But then where did the extraordinarily tender, charming and heart-warming sensations come from — the ones I could most certainly feel within me? Perhaps our joint efforts will manage to unravel the mystery through the aid of the following situation which I had the good fortune to witness.

CHAPTER SEVEN

Who's to blame?

Once when Anastasia was trying to explain something to me about lifestyles and faith, but couldn't find suitable, understandable words — which she no doubt very much wanted to find — a curious incident took place.

Anastasia quickly turned to face the ringing cedar, pressing the palms of her hands against its trunk. But then something inexplicable began happening to her. Lifting up her head and addressing either the cedar or Someone way up high, all at once she started speaking passionately and with concentrated attention in a combination of words and sounds.

She was evidently trying to show or explain something, or plead for something. From time to time her monologue seemed to be infused with tones of persistent demanding. The resonant ring of the cedar increased in volume. Its ray became brighter and thicker. And then Anastasia demanded sharply:

"Answer me! Answer! Explain! Give it to me, give it to me!" she said, shaking her head and even stamping her bare feet.

All at once the pale glow of the ringing cedar's tree-top became focused into a ray, and the ray suddenly broke off from the cedar and flew upward and dissolved into thin air. But at this point another ray appeared, coming down to the cedar from above. It seemed to consist of a bluish mist or cloud.

The needles of the cedar, pointing downward, were illuminated with similar misty rays, almost unnoticeable. And these rays pointed toward Anastasia, but didn't touch her — they seemed to disappear and dissolve in the air. And when she insistently stamped her feet and even slapped the ringing cedar's huge trunk with the palms of her hands, the glowing needles began stirring and their rays joined to form a single Ray of bluish mist. It aimed itself downward toward Anastasia, but didn't touch her. The Ray dissolved in the air, literally dissolved — at about a metre away from Anastasia at first, then at just half that distance.

I suddenly recalled with horror how Anastasia's parents had perished — very likely from just such a Ray.

Anastasia continued her stubborn pleading and demanding, much like a spoilt child insisting on some desired favour from its parents. And suddenly the Ray made a dash for *her*, as it were, illuminating her whole body like a flashbulb.

A cloud first formed around Anastasia and then began dissipating, ever so slowly. The ray from the Cedar dissolved, the rays from the needles were extinguished. The cloud around Anastasia continued to dissipate. It was either entering into her or dissolving in space.

Now radiant with a joyous smile, she turned and took a step in my direction. Then she stopped and began staring past me at something beyond. I turned around to see Anastasia's grandfather and great-grandfather coming into the glade. The tall, grey-bearded great-grandfather walked slowly, just ahead of his son. He was leaning on a stick that looked something like a shepherd's staff. Upon reaching my position, he stopped and fixed his gaze on me, as though staring into empty space. I couldn't even tell whether he actually saw me or not. Great-Grandfather stood silently for a moment. Then, after bowing ever so slightly, without uttering so much as a word of greeting, he headed over to Anastasia.

Even though Grandfather was a bit of a fussbudget, he was a very simple man. His whole demeanour pointed to a most kind and cheerful fellow. As he approached the spot where I was standing, he at once stopped and offered me a simple shake of his hand. He started to say something, but I can't recollect exactly what he said. For some reason both of us felt our attention and concern suddenly drawn to what was going on at the base of the cedar.

Great-Grandfather had stopped just a metre from Anastasia. They stood there for a while, silently staring at each other. Anastasia was standing before the bearded old man, her hands lowered to a vertical position, as though she were a schoolgirl or university applicant being confronted by a strict examiner. She looked like a child caught being naughty, and her anxiety was most evident.

The tense silence which had come over the scene was broken by the deep, clear, velvety tones of Great-Grandfather's voice. He did not say hello to Anastasia but proceeded at once to a stern questioning, every word slowly and distinctly pronounced:

"Who can make an appeal directly to Him without going through the light and rhythm that have been bestowed upon us?" Whereupon Anastasia responded without hesitation:

"Any Man can make an appeal to Him. From time immemorial He Himself has taken great pleasure in talking with Man. And this is what He wills right now."

"Are all paths outlined by Him in advance?" Great-Grandfather continued. "Are there many Earth-dwellers capable of discerning them? Are you capable of seeing these paths?"

"Yes. I have seen what has been outlined for mankind. I have seen how future events are dependent on the conscious awareness of those who are living today."

"Have His Sons and their enlightened followers who have perceived His Spirit, done enough to bring enlightenment to those living in the flesh?"

"They have done and are doing everything, not even taking thought for their own life. They have borne witness to the truth and are still bearing witness."

"Can one who has seen the truth have any doubt about His intellect, kindness and magnificence of Spirit?"

"He has no equals! He is One! But He does wish to communicate. He wants people to understand and love Him as He loves."

"In communicating with Him, is it permissible to be insolent and demanding?"

"He has given a particle of His Spirit and Mind to everyone living on the Earth. And if a small particle — His particle — in Man, does not agree with what is generally accepted, that means He — and I mean He — is not satisfied with everything as it has been outlined for the future. He is reflecting on it. Could one term His reflections insolence?"

"Who is permitted to hasten the pace of His reflections?"

"Only the One who *gives* permission."

"And just what are you asking for?"

"I am asking how to give understanding to those who do not understand, how to inculcate feeling in those who do not feel."

"Has the lot of those who fail to perceive Truth been determined?"

"The lot of those who fail to perceive Truth has been determined. But who is to blame for the lack of acceptance of truth — the one who does not accept the truth or the one from whom he receives it?"

"What? You mean, you..." Great-Grandfather said in agitation, and then fell silent.

He stood silently for a while, looking at Anastasia. Then, with the help of his staff-like cane, he got down on one knee and took Anastasia's hand. Inclining his silvery-grey head toward her, he kissed her hand and said:

"Hello, Anastasia."

Anastasia herself at once knelt down before her great-grandfather, and exclaimed with excitement and surprise:

"What do you mean, Grandpakins, treating me like a child? I'm grown up now."

Then she put her arms around his shoulders, snuggled her head against his beard-covered chest and held still. I knew she was listening to his heartbeat. That was something she had loved ever since her childhood.

The oldster continued kneeling, one hand resting on his cane, the other stroking Anastasia's golden hair.

Grandfather got excited, and rushed over to his father and granddaughter who were both still kneeling. He began strutting around them, throwing up his arms in some bewilderment. Then all of a sudden he too got down on his knees and embraced them both...

Grandfather was the first to rise to his feet. He then helped his father up. Great-Grandfather was still staring intently at Anastasia. Then he slowly turned around and started walking off. Grandfather in the meantime started muttering away, though it wasn't clear whether he was addressing anyone in particular:

"All the same, they're all spoiling her. Even He spoils her. Dear me, just look at where she's got to! She pokes her nose in wherever she feels like it. There's nobody to teach her a lesson. Who will now help the dachniks? Who, I say?!"

Great-Grandfather stopped in his tracks. He slowly turned around and said distinctly, in his deep velvety voice:

"Granddaughter dear, follow the dictates of your heart and soul. I myself shall help you with the dachniks."

Turning away once again, the majestic greybeard started on his way out of the glade.

"Do you see what I mean? — they're all spoiling her," Grandfather broke in again.

Picking up a short switch, he strutted over to Anastasia. Waving the switch about his head, he threatened: "I'm going to teach her a lesson, right now!"

"Oh, oh!" Anastasia threw up her hands in feigned fright. Then she gave a laugh and ran off, trying to elude her pursuing grandfather.

"So, she's even taken it into her head to run away from me. As if I couldn't catch up!" he muttered under his breath.

With unaccustomed ease and speed he intensified his pursuit. Anastasia ran laughing, weaving her way across the glade. And while Grandfather did not relax his pace, he was still unable to catch up to her.

Suddenly Grandfather gasped and sat down, grasping his leg. Anastasia quickly turned about, her face full of concern. She ran over to her grandfather and held out her hands to him. And all at once she stopped. Her infectious peals of laughter filled the glade. I paid particular attention to her grandfather's pose and realised the source of her mirth.

Grandfather was squatting down on one leg, holding his other leg out in front, not touching the ground. And here he was stroking the very leg he was squatting on, as though it had been injured. He had outsmarted Anastasia, but she was not deceived.

As it turned out later, she was supposed to have noticed right off the comic discrepancy in his pose. While Anastasia was laughing, Grandfather managed to seize her by the arm. He raised his switch and gave her a light spanking, like a child. Anastasia squealed, trying to pretend it was painful. And in spite of the endless laughter she was trying so hard to restrain, Grandfather put his arms around her shoulders and said:

"All, right, that's enough. Don't cry. You've learnt your lesson? You've got what was coming to you. You'll be more obedient in future.

"Listen, I've started training the eagle. It may be old, but it is still strong and remembers many things. And here she's insolently poking her nose into everything."

"Grandpakins! My dear, sweet Grandpakins! The eagle! That means you already know about the baby?!"

"The star, don't forget!..."

Anastasia didn't let her grandfather finish. Putting her arms around his waist, she lifted him off the ground and spun him around. When she returned him safely to the ground, Grandfather staggered a bit, and said, trying to appear strict:

"So that's the way you treat your elders? You see what I mean — you're spoilt!" And, continuing to wave the switch, he hurried to catch up with his father. As he reached the trees at the edge of the glade, Anastasia called after him:

"Thank you, Grandpakins, for the eagle. Thank you very much!"

Grandfather turned around and looked at her.

"Only just be, my dear child... please remember to be more —" His voice was too gentle. Breaking off his sentence, he added with a bit more severity:

"Watch out, or else..."

And he disappeared into the forest.

CHAPTER EIGHT

The answer

Once we found ourselves alone, I asked Anastasia:

"What's all the big excitement about some kind of eagle?"

"The eagle will be very much needed for the little one," she answered. "For our baby, Vladimir!"

"To play with?"

"Yes. Only play has a considerable significance for his future learning and feelings."

"I see."

I said this, even though I didn't fully understand this business of playing with a bird, even an eagle.

"But what were you doing with the cedar? Were you praying, or talking with someone? What happened with you and the cedar, and why did Great-Grandfather seem so severe when he talked with you?"

"Tell me, Vladimir, do you think there is, well, some kind of *intelligence* out there? Does there exist a Mind in the invisible world of the cosmic — in the Universe? What do you think?"

"I think it's true. You know, even scholars talk about that, as do mediums, and the Bible."

"And this *something* — what would you say is the best word to describe it? I need to know this so that you and I can agree upon a definition. Say, for example, Mind, Intelligence, Being, Forces of Light, Vacuum, Absolute, Rhythm, Spirit, God...?"

"Well, let's say 'God'."

"All right, then. Now tell me, does God attempt to communicate with Man, what do you think? I do not mean by a voice from heaven, but through people, through the Bible, let us say — to offer a hint on how to be more happy?"

"But the Bible was not necessarily dictated by God."

"Well, by whom, then, would you say?"

"People could have done that — people who wanted to invent religion. They sat down and wrote it collectively."

"You think it is that simple? People just sat down and wrote a book, and thought up narratives and laws? A book that has lasted for millennia and is the most popular and widely read book that has existed to date?! Over the centuries a whole multitude of other books have been written, but few of them can compare with the Bible. What does that mean to you?"

"I don't know," I admitted. "Ancient books, of course, have been around for a long time, but most people today prefer contemporary literature — novels, detective stories and all sorts of inferior stuff. Why is that so?"

"Because reading them hardly requires any thinking. In reading the Bible one is obliged to think at a faster pace and there are many questions one must answer for one's self. Only then will it become clear. It unfolds itself, so to speak, to one's consciousness. If one looks upon the Bible merely as a statement of dogma, then reading and memorising a few commandments is sufficient. But any dogma imposed from without and not grasped by one's inner being precludes taking advantage of the opportunities afforded Man as Creator."

"What questions do we need to answer when we read the Bible?"

"To begin with," replied Anastasia, "you might try to figure out why Pharaoh was unwilling to allow the children of Israel to leave Egypt."

"Well, what's there to think about? The Israelites were slaves in Egypt. Who would want to let his slaves go? They worked hard and brought Pharaoh a good income."

"The Bible says that more than once the Israelites brought a plague over the whole land of Egypt. They even killed people's first-born offspring, along with those of animals. Sorcerers were later burnt at the stake for such acts, but here Pharaoh simply refused to let them go. Now answer the question: where did the Israelite slaves get enough goods and cattle to spend forty years travelling? Where did they get the weapons to seize and destroy cities along their route?"

"What do you mean, where? Didn't God give them everything?"

"Do you think that was only God's doing?"

"Then who?"

"Man, Vladimir, has full freedom. He has the opportunity to make use of all the bright resources God gave him originally, but he can make use of other resources too. Man represents a union of opposites.

"See, Vladimir, how the Sun shines. That is God's creation. It is for everyone. For you and me, for the snakes, the grass and the flowers. But bees use the flowers to get honey, while the spider's power is to draw poison. Each of them has its own function and no bee and no spider can do otherwise. Only Man has a wider scope, only Man can act in more than one way! One Man can *rejoice* at the first rays of the Sun, while another might curse. Man, you see, can be both a bee and a spider."

"Does that mean God wasn't the only one helping the Israelites? How can you tell, then, what God actually *did*, as opposed to what was merely attributed to Him?"

"When something significant is created through Man," Anastasia explained, "there are always two opposites at work. Man exercises freedom of choice. Which he will accept more of depends upon his purity and conscious awareness."

"Well, all right, let's accept that. So, you were attempting to talk with Him when you were standing at the base of the cedar?"

"Yes, I wanted Him to answer me."

"And Great-Grandfather objected?"

"Great-Grandfather thought that I was speaking too irreverently, that I was too demanding."

"You really were demanding, I saw it. You were stamping your feet, and pleading. What on earth did you want?"

"I wanted to hear an answer."

"What sort of answer?"

"You see, Vladimir, God's essence is not in the flesh. He cannot yell down to everyone from heaven, telling them how to live. But He wants things to be fine and whole with everyone, and so he sends His Sons — people into whose mind and soul He has been able to break through at least to some extent.

"His Sons then go and talk with other people, they speak different languages. Sometimes through words, sometimes with the help of music or pictures, or various actions. Sometimes they are listened to, at other times they are persecuted and killed. Like Christ Jesus, for example. And still God is sending forth His Sons. But as always, it is only some of the people who pause and listen to them, while others who are called do not get the message at all. And they violate the laws of a happy existence."

"I see. And that's why God will punish mankind by a global catastrophe — some kind of fearful judgement?"

"God never punishes anyone, and He does not need catastrophes. God is Love. But that is the way it was planned from the very beginning. Created that way from above. When mankind reaches a specific point, one might say, in its unwillingness to accept the essence of truth. Once the elements of darkness manifest in Man reach that critical point, in order to avert total self-annihilation, a global catastrophe rushes in which takes away a great many people's lives and crushes the destructive life-support system of artificial creation. The catastrophe serves as a lesson to those who are left alive.

"Following a catastrophe there is a window of time in which mankind seems to go through a fearful hell. But it is a hell of their own making. It is those who are left alive that fall into this hell. Then for a while their children survive as in a pristine, original state, and they eventually reach a stage one could call Paradise. Then they fall away again, and it all starts over again in tears. This has been going on for billions of earthly years."

"If all this has been inevitably repeating itself for billions of years, what then were you asking for?"

"I wanted to find out how and by what means people could be made wiser without subjecting them to a catastrophe. You see, I have figured out that a catastrophe can be blamed not only on those who do not accept truth, but also on the absence of a sufficiently effective means of making the truth be seen, of making people alert to the truth. I was asking Him to find such a means. To reveal it, either to me or someone else. To whom, I feel, is not really important. What is important is that it is there to be seen, and that it works."

"And what did He tell you? What kind of voice does He have?"

"Nobody can tell what kind of voice He has. His answer takes form, as it were, in Man's discovery of a thought spontaneously occurring to himself. After all, He can speak only through His particle that is present in every Man, and this particle is already relaying information to every other part of the individual with the help of the rhythm of vibration. Hence the impression arises that Man is doing it all by himself. Though Man himself can actually do a great deal. After all, Man is God's likeness. In each Man there is a tiny particle breathed into him by God right at birth. He has given half of Himself to mankind upon the Earth. And the forces of darkness try by whatever means they can to prevent this God-reflected particle from acting out its high purpose, to distract Man from communication with it, and, through it, with God. It is much easier to fight with a small particle when it is all alone, especially if it is not connected to the Basic Force of the Universe.

"But if these particles unite amongst themselves in bright aspirations, it is much more difficult for the forces of darkness to hinder them. Even if one single particle, living in just one single Man, is in full contact with God, then it is impossible for the forces of darkness to overpower him, to defeat his spirit and mind."

"That means," I surmised, "you appealed to Him so that the answer would be given birth in you as to what to say to people, and how to say it, in order to avert a global catastrophe?"

"More or less."

"And what answer was given birth in you? What words must be spoken?"

"Words... just words alone, pronounced in the usual way, are not sufficient. So many words have been spoken already. Yet humanity on the whole continues to move toward its own perdition.

"You have no doubt heard words to the effect that smoking is bad, that alcoholic drinks are bad. And this is repeated by a number of sources, including your own physicians, in the language you best understand, yet you still go on doing it. You go on doing it without regard for the deterioration in your own health, and even painful sensations will not restrain either you or many other people from these destructive habits. God says to you: 'You should not do that.' And the message reaches you through pain. And it is not just your pain, but His too, and yet you take painkillers galore and go on doing your own thing as before. Again, you are not interested in thinking about what produces the pain.

"And all the other higher truths are known to mankind, but they are not being acted upon. Time after time they are rejected in favour of momentary illusory gratifications. It means another way must be revealed to allow them not only to know but also to feel other kinds of pleasure. Once Man has learnt of these, he can compare and realise everything for himself, he will unblock access to the God-bestowed particle within him. It is no good simply threatening Man with a catastrophe, it is no good simply blaming those who do not accept truth. Everyone who brings the truth to others must understand how needful it is to seek a more perfect method of explaining it. Great-Grandfather agreed with me."

"But that's not what he said."

"There was a lot that Great-Grandfather said that you did not hear."

"If you were able to communicate with each other without words, why then did you say the words that I *did* hear?"

"Would you not consider it offensive if people conversed using foreign words you could not understand, given that they knew your language too?"

Various thoughts ran through my mind: Either I believe everything she tells me or I don't. She herself, of course, believes. And it's not just that she *believes* it, she *acts* upon it. She takes it all so intensely — maybe I should try to somehow restrain her enthusiasm. So I tried to dampen her fervour by saying:

"You know what I think, Anastasia — maybe you don't need to take it so to heart and get so stirred up with your demands, as you were doing at the cedar tree. Even the blue glow or vapour from the cedar came crushing down on you. Your grandfather and great-grandfather were right to be concerned. It's probably very dangerous. If God has not given the answer to any of His Sons as to how to explain everything to people most effectively, that means there is no answer. It means that a global catastrophe is the most effective way of getting His message across. Maybe He's even annoyed with you for poking your nose in too far and will punish you so you won't do it again, just like your grandfather said."

"God is kind. He will not punish."

"But He isn't speaking to you either. Maybe He's not interested in listening to you, and meanwhile you're wasting so much energy."

"He is listening and He is answering."

"What is He answering? Is there something new you know now?"

"He has hinted at where to find the answer, where to search for it."

"He's 'hinted'? To you?! So, where is it?"

"In the union of opposites."

"What does that mean?"

"It happens, for example, when two opposite extremes of human thinking in the Avatamsaka commentary merge into a new dynamic whole. This was behind the philosophies of Hua-yen and Kegon,[1] which offer a world-view of even greater perfection, not unlike the models and theories in your modern physics."

"What was all that?"

"Oh, please do excuse me. I do not know what came over me. I completely forgot myself."

"What are you apologising for?"

"You must forgive me. I used words which are completely unfamiliar to you."

"You're right. They are unfamiliar. I have no idea what they mean."

"I shall try not to do that again. Please, do not be angry with me."

"Don't worry, I'm not angry. Only explain in ordinary words where and how you will go about searching for this answer."

[1] *Avatamsaka Sutra* (also known as the *Flower Garden* Sutra) — considered to be the most profound of the Buddhist *sutras* (sets of aphorisms), which holds that all manifestations of existence are self-created and mutually identical. It gave rise to the philosophical school known as *Hua-yen* in China and *Kegon* in Japan.

"I certainly cannot do it alone. It can only be known through the joint effort of the divine particles to be found in various people living on the Earth — people with opposite modes of thinking and comprehension. Only through a joint effort will it be seen, and then in a dimension invisible to the eye — the domain of thoughts. One can also call it the dimension of the forces of light. It exists *between* the material world, in which Man lives, and God.

"I shall see it, and many others will, too. Then it will be easier to attain a universal conscious awareness. It will be easier to bring mankind through the dark forces' window of time. And the catastrophes will not be repeated."

"Specifically, what do people need to do right now to make the answer appear?"

"It would be fine if a lot of people could wake up in the morning at a set time — six o'clock, say — and think about something good. What specifically they think about is not important. It is important that they come out with bright thoughts. They can think about their children, about their loved ones, about how to make everyone happy. If they could only think fifteen minutes like that. And the more people that do that, the quicker the answer will come. The Earth's time zones may be different, since the Earth is turning, but the images created by these people's bright yearnings will merge into a single, clear, fulfilled image of conscious awareness. The simultaneity of bright thoughts will intensify each person's ability many, many times."

"Oh, Anastasia, how naïve you are! Who in their right mind would wake up at six o'clock in the morning just to think for fifteen minutes? People will only get up that early if they have to go to work, or have a plane to catch, or are going on a business trip. Anybody else will decide: 'Leave the thinking to others, I'm going to get some more sleep!' I doubt you'll find many helpers that way."

"But you, Vladimir — could not *you*, at least, help me?"

"Me? I don't wake up that early unless I have to. But if I should somehow find myself waking up then, what good things should I think about?"

"Well, for example, you could think about the little son I will be giving birth to. Your son! Think how delighted he will be to be kissed by the Sun's rays, to see the pure and magnificent flowers all around him, and have the bushy-tailed squirrel play with him in this glade. Think how good it would be if all the other children in the world could forever be kissed by the warm Sun — then nothing would make them sad. Then think about who you might say something glad to or give a smile to during the day ahead. And how good it would be if this marvellous world lasted forever, and what you could do — you in particular — to bring this about."

"I'll think about our son. And I'll try to come out with other good thoughts. Only what's the point? You'll be thinking here, in the forest, while I'll be in an apartment in the city. That's only two of us. You say many people are needed. So until we get a lot of people involved, isn't it pointless for just the two of us to try?"

"Even one person, Vladimir, is more than none. Two together are more than two apart. Later, after you write your book, more people will come along. I shall feel them and delight in each one. We shall learn to catch each other's feelings of the heart, understand and help each other through the dimension of the forces of light."

"Everything you say still has to be believed. I myself don't completely believe in this 'bright dimension', this 'domain of thoughts'. You can't even prove it exists, because you can't touch it."

"Yet your scientists have come to the conclusion that thought *is* something tangible."

"They have, but since you still can't actually *touch* it, it's not something you can get completely set in your mind."

"But when you write your book, people will be able to touch it, they can hold it in their hands. Like a materialised thought."

"Again you're carrying on about that book! I've told you, I don't believe in *it* either. Even less in your claim that you, with the help of certain combinations of letters known only to you, can arouse feelings in the reader — bright feelings yet, that will help the reader make some sense of it all."

"I told you how it works."

"Yes, you told me. But it still doesn't make me believe. If I try to write, I shan't tell everything all at once. People will laugh at me... You know something, Anastasia, can I tell you in all honesty?"

"Yes, tell me in all honesty."

"Only don't be offended, okay?"

"I shall not be offended."

"Everything you've talked up to me I'm going to have to verify with our scholars, and see what they say about it in various religious and modern teachings. There's a lot of different courses out there now, a lot of preachers."

"Go ahead and verify, by all means."

"And still, I feel you're a very kind person. Your philosophy is interesting, quite unusual. But if you compare your actions with those of others who are concerned about the soul, about ecology, well, frankly, you're way behind the rest."

"Why should you conclude that?"

"Think about it. All the enlightened people, as you call them, have gone off by themselves at some point. Buddha went off for seven years into the forest and set up a whole doctrinal platform, and he has a lot of followers throughout the world. Christ Jesus went off just for forty days, and even now people are excited about his teachings."

"Christ Jesus went off by himself more than once," Anastasia pointed out. "And he did a lot of thinking when he was travelling about."

"So let's say *more* than forty days, let's say a year even. The elders, who are now considered saints, were ordinary people who went into the forest to live in isolation for a time, then later monasteries were built on these sites, and a lot of followers arose, right?"

"Yes, Vladimir, you are right."

"And here you've been living twenty-six years now in the forest, and you don't even have a single follower. You haven't come up with any platform. And here you're asking me to write a book. You're grasping at that like a straw. You dream of laying out your own combinations of signs in it. Well, if things aren't working out for you like with other leaders, maybe it's not even worth trying. There are others more capable than you who may well think up something without your input. Come on, why not get real and live more simply? I'll help you adapt in our world. Now, you're not offended, eh?"

"No, I am not offended."

"Then I'll tell you the whole truth, right to the end. To help you get a hold of yourself."

"Go on."

"You have some extraordinary abilities, Anastasia, there's no doubt about that. You can pick up any information you want as easily as counting one-two-three. But tell me now, when did you first become aware of that Ray of yours?"

"It was given to me right at the start, as it is to everybody. Only my awareness of it, and how to use it — that was something Great-Grandfather taught me by the time I was six."

"So. That means at six years of age you were already able to see what was going on in our lives? You could analyse situations, help people — even treat illnesses at a distance?"

"Yes, I could."

"Now, tell me, what have you been doing all the twenty years since?"

"I *have* been telling you and showing you. I have been working with the people you call dachniks. Trying to help them."

"All these twenty years, day in and day out?"

"Yes, sometimes even at night, if I was not too tired."

"So, you've been acting like an obsessed fanatic, stubbornly holding on to the dachniks all these years? Who made you do this?"

"Nobody can make me. I did it of my own free will. After Great-Grandfather suggested it to me, I realised for myself what a good thing, how important it was."

"You know, I think your great-grandfather suggested the dachniks to you because he felt sorry for you. After all, you grew up without your parents. He gave you the very easiest and simplest task. Now that he's seen you've begun to understand something greater, he's given you permission to work with other things. And to drop the dachniks."

"But this *other* is connected with the people you call dachniks. And I shall continue to help them. I love them very much and I shall never abandon them."

"Now *that's* what I call fanaticism. There's something in you that you don't have enough of to be a normal person. You must understand that. The dachniks are far from being the most important people in our society. They have absolutely no influence at all over social development. Dachas and vegetable gardens — they're just small subsistence plots. It's where people go to relax after their hard work or when they go into retirement. And that's all. You understand? That's it! And if you, with all your colossal knowledge and phenomenal abilities, are only interested in dachniks, then you must have some kind of psychological disorder. I think I ought to take you to a psychotherapist. If you can get that disorder cured, then just maybe you'll really be in a position to help society."

"I very much want to help society."

"So then, let's go — I'll take you to a practising psycho-therapist at a good private clinic. You yourself said a global catastrophe could happen. This way you'll be able to help ecological movements, you'll be able to help science."

"But I shall be an even greater help if I stay here."

"All right, you can come back here later and start getting involved in more serious issues."

"What do you mean, 'more serious'?"

"You decide. Probably something connected, for example, with heading off an ecological disaster or a global catastrophe. By the way, do you have any idea when the latter might occur?"

"There are localised disasters happening even now in various parts of the Earth. Mankind has been preparing everything and more for its own destruction for a long time now."

"But when will it happen on a global scale — when will the apocalypse come?"

"It might occur in 2002, for example. But it can be prevented, or delayed, as happened in 1992."

"You mean to say it might have come to pass in 1992?"

"Yes, but they delayed it."

"Who are 'they'? Who averted it? Who delayed it?"

"A catastrophe on a global scale in 1992 was averted thanks to the dachniks."

"Wha-a-at?!"

"There are all sorts of people all over the world who are working against global disaster. The 1992 catastrophe did not happen mainly thanks to the Russian dachniks."

"And you... that means you!... Even at six years old you were aware of the dachniks' significance? You foresaw it? You worked non-stop. You helped them."

"I understood the dachniks' significance, Vladimir."

CHAPTER NINE

Dachnik Day and an All-Earth holiday!

"But why Russian dachniks in particular? What's the connection here?"

"You see, Vladimir, even though the Earth is very large, it is very, very sensitive.

"Think of how big you are by comparison with a tiny mosquito. And yet, when a mosquito lands on you, you feel it through your skin. And the Earth also feels — everything. When people pave it over with concrete and asphalt, when they cut down trees and burn the forests growing on it, when they pick and poke at its innards and sprinkle it with powder called fertiliser, it feels the hurt. And yet still it loves people, as a mother loves her children.

"And the Earth tries to absorb into its depths all humanity's anger, and only when it no longer has the strength to hold it back, that anger explodes in the form of volcanic eruptions and earthquakes.

"The Earth needs our help. Tenderness and a loving attitude give it strength. The Earth may be large, but it is most sensitive. And it feels the tender caress of even a single human hand. Oh, how it feels and anticipates this touch!

"There was a time in Russia when the Earth[1] was deemed to belong to everyone and therefore nobody in particular. So

---

[1] *the Earth* (Russian: *Zemliá*) — in this case denoting the land, especially arable land. The reference here is to the early Soviet period of Russian history, when the Bolshevik government took the country's farmland out of

people did not think of it as their own. Then changes came in Russia. They began giving out tiny private plots to people to go with their dachas.

"It was no coincidence at all that these plots were extremely small, too small to cultivate with mechanised equipment. But Russians, yearning for contact with the Earth, took to them with joyous enthusiasm. They went to people both poor and rich. Because nothing can break Man's connection with the Earth!

"After obtaining their little plots of land, people intuitively felt their worth. And millions of pairs of human hands began touching the Earth with love. With their hands, you understand, not with mechanised tools, lots and lots of people touched the ground caressingly on these little plots. And the Earth felt this, it felt it very much. It felt the blessing touch of each individual hand upon it. And the Earth found new strength to carry on."

"So, what now?" I queried. "Should we erect a monument to every dachnik as the saviour of the planet?"

"Yes, Vladimir, they are saviours indeed."

"But that would be far too many monuments! I have it! Why not set up a one- or two-day national holiday? *Dachnik Day,* or *an All-Earth Day,* it could be designated in the calendar."

"Oooh, a holiday!" Anastasia threw up her arms in elation. "What a terrific idea indeed! A celebration! A happy and cheerful holiday — that is something we definitely need!"

"And you with that Ray of yours can suggest to our government, to our deputies in the State Duma,[2] that they pass the required legislation."

---

the hands of its individual peasant owners and declared it state property. It was not until 1993 that the right to private ownership of land was restored in Russia's new Constitution.

[2]*Duma* (pronounced *DOO-ma*) — Russia's national parliament.

"I cannot get through to them. They are too busy with their daily routine. They have so many decisions to make, they have absolutely no time to think. Besides, there is not much point in my attempting to raise their conscious awareness. It would be difficult for them to accept a complete conscious picture of reality. They are not allowed to make any better resolutions than those they are passing at the moment."

"Who can stop the government or the president from so doing?"

"You. The masses. The majority. As for correct decisions, they are what you call 'unpopular measures'."

"Yes, you're right. We have democracy. The most important decisions are taken by the majority. The majority is always right."

"The greatest conscious awareness is always achieved first by individuals, Vladimir. It always takes the majority a space of time to catch on."

"If that's true, then why do we need democracy, referendums?"

"They are needed to serve as a shock-absorber, to avoid sudden jerks. When these shock-absorbers do not work, revolution occurs. A revolutionary period is always a challenge for the majority."

"But a *Dachnik Day?* — that's not revolution. What's wrong with *it?*"

"A holiday like that is fine. It is needed. Definitely needed. It should be set up as quickly as possible. I shall think about how it can be done as quickly as possible."

"I'll help you. I know better which levers to pull in our world for the most effective results. I'll write to the papers... No, better still, I'll write about the dachniks in that book of yours and ask people to send telegrams to the government and the Duma, requesting the establishment of a Dachnik Day as an All-Earth holiday. Only what date should it be?"

"The 23rd of July."

"Why the 23rd?"

"It is an appropriate day. Also because it is your birthday, Vladimir. After all, this fantastic idea is all yours!"

"That's great. So, we'll ask people to send telegrams asking for legislation setting up the 23rd of July as Dachnik Day and an All-Earth holiday. And as soon as the telegrams start arriving at the Duma and people begin to wonder why people are sending them, you burst in with your Ray!"

"Burst in I shall! I shall burst in with all my might! And it will be a fine, bright and beautiful holiday! For everyone! Everyone will have such a good time and the whole Earth will rejoice in its light!"

"Why does *everybody* have to have a good time? This holiday's only for dachniks, isn't it?"

"We must see that *everyone* has a good time. This holiday will indeed begin in Russia. But then it will become the most fantastic holiday for the world as a whole. A marvellous holiday for the soul."

"And how will it be celebrated the first time in Russia?" I enquired. "Nobody will know what to make of it."

"Each one's heart will suggest on that day what he should do and how. I can visualise a general outline right now."

Then Anastasia began talking, clearly enunciating each word. She talked with both speed and inspiration. It was all most extraordinary — the rhythm of her speech, the arrangement of her phrases, the pronunciation of her words:

May all of Russia wake that day at dawn. May people alone, or with friends and family, come to the land and stand upon it with bare feet. Those who have their little plot of land, let them greet with praise the first rays of the Sun amidst the shoots and seedlings they have planted. And touch each species with caressing hands.

As the Sun rises in the sky, let them pick and taste the fruit of their plantings, one from each variety, and that should suffice them up 'til the mid-day meal.

Before the meal let them tend their plots anew. Let each one ponder, their life and joy, and what they are destined to do.

Let each remember their family and friends with love. And ponder why their planted seeds are growing, and designate the purpose of every plant.

And even before the mid-day feast everyone should spend at least an hour by themselves. It is not important how or where or exactly when, but they should be alone for a spell. To spend at least an hour in an effort to look within themselves.

Let the whole family gather for the meal in the middle of the day. Those living at home and those who have come from far away. Let dinner be prepared from what the Earth has borne for the hour of repast. Let every one bring to the whole table whatever is desired by his heart and soul. Let all the family members look each other lovingly in the eye. And let the eldest bless the table together with the youngest. And let the table all around with quiet conversation resound. There should be good words spoken. About all those who sit beside you.

The scene Anastasia described was so extraordinarily vivid that I could feel myself sitting at the table, with people all around. I found myself caught up in the celebration — I was believing in it or, rather, I was participating in it. And I felt led to contribute a feature of my own:

"There should be a toast before dinner. Everyone raise their glass. Let's drink to the Earth, let's drink to love!"

I actually felt I was holding the glass in my hand.

Then suddenly she broke into my reverie:

"Vladimir, please let there be no alcoholic poison on the table."

The glass vanished from my hand.

"Stop it, Anastasia! Don't spoil the celebration!"

"Well, since you have your mind set on it, let there be some wine from berries, but this must be imbibed in very small sips."

"All right, wine it is, then. Just so as not to change our habits all at once. And after the dinner, then what shall we do?"

Let the people return to the cities and towns, having gathered the fruit they have grown on their little plots of ground. Let them bear it in baskets and share it with everyone at home who do not have plots of their own.

Oh, how many positive feelings will come from this day! They will bring about healings of many people's diseases. Diseases which threatened with death and those not erased by time will simply vanish. Let those who are incurably or even slightly ill go out and meet the flood of dachniks returning from their plots. The rays of Love and of good, along with the fruits of their labours will heal diseases.

Look and see! Look at the city's main railway station, where floods of people are arriving with baskets of flowers. Look and see the people's eyes glimmering with kindness, joy and peace.

Anastasia was virtually glowing with a radiance, as she became more and more inspired with the idea of the holiday. Her eyes were no longer merely shining with joy, they were literally sparkling with a pale-blue luminescence. The expression on her face was changing, yet still remained joyful, as though a mighty flood of images of this celebration were rushing through her brain.

All at once she fell silent. Then, bending one leg at the knee and lifting up her right arm, she sprang from the ground with a tremendous recoil, virtually taking flight like an arrow shot from the Earth. She leapt almost as high as the bottom branches of the cedars. Upon landing, she waved her arm, clapped her hands, and a bluish glow flooded the glade. All the words Anastasia now uttered seemed to be echoed by each tiny bug and blade of grass and each majestic cedar. Her voice sounded as though it were being reinforced by a hidden power. Even though her words were not that loud, it seemed as though they could be heard by every vein running through the unfathomable expanse of the Universe.

Mother Russia will greet crowds of guests on that day! They are all of the Earth as Atlanteans born! As prodigal sons they shall return.

On that day, all over Russia, let everyone awake and greet the dawn. Let all the strings of the harp of the Universe make cheerful melody and swell with resonant sound. Let all the bards sing and tell with joyful tongue and play guitars in all the streets, in every yard around. And he who is too old will once again be young, as many, many years ago.

"And I, Anastasia, will I be young once more?"

Both you and I, Vladimir, shall be young, and people will feel young for the very first time. And the old shall write letters to their children. And children to their parents. And infants taking their very first steps on Earth shall enter a better world of joy and mirth. And on that day no child shall feel insulted. For adults shall treat children as their equals.

And all the gods on high will to the Earth descend. And will commend themselves to take on simple forms.

And God Himself, the Universal God will be delighted. May You rejoice too in Love, making all the Earth so bright!

Anastasia was really getting carried away with images of the holiday. She was whirling around the glade in a fiery dance, becoming more and more inspired at every step.

"Stop! Stop!" I cried to Anastasia, suddenly realising that she was taking it all too seriously. She was not merely uttering words. I now realised her every word and novel turn of phrase was actually a visualisation! She was visualising images of the celebration! And with her typical stubbornness she will go on visualising and dreaming about it until the dream turns into reality. Like a diehard fanatic she will dream! She will give her *all* to those dachniks, just as she has done for the past twenty years. And I cried out to stop her:

"What's going on? Don't you understand? All that stuff about a holiday — it's all just in fun! I was just teasing!"

Anastasia suddenly stopped in her tracks. No sooner did I catch a glimpse of her than I felt a big lump in my throat from the look on her face. Her face looked bewildered like that of a child. She looked at me with pain and pity, as though I were an unremitting attacker. And almost in a whisper she started saying:

Vladimir, I took it seriously. I have already visualised it all. And to life's chain of events people's forthcoming telegrams have already interwoven a link. The order of events will be broken without them. I have accepted your words, believed them and brought them to pass. I perceived you were speaking of the holiday and telegrams sincerely. Do not take back the words that you have spoken. Just help me with the telegrams, so that I may, as you said, offer assistance with my Ray.

"Okay, I'll try, only don't panic, — maybe it'll end up that nobody will even want to send the telegrams."

There will be people who will comprehend. They will feel it in the government and in your Duma as well. And a holiday there will be! It will arise! Time will tell! Look here!

And once again celebration images passed before my eyes.

There! — I've written about it. Now you can go and do as your heart and soul dictates.[3]

[3]In 1998, one year after this book was first published in Russian, the governor of St. Petersburg, Vladimir Yakovlev, instituted a *Gardeners' Day*, giving the residents of St. Petersburg and the surrounding region an additional day off to spend on their garden-plots. Since then this example has been followed by many regional authorities and — while not yet instituted on the national level — the holiday is officially celebrated in dozens of cities and regions throughout Russia. The date of the holiday varies from region to region.

CHAPTER TEN

The ringing sword of the bard

"What do you mean, Anastasia, by such extraordinary turns of phrase in speaking about the holiday? You pronounced each word in such a tone that every sound was crystal clear on its own!"

"I tried to reproduce a picture of the holiday with precision, to use detailed images."

"But what about the words? What particular significance do *they* have?"

"Upon each word was borne a multitude of happy pictures and events. And now they will all come true. For thought and word, you understand, are the principle instrument of the Grand Creator. An instrument bestowed not on all that grows with flesh and bones, but just alone to Man."

"Then why doesn't *everything* that people say come to pass?"

"When the thread between the spoken word and the soul is broken, when the soul is found empty and the image dulled, then what is said, though it be plenty, is as empty as chaotic sound. And nothing can it betoken."

"That's sheer fantasy! Come on now, you let yourself believe in everything, like a naïve child."

"How can it be a fantasy, Vladimir?! After all, I could give hundreds of examples from the world you live in, and even from your own life, as to what power a word has when it projects the image connected with it!"

"Then give me an example I can understand."

"An example? Here is one. A person is standing on the stage before an audience and speaking words. An actor, for instance. He will repeat the same words people have heard many times before, but there is only one actor people will listen to with bated breath. Another they will not adore. The words are the same, but there is a vast difference in how they are declaimed. What do you think? Why does that happen?"

"Well, that's actors for you. They spend years studying at drama school — some are outstanding in their profession, others just so-so. They memorise their lines at rehearsals so that they can say them with expression."

"They are taught at drama school, Vladimir, how to get inside the image that underlies the word. Then they try to reproduce that image during rehearsals. And if an actor succeeds in projecting even ten percent of the invisible images underlying the words he utters, the audience will then listen with their whole attention. And if he should succeed in projecting the images behind *half* of his words, you will indeed call that actor a genius. For his soul is speaking directly with the souls of those sitting or standing in the auditorium. And during the play people will laugh or cry as they feel in their soul what the actor desires to convey. Such is the instrument of the Grand Creator."

"And you, whenever *you* speak, with how many words can you project the corresponding image — ten percent, or fifty?"

"With *all* of them. That is the way Great-Grandfather taught me."

"All of them? Really?! All the words?!"

"Great-Grandfather said it is even possible to project the images contained in the letters of the alphabet. And I learnt how to come up with an image for each letter."

"Why letters? Letters don't mean anything."

"Letters *do* mean something! Behind every letter in Sanskrit, for example, there are words, even whole phrases.

There are letters there too, and beyond them many written words, so that infinity is hidden in every letter."

"Well isn't that something?! And we just splutter out our words."

"Yes, that is what happens to words that have been passed down to us over thousands of years. They have passed through and penetrated time and space. And the forgotten images underlying them still today are once more attempting to knock on the door of the human race. And they watch out for our souls, and even go to war on their behalf."

"And what kind of words are these? Is there at least one that might be familiar to me?"

"Of course there is. At least as a sound you have heard. But people have forgotten what underlies these words."

Anastasia lowered her eyelids and sat silent for a while. Then, very quietly, almost in a whisper, she asked me:

"Vladimir, please pronounce the word *bard*."

"*Bard*," I said.

She shuddered, almost as though in pain, and said:

"Oh, the indifference and banality in your pronunciation of that majestic word! You blew a cold gust of emptiness and neglect upon the candle's restless flickering flame. A flame that has been connected through the centuries and possibly even addressed to you or someone else living today by a distant forebear. Forgetfulness of our derivation is the cause of our modern devastation."

"And just what didn't you like about my pronunciation? What should I be remembering in connection with that word?"

Anastasia fell silent. Then in a quiet voice she began uttering phrases straight out of antiquity:

"Long before Christ's birth there lived certain people on the Earth — our forefathers, who were called Celts. Their wise teachers were known as Druids. Many peoples inhabiting the Earth at that time knelt before the Druids' knowledge of the material and spiritual worlds. Not a single Celtic warrior would dare unsheathe his sword in the presence of a Druid. To be awarded the title of Druid even at the starting level, they had to undergo at least twenty years of arduous training at the hands of a spiritual teacher — a Druid priest. Those who were consecrated in this domain were known as *Bards*. They alone had the moral authority to go out among the people and sing about and inculcate the light and truth contained in their song, using words to project images and heal people's hearts.

"The Celts fell subject to attacks by Roman legions. Their last battle took place at a river. The Romans noticed that there were women walking among the Celtic warriors — women with long, flowing hair. Experienced Roman commanders, though knowing what this meant — that they would have to outnumber the Celts six to one in order to defeat them, were unaware of the reason why. Nor do modern historians and researchers have a complete explanation. It all had to do with these unarmed women with their long, flowing hair.

"The Romans surged in with a mighty force, outnumbering the Celts nine to one. Aligned with their backs up against the river, the last family of fighting Celts was on the verge of defeat.

"They stood strong in a semicircle. Behind them was a young woman, breast-feeding a wee baby girl, and singing. The young mother sang a bright and cheerful song, so as not to instil doleful fear in the little one's soul — so that she would be left with images of light.

"Whenever the little one tore herself away from her mother's breast, their eyes would meet. The woman would cease her singing and each time tenderly utter her baby's name: *Barda*.

"Soon there was no longer any semicircle to defend the pair. All that stood between the nursing mother and the flood of Roman legionnaires making their way along the narrow path was a young and blood-gored Bard armed only with a sword. He turned to look at the woman, their eyes met and they smiled at each other.

"The wounded Bard managed to stave off the Romans while the woman went down to the river and put her wee baby girl into a little boat and pushed it away from the riverbank.

"With one last great effort of will-power, the bleeding Bard threw down his weapon at the woman's feet. She took up his sword, and fought for four hours straight with the legionnaires on the narrow path, preventing them from reaching the shore. Their strength became spent and they spelled each other off on the narrow path.

"The Roman commanders looked on in silent astonishment, but could not understand how strong and experienced soldiers could not come close enough to even scratch the woman's body.

"For four bruising hours she fought the flood of Roman attackers. Then the woman's lungs gave out, dried up with dehydration as no liquid had touched her tongue, and drips of blood began oozing from her cracked, beautiful lips.

"Slowly sinking to her knees, her strength waning all the while, she still managed one more faint smile in the direction of the little boat carrying away her wee Barda, a future songstress, downstream with the current. And one more gleam of the word and its image which have been carried down through the millennia for the benefit of many living upon the Earth today.

"Man's being is not only in the flesh. Man's invisible feelings, aspirations and sensations are immeasurably sharper and greater than what can be discerned by the eye or ear. As in a mirror, they are but partially reflected in the visible material state.

"The baby Barda grew into girlhood, and later became a woman and a mother. She lived on the Earth and sang. Her songs imparted to people only bright feelings and, like the all-healing Ray, helped them chase away the gloominess of the heart. Many of life's afflictions and deprivations tried to extinguish the source of this Ray. The hidden forces of darkness tried to break through to it, but could not overcome the one obstacle in their way, the Bard and his wife who stood looming before them on the narrow path.

"Man's essence is not in the flesh, Vladimir. The Bard's bleeding body projected into eternity the smile of his soul's blessed light, reflecting the unseen essence of Man.

"And the lungs of the young mother holding the sword gave out after a while, blood dripped, then poured from the cracks in her lips, which had caught the Bard's bright smile.

"And now, Vladimir, believe in me. Understand and see! And you will hear the ring of the invisible sword of the Bard, beating back the attack of the dark and angry forces on the path to the hearts of his descendants today.

"Now, please pronounce the word *Bard* once again, Vladimir."

"I can't. Not until I can say it with the proper meaning. Then I shall most certainly pronounce it."

"Thank you for not attempting it, Vladimir."

"Tell me, Anastasia — after all, *you* are able to tell. Who among those living today are the direct descendants of that nursing mother and the girl — the songstress Barda? Of the Bard-warrior who stood on the narrow path? Who can forget something as important as his ancestry?"

"Tell me, Vladimir, why this question came to your thought."

"I want to get a good look at that person or persons who have forgot such things. Those who do not remember where they came from. Those without feeling for the same."

"Perhaps you want to make certain that *you* are not the one who is forgetting?"

"Now what does that...? Never mind, Anastasia, I've got it now. You needn't give it another thought. Let each person figure it out for themselves."

"Fine," she replied and fell silent, looking at me.

And I too kept silent for a time, reflecting on the pictures Anastasia had painted, and then I asked her:

"Why did you choose that particular word as an example?"

"To show you how the images underlying it in the real world will soon take visible form. Guitar strings in swarms are now vibrating under the fingers of today's Russian bards. Even back when I was dreaming about it all in the taiga, these bards were the first to feel the images. Their hearts and their souls...

"At first it was only in one of them that flared a flickering burning flame and the delicate resonance of a guitar string, but then the souls of others caught the rhythm and joined in. Soon their songs will be heard by many both near and far. These are the bards who will help us behold the new dawn. The dawn of enlightenment of human hearts and souls. You shall hear their songs. And these will be new songs, songs of the awakening dawn."[1]

---

[1]Since this book was first published in 1997, Russian bards have written *hundreds* of songs inspired by Anastasia. Numerous song festivals have taken place throughout Russia, and multiple song albums have appeared. Many of the bards have become wanderers, travelling in groups of up to fifty singers and giving free concerts all over Russia, spreading the message of light, happiness and the healing of the Earth.

CHAPTER ELEVEN

A sharp about-turn

Returning to the ship after my three-day stay with Anastasia, it was some time before I was in a frame of mind to take charge of company business. At first I was unable either to decide on the ship's next destination or answer the many radiograms coming in from Novosibirsk. And the hired workers, and even some of my crew, apparently sensed my inattention to the daily routine and began stealing. They were arrested by the police from Surgut (the town where the ship was docked) working with my bodyguards, and detention papers were drawn up, but even this was not something I felt like delving into at the time.

It's hard to say at the moment just why my talks with Anastasia had such a strong effect on me.

Before this my firm had received many visits from representatives of all sorts of religious denominations. They claimed they wanted to do something good for society and always asked for money. Sometimes I would oblige just so they would go away, without looking too deeply into the cause they were collecting for. And what was the point of asking them more questions if the conversation always ended up with a request for money?

In contrast to all these so-called 'religious' people, Anastasia never asked for money. In any case, I couldn't even imagine what I could give her. Outwardly it seemed she had nothing, and yet I gradually got the impression that she had everything. I gave orders for the ship to proceed full speed to Novosibirsk and holed myself away in my cabin to think.

My more than ten years' experience in business and team-management had taught me a lot. The highs and lows I had gone through had given me the skills I needed to seek and find a way out of all sorts of tricky situations. This time, however, I felt I was at rock bottom. All the troubles imaginable came upon me simultaneously. The failure of the firm appeared imminent. One of the so-called 'well-wishers' had already started a rumour, now increasing in currency, that something had happened to me and that I was no longer capable of making sound business decisions. So, people concluded, it was *sauve qui peut,* every man for himself. And that's exactly what happened. Upon my return I saw how people were saving themselves. Even my relatives had their hand in it, pilfering what they could from the company. "It's all going to go broke anyway!" they figured.

There was just one small group of my long-time employees who had tried to withstand the onslaught. But after the arrival of the lead ship, upon seeing what kind of literature I had my nose into, even they became worried about my mental state.

I myself had a perfectly clear and sober perspective on what was happening. I was fully aware that I was no longer in any position to manage this team effectively. Even those I had earlier trusted as my tried and true supporters were now starting to cast doubt upon any decision I took.

Even though I very much wanted to tell everyone who would listen about Anastasia, it hardly seemed possible to count on anybody's understanding. It might even land me in the loony bin. My family were already starting to talk about what kind of treatment I needed.

Without saying so in so many words, those around me were demanding I get back down to earth and come up with a business plan, and a successful one at that. They dismissed my latest distraction as either madness or a nervous breakdown.

I had really begun thinking about all sorts of things in this life of ours.

"What's going on here?" I thought. "You hustle through one commercial operation and even earn big money, but where's the satisfaction? You immediately want more. And it's been going on like that for over ten years now! Where's the guarantee that this race won't last my whole life long without so much as a whiff of satisfaction?! One person gets upset because he doesn't have enough money for a bottle of vodka. A billionaire gets upset because he doesn't have enough for some major acquisition or another. Maybe it's not the amount of money that counts?"

One morning two old acquaintances of mine — both entrepreneurs in charge of big commercial firms — came to see me at my office. I started talking with them about setting up a commonwealth of pure-minded entrepreneurs, about the purpose and goals of our business activities. After all, I just had to share all this with *somebody*. They played along, nodding now and then in agreement. It was a long conversation, and I ended up thinking to myself: can it be that they actually grasped it? — they did spend a lot of time discussing it, after all! Later my driver told me:

"You know, Vladimir Nikolaevich,[1] they were *asked* to come and see you. By people concerned about your health. They wanted to know what you've been preoccupied with all this time, what's been on your mind. In short, to make sure you haven't lost your mind. They wanted to know whether they should call in a psychiatrist or simply wait and let it pass."

----

[1]*Nikolaevich* (most often pronounced *ni-ka-LIE-yitch*) — Vladimir Megré's patronymic (a middle name derived from one's father's first name). In Russian the combination of the first name and patronymic is the standard polite form of address among business acquaintances, especially to a superior.

"And what do *you* think of my mental state?"

He fell silent for a while, and then said quietly:

"For ten years your work's gone along just great. Many in the city have said you're a successful businessman. But now all your employees are afraid they may be left without a paycheque."

It was only then I realised the extent of people's concern about me, and I said to the driver:

"Turn the car around."

I went back to the office. I called an emergency staff meeting. I appointed supervisors for the company's various activities and gave them full authority to act in my absence. I then told the driver to pick me up early the next morning and take me to the airport. Just as I was about to go through the boarding gate, he handed me something wrapped in a towel. It was warm. I asked:

"What is it?"

"*Pirozhki.*"[2]

"So, you're giving me these out of compassion for a crazy person, eh?"

"They're from my wife, Vladimir Nikolaevich. She couldn't sleep, and baked all night. She's never baked anything before, she's still a pretty young woman, but last night she plunged right in. She insisted I give them to you. She wrapped them in a towel — they're still warm. She says... you won't be back for a while. If you come back at all... This is good-bye."

"All right, then. Thank you very much."

He resigned from the firm a few days later.

---

[2] *Pirozhki* (pronounced *pee-rash-KEE*) — Russian pastry with a filling, akin to Ukrainian pierogies. A quintessentially home-made dish, *pirozhki* are often the highlights of family gatherings and celebrations. A gift of *pirozhki* denotes a loving attitude on the part of the giver.

Chapter Twelve

Who sets the course?

Seated on the airplane I closed my eyes. The plane's course was set with precision. It was headed for Moscow. The course of the rest of my life was still to be set. But I was thinking more about entrepreneurs.

Many people today still tend to regard entrepreneurs as people who are constantly working out business deals, having amassed their initial capital by some illegal means and multiplying it at the expense of those around them. Naturally, just as in any other segment of our society, there are entrepreneurs and then there are entrepreneurs. However, having been right at the centre of entrepreneurial life in our country from the very beginning of *perestroika*, I can tell you that the majority of the first wave of post-communist entrepreneurs made their initial capital by looking for unorthodox solutions for producing new merchandise or goods which had been in short supply, and finding more efficient ways of structuring manufacturing operations.

It was a peculiar characteristic of Soviet and Russian entrepreneurs to make money from scratch — i.e., starting with nothing, not even credit. After all, the first wave of entrepreneurs had no access to privatised factories that the next wave enjoyed. They had to fly by the seat of their pants and hope they would be lucky. And they did make money from scratch. By way of proof, let me cite an example from my own experience.

CHAPTER THIRTEEN

Money from scratch

Back before *perestroika* I was in charge of a small unit in a photographic collective. It included lab technicians and a number of roving photographers. Everyone had both a salary and additional perks, which allowed us to make a fairly decent living for the time. Each member of our unit received a percentage of the total profits. Naturally we wanted more. But for that we had to find more clients. I managed to hit upon a solution. Anyone who wishes is free to copy it, even today.

One day while I was travelling on a highway in my humpbacked Zaporozhets[1] I got a tyre puncture. While getting the tyre repaired I watched the cars passing by one after another and thought to myself: "If only we could give all these drivers a chance to have their photo taken, there would be huge profits to be made!"

It took but a few minutes to formulate a plan of action in my head — a plan whose realisation in practice would soon quadruple our unit's profits. It worked this way: one of our photographers would stand at the side of the highway with a camera. He had two assistants with green armbands bearing the *SB*[2] insignia and brandishing batons like those used

[1] *Zaporozhets* — a popular and (relatively) inexpensive car manufactured during the Soviet period in the Ukrainian city of Zaporozhye. Its small size, low power, old-fashioned design and proclivity to break-downs have given it a reputation as an "inferior" vehicle, and both the car and its owners have become the butt of numerous jokes.

[2] *SB* — Initials for *Sluzhba byta,* the common designation for service industries in Russia.

by the traffic police. Motorists would stop, thinking it was the "Green" or some other patrol.[3] Upon learning that it was simply a photo service being offered and that nobody was about to pounce on them or fine them or inspect their vehicle, drivers were happy to stand in front of their car (next to the licence plate) and have their picture taken. They gave the addresses where they would like the photos to be sent C.O.D. The licence-plate had to be showing just in case there was a mix-up in the addresses.

We ended up offering this service on all the major highways leading to Novosibirsk over a six-month period. Then more and more we started encountering motorists who had already used the service. But during these six months our unit managed to realise a fairly decent income.

Later I thought of starting a photo campaign to take pictures of residential houses, adding postcard phrases like "I live here", "Home sweet home", etc.

People from our unit took pictures of thousands of houses. The demand turned out to be enormous. It got so that the photographers didn't bother asking which residents wanted it — they would simply walk along and take pictures of every house on the street. A few days later the postal service would deliver the photos to each dwelling and collect payment. People would send these snapshots to their children. Many said the pictures inspired the kids to come home for a visit.

Before long the collective started having problems paying the members of our unit their salaries which, in the opinion of the management of the day, had exceeded all reasonable bounds. But there was little they could do about it, since everyone in the collective was entitled to an equal share of their unit's profits.

[3]*Green patrol* — referring to teams of environmental control officers, set up to help abate air pollution in Russia's largest cities, and responsible for checking automobiles' exhaust emissions (CO, CO_2, CH, NO etc.).

During the early days of *perestroika,* our unit detached itself from the collective and formed an independent co-operative. I was chosen its first chairman.

This way we enjoyed greater freedom of movement. We had the opportunity to gather some seed money together and expand the scope of our operations. I began to think about new ventures to increase company profits.

One day I happened to have a conversation with an acquaintance of mine who worked at the Institute of Theoretical and Applied Mechanics. He was complaining that wages were being delayed or not paid at all, and that the lab unit was being threatened with dissolution. Where could they go, what could they do? They weren't needed by anyone, it seemed.

"What did your lab do before?" I asked him.

"We made thermal gauge tape. Nobody needs it anymore."

"What was it used for?"

"All sorts of things," he replied. He took a piece of a black tape out of his pocket and handed it to me."

"See for yourself," he said.

I took the piece in my hand, and all at once it turned green as I fingered it. I even threw it on the ground.

"What kind of junk is that? It turns green! Now I've got to wash my hands," I told him. To which he replied:

"Don't worry, it simply changed colour from the warmth of your hand. It's supposed to react to changes in temperature. If the temperature of your hands had been above normal, it would have turned red. The green colour indicates a normal temperature."

The concept took off quickly. Our company began producing flat thermometers and stress-indicators.

A piece of the tape was stuck onto a sheet of cardboard with bright coloured squares, each with a number beside it indicating degrees of temperature, and, *presto!* — a new product was born. We had it distributed through the state warehousing agency to many regions of the old Soviet Union (this was before the collapse of the USSR in 1991).

Our production staff increased and everyone made a fairly decent living. Our seed capital was growing. The lab also came out of the red, since a share of the profits accrued to the Institute.

Our co-operative acquired new equipment along with two vehicles. And then something happened which gave us an incredible boost.

One afternoon I arrived at the company office and noticed both our telephones in use. My secretary was on one of them, listening and taking down notes. The other telephone was being manned by the cleaning lady. No sooner had one of the phones been hung up than it started ringing again. At one point my secretary managed to tell me:

"They've been ringing off the hook for over two hours already! One call after another non-stop! Everybody's asking for our thermometers and stress-indicators. One fellow cursed us, calling us pre-*perestroika* dimwits. If we were willing to raise our prices, he said, he would buy them from us wholesale — at the higher price. They're all placing bulk orders. They're even ready to give us advance deposits."

During the early days of *perestroika* in our country, if you remember, there was quite a proliferation of manufactured kitsch on the market — plastic clip-on earrings, posters and calendars featuring semi-nude girls. Everyone snapped these things up like crazy.

Against that background what we produced looked like a super novelty. But after six months of production, sales suddenly took off with a bang. Something had happened, but what?

It turned out that on a TV broadcast the previous night, foreign-affairs correspondent Vladimir Tsvetov was commenting on how innovative the Japanese were, and showed a Japanese stress-indicator as an example. It looked just like ours. It was then that I realised for the first time the power of advertising and the nature of this beast called luck!

Our staff began working three shifts a day round the clock. We hired workers to do the packing, trimming and finishing in their own homes. Profits steadily increased. We acquired a small passenger ship. I also decided to manufacture seeding equipment for independent farmers. I even chartered a large cruise ship to organise business tours and trade expeditions to the regions of the Russian Far North.

CHAPTER FOURTEEN

A destructive force

As head of my very own co-operative I got to know first-hand what a destructive force — one capable of crushing any material state of well-being — impatience toward each other and the break-down of mutual understanding can be. Later I learnt that this is the very reason behind the failure of many collectives. And it can all start over a trifle.

Indeed, that's how it happened with my first co-operative. Not only was it torn apart itself, but several families were destroyed in the process. Even today I still don't know how to counteract this force which erupts spontaneously and is not subject to common sense!

It all began when I decided to procure for our firm a country house with its own estate. I entrusted the details to our acting inventory and supply manager Alexey Mishunin. He drew up all the necessary sale-purchase documents, while I went to take a look at the property. It included a large house, a fifth of a hectare of land, a bath-house, garage and greenhouse. We even got a cow and a flock of sheep in the bargain — not exactly a priority, but Mishunin said the owners had to go away and wanted to sell everything all at once. There was feed for the cow, and he had already arranged for a woman from the village to come in and do the milking.

A couple of days later I called a meeting of the members of the co-operative to tell them about our acquisition. I explained it was intended for entertaining guests, as well as being a place where the members of the co-operative could relax and celebrate special occasions. We would all have to work together to fix up the place, do some renovations and modernise the kitchen.

The male half of the co-operative greeted the idea with great enthusiasm. But the women began whispering among themselves. It wasn't clear who the ringleader was, but my wife took on the role of spokesperson, saying the men had overstepped all recognised bounds of decency in respect to the women.

"We work with you as equals here," she declared. "After that we go home every day and clean house, cook meals and take care of the children. Does that seem trifling to you? And now you want us, in addition to all that, to work our asses off at this country house of yours, do renovations, and then be cooks and waitresses for your receptions and drinking parties?!"

That was when all hell broke loose. The women poured out on the men all their personal and family grievances and other pet peeves. I realised this when one of them cried out:

"All you do is fool around with dominoes and stare at the tube the whole evening long!"

I knew that none of the men at the co-operative played dominoes. It was her husband, a firefighter, who played. He didn't even work for us. But wives of the co-operative workers were especially 'pissed off'. One of them stupidly blurted out to her husband in front of everyone:

"You always smell of sweat and cheap cigarettes," — he was especially fond of the Prima brand — "and now you're going to be smelling of cow-dung too?!"

A silence hung over the room. The husband took a deep gulp of air, blushed and retorted:

"I shall especially smell of cow-dung. Especially so that you won't come near me, you slut!"

At this she burst into tears. The women gathered around to console her. And it made them even more 'pissed off'. They started hurling all sorts of insults. One of our workers was named Zhenya Kolpakov — he'd invented all sorts of devices to increase productivity, and could fix anything that needed fixing. But now they told him:

"We have inventors here, but it takes a whole year to clean up after them!"

Then the discussion turned to politics:

"Gorbachev goes on television, but it's Raisa Maximovna[1] who makes all the decisions."

I declared a recess. I thought everyone somehow might come to their senses. After the break they all took their seats again, the outward restraint barely masking the inner tension. Once again my wife spoke in the name of the women. With a contrived tranquillity she threw out a venomous ultimatum:

"Of course, if you really want a country residence, go ahead, but not one of us women will step foot in it. In other words, it'll be yours alone. And since we share our funds in common and you have no right to spend them without our consent, as compensation we demand you give us one of the company cars with a driver, specially for our household use. We'll take turns using it."

"Great," came a chorus of male voices, "go ahead and choke yourselves! We'll give you anything you like as long as you promise not to show up there!"

"They're bound to find some farm hussies out there," one of the women observed.

"Let them look," retorted another. "Those hussies'll soon make themselves scarce. Who needs them?"

---

[1]*Raisa Maximovna Gorbacheva (née Titorenko;* 1932–1999) — wife of the last Soviet leader (General Secretary of the Communist Party and President of the USSR) *Mikhail Sergeevich Gorbachev* (1931–). In contrast to the wives of Gorbachev's predecessors, Raisa Maximovna played an active role in the political life of the Soviet Union and was rumoured to 'run the country' from behind her husband's back.

None of the men whose wives worked at the co-operative went home that night. It was Friday, and we headed out to our 'hacienda'.

We took a good look around, and started making plans for settling in. The next day we heated up the bath-house. At Mishunin's request the village woman came to milk the cow. We watched how she did it. It was a pleasant time. The cow was quiet, not restless. She was ours now. The woman advised that she wouldn't always be able to come to do the milking. We'd need to look up somebody else.

After an early-evening cleansing at the bath-house, we cooked ourselves supper. It turned out we had quite a feast! Mishunin fried some fish. We put out bottles of beer and vodka, and sat down at the table. And all at once: "Moo-o-oo!"

It was the cow. We got up and headed for the barn. It was milking time, and there was no milkmaid around. We stood there — eight men — in front of the cow and had no idea what to do.

In any case, who can explain what sometimes happens to people at the sight of an animal? You live your life day after day without the slightest thought for non-human creatures. And then all at once you find yourself in a situation where one of them's in your home: a cat, or a dog, or some other animal, and you find you have the same kind of feelings come over you that you'd have in the presence of a child. You're nervous, you worry. Why is that? Maybe it's really true that the first man, Adam, when God gave him the job of naming all the creatures, looked upon each one with *love,* and this love is something we've all inherited — it hides for the most part deep down inside us and makes an appearance only from time to time. Nobody can say for certain whether that's true or not. Only each one of us, I'm telling you, had *some* sort of feeling for that cow, and I'm positive it felt something for us, too.

And this is what came out of it. Seryozha Khodokov said:

"The milk's likely bursting her udder. We've got to do something."

We started in pestering Mishunin. Why on earth, we said, did you buy a cow? And yet at the same time we felt bad about selling it — it had only been one day but we had somehow taken to it like one of our own.

The cow looked at us with her sorrowful eyes, silently. Then she stretched her head out toward me and let out a loud "Moo-o-oo!" She was mooing so pleadingly, and I told Mishunin:

"Better get to the milking right away, since you were the one who bought her!"

Mishunin quickly fetched the milk-pail, tied the kerchief around his head (the kerchief the milkmaid had left behind), and climbed into the cow's stall. He asked us not to leave, as God knows what this cow might do. She let him approach and start milking her. We brought the cow some water to drink, put fresh hay into her stall and gave her some bread.

Mishunin went on milking. At first he wasn't very successful — only very thin streams of milk came out and even they sometimes missed the pail, but then it got a little better. After fifteen minutes the milk was still coming. Mishunin said, whispering for some reason:

"Sweat. My sweat's getting in the way."

"We gathered up handkerchiefs from whoever had them, and Seryozha Khodokov climbed into the stall to wipe the perspiration from Alexey's forehead. He squatted down beside him to see how the milking was going, from time to time wiping the sweat from Alexey's face. And suddenly we could hear Seryozha's agitated whisper:

"What are you doing? You're hurting her! You've got a good stream coming from your right hand, but only a third of that from your left. You can permanently damage her udder that way."

"It's my fingers," Mishunin whispered. "It's 'cause my fingers have gone numb on my left hand. Maybe you'd better help."

Seryozha Khodokov approached the cow from the other side and they began milking together simultaneously.

After half an hour, maybe more, they had milked a whole pailful.

That night at supper we drank fresh milk, and I swear it was the best-tasting milk we'd ever had in our lives.

Early the next morning we were awakened by the milkmaid, who told us with some astonishment that she had tried milking the cow that morning, but for some unknown reason the cow wouldn't let her anywhere close to her.

Once again we trotted off to the barn. We did everything just the way we had the night before, and the cow started milking.

"Well ain't that the limit!" exclaimed the woman. "Since the cow seems to like you so much, *you* can milk her from now on. Happens that way, y'know. A cow can let some people come close, but others she jolly well won't."

Our cow, it turned out, was quite picky. Not only did she not let any of the hired milkmaids near her, whenever she was milked she demanded that one of us stand by her muzzle and feed her, and talk to her, while the milking had to be a joint effort on the part of two men together. That meant three of us had to go for each milking session. So that's how we drew up the schedule — three at a time. At least until we sold the cow, we thought. But it wasn't long before the rumours about our picky cow began flying around. Buyers would come and try milking her themselves, and nothing happened. And they'd refuse to take her, even for a pittance. Granted, I did make one condition — that she wasn't to be slaughtered for meat.

We called in a veterinarian, and he told us:

"That does happen, fellows. An animal gets used to some-one, and may reject others for a long time. But tell me, what on earth possessed you to domesticate her that way?"

He didn't have any real advice to offer us, apart from tell-ing us that our cow was calving — meaning she was pregnant. When the time came we would have to prepare for the birth-ing. The vet indicated the approximate date. We would know when the time was near when she stopped giving milk.

Since the men were obliged to keep watch three at once, we ended up spending a lot of time at our 'hacienda' — even staying overnight there.

Our wives had a hard time accepting that we were really having problems with the cow, since they had sworn never to set foot in our 'hacienda' themselves, and looked upon this whole story of the cow as a convenient excuse. The wom-en and wives working at the co-operative completely lost all sense of self-control. They started telling obscene jokes. The one who complained about her husband's bad smell said:

"Only a sexual pervert could attract such a perverted cow!"

To which he retorted:

"I'd rather spend my whole life milking a silent cow than listening to your dumb remarks."

Soon afterward he moved out completely to live in the 'haci-enda' and later got a divorce from his wife. He married a young country girl with a child and became quite a decent farmer.

Then the day came when the cow stopped giving milk. On the vet's advice we got everything ready for the birthing. But the cow gave birth all by herself and without incident. She bore a little bull-calf. A handsome son-of-a-gun. When we called the vet, he took one look at the pair and said:

"Well, that's great! Nothing more to be done here. She's taken care of it all by herself. Just keep the place clean. Make sure she's well fed."

Some time later we managed to find a good home for both the cow and her bull-calf. One day we went over to see what a handsome creature he'd turned into, our little bull. And everything was arranged nicely for his mother. Even now I still think of her. I wonder whether she remembers us. But while we got things settled for the cow, we didn't manage to restore a sense of harmony and mutual understanding in the co-operative.

So I ended up dividing the co-operative in two, reorganising part of it under a different name. I began using the chartered ship to make long trading voyages to the North along the River Ob. In between such voyages I conducted business cruises for Russian and foreign entrepreneurs.

I took the lesson home that one indispensable condition of success, among others, is a sense of mutual understanding and respect in a collective. You must have faith not only in your own abilities but in everyone's. Any kind of ability you have is multiplied by your faith in the people around you.

CHAPTER FIFTEEN

'Herbalife' entrepreneurs

It was only upon arriving at Moscow's Vnukovo airport that I realised my funds were rather low — I had only 5 million roubles ($1,000) left, and I did not even have a specific plan of action. It was hardly likely that either my employees or my family would be able to cope with my accumulated debts; they would have to sell the company's assets, meaning I could not look to home for any assistance. Had I remained in Novosibirsk, of course, I could have worked things out. But that would have meant concentrating all my attention on the daily affairs of my business — something that was impossible after what had happened in the taiga and the promises I had made both to Anastasia and to myself.

Indeed, by this time it was hard to determine whether my actions were being guided by my own awareness and desire or by Anastasia's influence.

One thing was crystal clear: I was bankrupt. Having witnessed countless similar situations among my colleagues, I knew there was nobody I could turn to — either friends, relatives, or former employees. They would all avoid you like the plague. You can spend ten years of your life being a hero and then just one little mistake can put you in the doghouse and make you a non-person, despised by everyone you know. It's happened to a lot of prominent entrepreneurs. In a situation like this you can only hope in yourself and your own ability to find a way out of a dead-end predicament.

After leaving my bag (containing a sweater, some shirts and a few other trifles) at a hotel, I started tramping around the streets of Moscow. I tried figuring out what it all meant — everything Anastasia had said about Russia's entrepreneurs.

The first thing that struck my eye in Moscow this time was the activity of the so-called 'Herbalifers'.

Neatly dressed people stood in the tunnels leading to metro[1] stations in the city centre, haranguing passers-by with job offers. "With a foreign firm," as they said. They were luring them with promises of huge earnings and opportunity for promotion. The word *Herbalife* wasn't even mentioned — probably because almost every classified advertisement in the papers posted by a job-seeker ended with the words: "No Herbalife offers."

Still they stood there, wearing "Work for you" buttons and handing out flyers from some foreign firm, stubbornly urging people to at least come for an interview. Later I learnt that those responding were subjected to intense psychological conditioning, with special emphasis on two points dear to the heart of the average Russian.

First, seminar speakers would make a big thing of telling how they or their relatives, for example, received a fantastic healing with the help of this 'Herbalife' from overseas, with the implication that any potential distributor could also engage in the noble practice of treating people's ailments. The system was so miraculous, they declared, that no medical courses were needed, just two or three training sessions, even if you were a simple painter or plasterer, and, presto, you are qualified to act as a consultant to ailing consumers.

Secondly, they made a point of telling stories with examples of how one could get rich through promoting and distributing 'Herbalife' products. This meant buying at least one package for starters (with your own money), then finding someone

---

[1]*metro* — i.e., the *Metropolitan,* referring to the underground or subway system operating in Moscow and many other Russian cities.

else and convincing him in a one-on-one conversation of the fantastic benefits of using 'Herbalife', then selling it to him at a slightly higher price. At the same time you needed to keep recruiting more distributors, getting a percentage from each new recruit. The more recruits you attracted, the higher you would rise in the hierarchy and the more money would accrue to you. You would reach a point where you yourself wouldn't have to do any of the actual distribution work.

As an entrepreneur, I soon realised one thing very clearly: money *did* come showering down in a rain of gold, but only for the person at the very top of this pyramidal system and his closest collaborators. The whole long chain of distributors, divided into so-called levels, survived only thanks to each level benefiting from its own price mark-up, and it was all paid for by the one at the very bottom — the consumer who believed in the miracle properties of the product.

In some cases the price increased by twelve times!! The actual distribution keeps rolling along non-stop, thanks to the huge number of agents using their own accounts of healing to win the trust of their fellow-Russians and make them believe in the miracle properties of 'Herbalife'. A system like this is capable of selling even the ashes from one's stove. Any complainers are simply told that they have somehow misunderstood the instructions on the label or not followed them closely enough.

This system is especially effective in our country, where people are accustomed to getting the most reliable information from trusted friends and acquaintances rather than through official channels.

There is no point whatsoever in discussing the advantages or disadvantages of the 'Herbalife' products themselves. That is a long story. I can say only one thing with absolute certainty: all the fervour of the distributors telling about their own healings disappears as soon as they realise they're not going to get any money from you. In that case you'll start hearing a whole string of counter-examples, such as "It's nothing but a load of crap!"

This distribution system was invented in the West. Managed from the West, it lures in all sorts of unemployed Russians. But these are not *our* entrepreneurs. And now I shall tell you of yet another gimmick invented by Western businessmen.

CHAPTER SIXTEEN

Free holidays in Hawaii

If you should be stopped on a crowded Moscow street by smartly dressed young people (some of whom speak with an accent) inviting you to a presentation by a foreign firm with your own reserved table and free lottery tickets, offering you the opportunity to win a gold watch or even a free trip to Hawaii, you can be sure that you will be guaranteed a free trip. But it is best to bear in mind the old saying: "The only free cheese is in a mousetrap."

It's not hard to figure out just how this particular mousetrap works.

What you get 'for free' is the opportunity to stay in elegant lodgings. Upon arriving you discover that they really do look like the photos in the brochures. The catch is, you have to pay for the airline ticket, your food and all the 'incidentals'.

A few days into your stay you realise that this 'free' vacation is ending up costing you quite a bit more than the full price of a stay at some other comparable resort. It's all very simple: your 'free stay' is paid for by a host of surcharges on a range of food and other services. These surcharges cover, by the way, the agents standing on the street-corners and the so-called 'free' presentation, the colour brochures they hand you, not to mention the company's profit.

Of course, for those with lots of money to spare, it doesn't make too much difference. The only bad thing you might feel is the unpleasant sensation of being made a fool of. It is quite a different matter when an average Russian wage-earner of modest means, one who has spent a whole year saving for such a trip, takes the bait and, instead of going to see his mother or for a holiday at a Russian resort, hands over his hard-earned savings to these foreign smart-asses and like a fool spends two weeks in lodgings designed for fools like him.

Gentlemen from abroad, where did this attitude of disrespect for us Russians come from? As I was looking at the sales kiosks on our streets filled with imported goods, even imported bottled water, I remembered how it had been the same way on my ships, but back then I had never really thought about what was behind it. I was listening to radio reports about the suspicious quality of the chicken legs on sale all over the country, as well as about bottled water with fancy labels promoting its healing mineral properties, belying the fact that this stuff, sold in our stores, was simply tap water with suspicious additives. I was noticing the huge number of signs advertising how you could refresh your strength with a 'hot dog', as if all of Moscow and even all of Russia had suddenly made these rubber sausages their national dish, and wondering why this had never struck me before as it did now.

I remembered the respect and enthusiasm with which we'd greeted visiting entrepreneurs from abroad at the beginning of *perestroika*. I remembered how I'd organised business cruises down the River Ob for them on my ship, and how the Siberian entrepreneurs tried as hard as they could to provide them with the highest-quality service. Of course not all the visitors were the same, but what did we gain in the long term?

So, where are you, entrepreneurs of Russia? The ones that should be making our country flourish?!

Chapter Seventeen

The beginning of perestroika

At the very beginning of *perestroika,* when the first law on co-operatives in the USSR was enacted, many saw it as a call to action. And a lot of young people, as well as many not so young but invariably full of energy and desire to really do something for themselves and their country, literally threw themselves into the fray. And immediately found themselves surrounded by a hostile, pestering crowd.

"Down with them!" the crowd shouted. "Bourgeois smart-asses! What did we fight for, anyway?"

And even though many of Russia's pioneer entrepreneurs ended up working round the clock, pouring in a colossal amount of energy, not to mention their unique wit and inventiveness, hardly any of their efforts met with so much as a 'thank you'. The modicum of support they required was usually provided only by intercommunication and interaction with each other.

Then a concept was born — it literally came out of thin air — the idea of creating a Union of USSR Co-operators. I was part of the pilot group initiating the project, along with the well-known Russian entrepreneur Artem Tarasov.[1]

---

[1] *Artem* [pronounced: *art-YOM*] *Mikhailovich Tarasov* (1950–) — a prominent Russian entrepreneur, one of the first Soviet 'co-operators'. An engineer by profession, in 1989 he proclaimed himself the first legal millionaire in the USSR, and the following year he was elected as a deputy of Russia's Supreme Soviet (nominal Parliament). He founded dozens of business ventures, including Russia's leading business newspaper *Kommersant* and the *Transaero* airline. After years of suppression by the state, Tarasov emigrated to London. In 2004 he published a book of memoirs entitled *The millionaire*, exposing the corruption of Russia's ruling élite.

Most of us at the time were Communists. At the first entrepreneurs' congress I was elected secretary of the congress's Party Committee. I tried to explain to our overseer from the Communist Party Central Committee, Comrade Kolosovsky, that it was incredibly difficult for entrepreneurs to work under such pestering. We needed first and foremost the Party's moral support. But I soon realised that we were going to be facing hostility and pestering from a segment of the ordinary public, as well as high- and low-ranking officials, for a long time to come. We could not look to the higher echelons of the Central Committee for any outward show of support, since they were afraid of losing popularity — already their power was greatly diminished compared to the heyday of Soviet communism. An internal struggle had apparently begun and was now in full swing.

In addition, entrepreneurs had begun to feel mounting pressure from a tax squeeze. And today, with maybe one or two exceptions, not a single business can keep afloat if it dutifully pays all the required taxes. Realising this, many of them have managed to escape the tax squeeze by using all sorts of tricky loop-holes. But in doing this they have landed themselves in an even more precarious situation — being outside the law. Attempt after attempt to make officials on various levels see the absurdity of the prevailing tax system have not exactly been crowned with success. Indeed, they could not be, since the ones who initiated the system (and this is my own personal assumption) understand better than anyone else the impossibility of paying all the taxes, but this was exactly what they needed. Needed for what? For power, of course! For extortion!

One false step and you can be instantly ground to powder, outlawed by tax police and inspectors.

I felt sorry for the first entrepreneurs of *perestroika*, as well as for Russia's current crop of businessmen. I decided to do for them whatever lay within my powers. I went to the League of Russian Co-operators and Entrepreneurs, originally headed by Vladimir Alexandrovich Tikhonov,[2] whom we had elected to the post in *perestroika*'s early days. The League's executive Presidium still maintained a headquarters, but many of the offices were empty. Vladimir Alexandrovich had died a year and a half earlier. I was told that the Chairman of the Russian Business Round Table, Ivan Kivilidi,[3] had been poisoned, together with his secretary, just six months ago. Artem Tarasov had resigned from the League, and the organisation's membership was only a shadow of its former self.

Thanks to my acquaintance with one of three remaining League executives, my request for space in one of the empty offices was granted, along with two telephones, a computer and a fax machine. Since the League had no organisational funds available, I was pretty much on my own. To save time and hotel expenses, I used the office for my sleeping quarters as well. I was awakened every morning at six o'clock by the arrival of the cleaning lady, and the absence of a TV allowed me to work most evenings right up 'til midnight. This sudden shift in living conditions — from a luxury ship's cabin (where anything I wanted to eat or drink was only a bell ring away) to a drab office not designed for living accommodation — in no way embarrassed me. In many respects it actually afforded me greater opportunities to pursue my work.

[2] *Vladimir Alexandrovich Tikhonov* (1927–1994) — academician of the Lenin Agricultural Academy and co-author of the innovative legislation on Russian co-operatives mentioned above.

[3] *Ivan Kharlampievich Kivilidi* (1949–1995) — an entrepreneur of Greek descent, at one time said to be the richest man in Russia. Kivilidi was an outspoken advocate of political and economic reform. In 1993 he founded an influential "Russian Business Round Table" to forward the interests of Russian entrepreneurial élite in the political arena. The poison which killed him and his secretary was delivered by a breath-activated substance placed in his office telephone receivers.

I spent my time thinking out and drafting a constitution for a Fellowship of Entrepreneurs, along with compiling letters of appeal — these I sent out by fax in the early hours of the morning, when the communication lines weren't as busy. By hook or by crook, making use of both newspaper adverts and chance encounters, I gathered together a secretariat of various Moscow professionals who shared my enthusiasm for the project and realised its significance.

The secretariat also included three Moscow university students. First there came Anton Nikolaikin, who had been called in to fix a broken computer. Later, after learning of our work on organising the Fellowship, he brought along two of his friends, Artem Semenov and Alexey Novichkov. They immediately began work on encoding the electronic version of the *Golden Catalogue of Russia,*[4] for which they were able to put together a highly professional computer programme.

---

[4]*Golden Catalogue of Russia* (in Russian: *Zolotoi katalog Rossii*) — a reference to the Fellowship's proposed directory of member enterprises.

Chapter Eighteen

Fellowship of Russian entrepreneurs

The idea of a Fellowship meant that it would be open to any entrepreneurs who had been active in the Russian market for at least a year, and were sincerely striving to develop honest relationships not only with each other but with their clients and employees. Representatives of various non-profit societies tried to persuade me that today's entrepreneurs were cool to the idea of any form of organisation, that the age of faith-based euphoria had passed, and that membership in societies one could join simply by paying a modest fee had diminished catastrophically. They argued, furthermore, that the idea of organising a Fellowship with additional requirements involving the ethical standards of both the entrepreneur and the enterprise was simply absurd.

My old friend Artem Tarasov, having heard about my arrival in Moscow and what I was up to, came to one of the 'round tables'. He set to work on drafting documents, including an appeal to entrepreneurs. He laid out several thousands of dollars so I could make up glossy brochures to give out to delegates at a small-business congress[1] being organised in Moscow.

[1] *small-business congress* — a reference to the First All-Russian Congress of Small Business Representatives held on 19–21 February 1996 in the prestigious Kremlin Palace of Congresses in Moscow. This high-profile event, organised by several government agencies and the Chamber of Commerce of the Russian Federation, featured an address by Russian president Boris Yeltsin. To the entrepreneurs' disappointment, however, many of the promises of government support to small business voiced during the congress were never fulfilled.

But the congress organisers decided not to allow any brochures on the Fellowship to be handed out, no doubt fearing competition from us. As a result, secretarial staff and students positioned themselves just outside the entrances to the Rossiya Hotel,[2] trying to hand delegates folders containing the brochures. They stood there withstanding both the cold and attempts to chase them away by the militia, who thought some kind of illegal selling might be taking place. Artem Tarasov still managed to take a package of brochures into the Kremlin Palace of Congresses, where the congress was being held — though, unfortunately, only a rather small quantity.

The operation we had placed so many of our hopes on ended in failure. Organising the Fellowship was proving to be an impossibility. The difficulty was that getting the necessary information out to all the entrepreneurs across the country required a huge outlay of roubles on printing and postage costs, since favourable responses were coming in from only ten percent of the people we managed to reach. The required funds were simply not available.

Besides, the League executive kept back a portion of the membership fees as office-space rent, as they had no other source of funds. Sensing some sort of snag, the League stopped giving out money for organisational expenses altogether, in spite of the fact that the membership fees had been specifically earmarked for organisational expenses.

The League needed to use the entrepreneurs' membership fees just to cover operating costs, they explained. Then they began holding back wage payments for the secretarial staff. I was obliged to vacate the League's premises, leaving behind my second computer which had been purchased with funds from the entrepreneurs who had joined the Fellowship.

---

[2]*Rossiya Hotel* — a large hotel complex in downtown Moscow, across from the Kremlin and Red Square, overlooking the Moskva River.

"How come?" queried the students in bewilderment — students who had spent hours working out computer programmes at their own expense. "We've been doing the work which this non-profit organisation, according to its own constitution, is supposed to carry out, and here they're treating us like tenants, and spitting on the entrepreneurs in the process."

The League executive argued: "The office rent must be paid."

With what was left of the secretarial staff, I tried to carry on the work out of one of the entrepreneurial trades union offices, but the same situation repeated itself there.

After getting to know the leaders of several non-profit organisations, I suddenly realised that they all had titles, but no membership, something like the so-called 'sofa parties',[3] existing only for the benefit of their executives. While this was not true of the Farmers and Peasants Association, headed by Vladimir Bashmachnikov (and there may be other exceptions), this was the general state of affairs at the time.

Even today there is no non-profit organisation in Russia bringing together any significant number of entrepreneurs, and those that do exist are of the 'sofa party' variety. Why? Among the possible causes I would include the anonymity of membership fees.

For some reason it always happens that once an executive body is created, it starts making decisions on behalf of entrepreneurs without consulting the majority.

Walking away from the trades-union office, I now found myself without any means of communication and without anything to live on. Artem Tarasov had by this time emigrated to London. He had tried to get himself on the ballot for the

---

[3] *sofa parties* (in Russian: *divannye partii*) — political parties (or non-profit societies) with the trappings of a registered organisation, but created merely to advance the interests of one individual or a small group.

Russian presidency and had spent billions of roubles collecting the required signatures, but when the Central Election Committee invalidated most of those signatures, Artem was obliged to look after repairing his own financial affairs.

The local residents working in the secretariat, not receiving any pay, were obliged to quit.

I was left all alone. Or rather, I thought I had been left all alone. But three Moscow students weren't about to abandon the work they had started: Anton, Artem and Lyosha. Anton actually used his own holiday savings to pay the monthly rent on an apartment for me. They were willing to wait until I sought and found a way out of my present circumstances and could continue my work on creating the Fellowship. They had got caught up by the whole idea. They believed in it. But I could see nothing ahead but a dead end.

It was right at this time that some news arrived from Novosibirsk.

CHAPTER NINETEEN

Suicide?

One evening a man from Novosibirsk dropped by to see me. He was in Moscow on some business of his own. He brought along a bottle of vodka and some light snacks. We sat in the kitchen of my one-room flat, and he told me about how things stood with my family and my company.

The situation was indeed deplorable. My firm had had to give up one of its offices in the centre of the city for lack of funds to pay the rent. Our automobile spare-parts store had had to close. The workers there tried selling shoes, but their debts only increased. The entire responsibility fell on my shoulders.

"And here you're up to goodness-knows-what. A lot of people are saying you've gone mad. You should have worked out things at the company first and then gone off and done your own thing, whatever it is. Nobody there has faith in you any more."

As we were finishing off the bottle, he asked me:

"You want me to tell you my honest opinion — what they expect of you?"

"Go ahead," I replied.

"They would like you to do away with yourself, or at least disappear for good. You be the judge — it's impossible to start anything now without any seed capital, and here not only do you not have any seed capital, you don't even have enough to live on. And your debts have been building up like crazy.

"You know, nobody's ever heard of someone climbing out of a hole like that. But with you out of the picture, your death will settle everything, and they can divide up what's left of your estate.

"Your wife says that according to the horoscope you're a Leo, and you've just been wasting your whole life away, so you *should* die in poverty, just like in the horoscope.

"Come on, now, why did you undertake that second expedition? Nobody can figure it out."

In spite of the fact that we were both pretty drunk, when I awoke the next morning I had a clear recollection of the whole conversation. His arguments were forceful and convincing. Novosibirsk was a dead end; there was a dead-end situation here in Moscow too. People who had worked alongside me were suffering, my family was suffering. I couldn't possibly find a way out and fix everything — there was simply no way out. Only my death could put an end to the suffering.

Of course suicide is never the right thing to do. But according to the logic of events, my suicide would relieve the suffering of others, and if that was the case, then he was right, and I had no right to live. And so I decided to do away with myself. The thought of it even brought comfort to me. I was freed from the need to undertake a torturous search for a way out of my present situation, since I agreed that death *was* the way out.

I cleaned up the apartment a bit and wrote the landlady a note to say I wouldn't be back. I decided to go to the trades-union office to put the Fellowship files in order. Someone — okay, maybe not now, but later, perhaps — would carry on with the work.

The only question was: how would I do away with myself when I didn't even have enough money to buy the poison? Then I really began thinking: maybe it shouldn't *look* like suicide... Maybe I'll go take a dip in the river, just like the 'walruses',[1] and I'll jump through a hole in the ice and drown. So I headed off toward the Moskva River.

---

[1] *walruses* — the name given to the many hardy souls who brave the icy waters of Russia's lakes and rivers in the middle of winter (akin to 'Polar Bears' in Canada and America).

As I was making my way through an underground passage-way at the Pushkinskaya metro station, my ear all at once caught a familiar melody. It was being played by two young girls on their violins. An open violin-case lay on the pave-ment in front of them and passers-by were tossing in money. A lot of buskers make extra money like that at metro stations. But the way these two girls were playing their sweet melody amidst the bustle of noisy pedestrians and the screeching of trains in the background caused many a passer-by to slow down and listen. As for me, I couldn't help but stop dead in my tracks. The violin bows were echoing a melody I had heard only once before — in the Siberian taiga — a melody sung by Anastasia.

Back there in the taiga, I had once asked her to sing some-thing of her own — a song I'd never heard before, and she came out with this extraordinary, unusual captivating melody with-out words. She started by screaming like a newborn baby. Then her voice began sounding ever so quiet and tender. She stood beneath a tree, her hands clasped to her breast, and it seemed as though her voice was a lullaby, gently caressing a little baby, trying to tell him something. Her voice was so quiet it caused everything around to be still and listen. Then she seemed to be filled with delight at the little one waking from sleep, and her voice took off with rejoicing. The incredibly high-pitched sounds and cascading trills soared and took flight to the heav-ens, radiating through space and delighting all around...

I asked the girls:

"What were you playing?"

They exchanged glances and one of them said:

"I was just sort of improvising."

And the other chimed in:

"And I was just playing along."

Here in Moscow, caught up as I was with the idea of set-ting up the Fellowship of Entrepreneurs, which had become the main focus of my life, I had almost completely forgotten about Anastasia. And now, on the last day of my life, as though to say farewell, here she was reminding me of her existence.

"Please, play some more, the way you were playing before!" I asked the girls.

"We'll try," the older one replied.

And there I stood in the metro station passageway, listening to the captivating melody of the violins and remembering the glade in the taiga and thinking:

Anastasia! Anastasia! It's much too complicated to make all that you thought up come true in real life. It's one thing to dream — quite another to turn the dream into reality. Some sort of mistake must have crept in as you were working out your plan: organise a fellowship of entrepreneurs, write a book...

I felt as though a flood had hit me. Repeating these last two phrases over and over again, I felt there was something out of place there, something wasn't right. Back there in the taiga — in the taiga... the words had been spoken not quite the same way, but how? How else could they have been said? As I continued repeating them, I happened to switch the word order and heard myself saying: "Write a book, organise a fellowship of entrepreneurs."

But of course! The book should have been written *first!* The book was supposed to settle all these questions and, most importantly, spread *information* about the fellowship! Yikes, how much time I realised I'd wasted and, in the meantime, look at how complicated my personal life had become!

All right, then. *I'll get busy,* I thought. At least now it's clear just what I should be busy *at.* It's absurd, of course — someone who doesn't know how to write, writing a book, especially one he expects people to actually read! But Anastasia had faith it would work out. She kept trying to convince me. Okay. That means I've really, *really* got to try now. And I've got to see it through to the end!

CHAPTER TWENTY

The Ringing Cedars of Russia

I decided to go back to my apartment. Moscow was already feeling the touch of spring. All that remained in the kitchen was half a bottle of sunflower-seed oil and some sugar. I needed to replenish my larder and decided to sell my winter *shapka,*[1] which was made of mink. It was a real mink hat, not imitation, and cost a great deal.

Of course, the winter weather was almost over now, but I thought I might get at least something for it, so I headed for one of Moscow's many outdoor markets. I went up to various merchants selling fruit and other goods. They looked at the *shapka,* but were in no hurry to buy it. I had already decided to lower the price when two men approached me. They turned the *shapka* over in their hands, feeling the fur.

"I need to try it on. Go see if you can borrow a mirror somewhere," one of them said to his companion and suggested I follow him off to one side.

We reached a secluded spot at the end of a row of stalls and stopped to wait for his companion with the mirror. We didn't have to wait long. He crept up stealthily from behind, and the blow on the back of my head first caused me to see stars, then my whole vision went blurry. I managed to grab hold of a fence to stop myself from falling to the ground, but when I came to, my 'buyers' were nowhere to be seen. The *shapka,*

---

[1]*shapka* — a warm fur hat, often with ear-flaps (tied up on top when not too cold); the commonest form of headgear during Russian winters.

too, was gone. Only a couple of women were there, making sympathetic *oohs* and *ahs*.

"Are you okay? Awful bastards, those. Here's a crate — you can sit down for a bit."

I stayed standing against the fence for a while longer and then slowly made my way out of the market area. A spring drizzle was falling. I was about to cross a street and stopped on the kerb to look both ways. There was a painful ringing in my head. I wasn't watching, and a passing car sprayed me with water from a puddle, thoroughly wetting my trousers and windbreaker flaps.

I was trying to figure out what to do next when a truck whizzed by, covering me with more spray from the same puddle, and this time the spray flew right into my face. I stepped back from the kerb and took refuge from the rain under the awning of one of the commercial kiosks, and tried to think my next plan of action.

There was no way, I realised, I could get into a metro station looking like this. It was three stops to my apartment. Sure I could walk it, but the way I looked I still might get picked up by the police, thinking I was a drunk, or a tramp, or just a suspicious person. Then you stand there, trying to explain and justify yourself while they investigate your case. What could I tell them anyway? Who am I now?

And then I saw this man.

He was shuffling slowly along the sidewalk, carrying two cases of empty bottles. He looked like one of those tramps or boozers who often circulate among kiosks that sell spirits on tap. Our eyes met. He stopped, put down his cases on the sidewalk and struck up a conversation with me.

"What are you standing there looking at? This is *my* territory. On your way!" he said quietly, though not without an air of authority.

Not wanting to argue with him or cross him — indeed, not

having the strength to do so, I replied:

"I don't need your territory. I'll just gather myself together and leave."

But he continued:

"And where will you go?"

"None of your business where I'm going. I'll just leave. That's it."

"And will you make it?"

"I'll make it, if I'm not interfered with. Leave me alone!"

"The way you look you won't either stand very long or walk very far."

"What's that to you?"

"You haven't got a home to go to?"

"What?"

"A novice, eh? Okay, wait here a moment."

He picked up his cases and walked off. He came back a moment later with a wrapped parcel and again started speaking to me.

"Follow me."

"Where are we going?"

"To a place where you can rest for a couple of hours, or maybe 'til morning. You can get yourself dried out. Then you can proceed on your way."

Following after him, I asked:

"Is your apartment close by?"

Without turning his head he responded:

"You couldn't get to my 'apartment' if you walked your whole life long. I don't have any apartment. I have my 'deployment quarters'."

We walked up to a door leading to the basement of a multistorey block of flats. He told me to stand over to one side while he looked around, waiting until none of the tenants were to be seen, then stuck something that looked like a key in the lock and opened the door.

It was warmer in the basement than on the street. Heat came from hot-water pipes which had been deliberately stripped of their insulation, probably by tramps. On the floor in one corner stood a pile of rags, illuminated by a dim light filtering in through a dust-covered basement window. But we went on past them into a far corner which stood empty.

He unwrapped the parcel and brought out a bottle of mineral water and uncapped it. Taking a swallow of water in his mouth, he sprayed it all around, as though from an atomiser.

"That's to keep the dust down!" he explained.

Then he slightly moved a divider standing in the corner to one side. From the narrow space between the divider and the wall he took out two sheets of plywood covered with plastic, along with several pieces of plastic-covered cardboard. He used them to lay out two makeshift bunks on the floor. Taking an old food tin from the corner, he lit the candle it was holding. The lid of the tin was not completely detached; it was clean and bent slightly upward in a semicircle to serve as a reflector. This primitive device illuminated the edges of the bunks and the half-metre of space between them. Here he spread out a sheet of newspaper, on which he started laying the contents of the parcel — cheese, bread and two packages of *kefir.*[2]

Neatly slicing the cheese, he issued an invitation:

"What are you standing there for? Come on, sit down. Take off your jacket, hang it over the pipe. When it dries out, we'll clean it. I've got a brush. Your trousers will dry out without taking them off. Try not to wrinkle them."

Then he brought out two drams[3] of vodka, and we sat down to eat. In contrast to the dirty basement floor all around us, the corner my companion had managed to set up for himself had an air of cleanliness and coziness.

---

[2]*kefir* — a popular drink made of thick fermented cow's or goat's milk, often sold in cardboard packages.

After we clinked glasses, he introduced himself:

"Call me Ivan. Nobody here bothers with patronymics."

The way he improvised the bunks and set out the food on the newspaper, despite the dirty floor, created a clean and cozy atmosphere in his basement corner.

"I don't suppose you have anything softer to lie on?" I asked after supper.

"You can't even keep rags down here — they only get dirty, and then they start to smell... I've got neighbours over in that corner. Two of them... they show up from time to time. They've made one hell of a dirty mess."

We got involved in conversation. I started answering his questions, and in doing so I ended up inadvertently telling him about my meeting with Anastasia — her lifestyle and her abilities — about her ray, her dreams and aspirations.

He was the first person I had talked with about Anastasia! I myself don't know why I told him about all her eccentricities, about her dream and how I promised to help her. I had indeed tried to set up a fellowship of pure-minded entrepreneurs, but had made a major mistake. I should have written a book first.

"Now I'll set about writing one and try to get it published," I affirmed. "Anastasia said the book would be needed first."

"Are you really confident you can write it and get it published without any funds?"

"I don't know whether I'm confident or not. But I shall certainly work in that direction."

"That means you have a goal, and you're going to go for it?"

---

[3]In the mid-1990s 'drams' of vodka were actually sold in what appeared to be plastic yoghurt cups, complete with a metal foil cover. This packaging enabled heavy drinkers to dispense with the need for a glass or to find a co-drinker to split the cost of a bottle, and thereby gained tremendous popularity.

"I'm going to try."

"And you're sure you'll make it?"

"I'm going to try."

"Yeah, a book. You'll be needing a good artist to do the cover. Someone who can do it with heart. In line with the meaning of the book, with the goal. And where're you going to find an artist if you haven't got any money?"

"I'll have to do without an artist. Without a fancy cover."

"You should do it up brown, with a cover that really fits in with the book. If I had good paper, brushes and paints, I'd help you. Only those things cost a lot now."

"You mean to say you're an artist? Professional?"

"I'm an officer. But I've loved drawing and painting since childhood. I joined various art groups. Whenever I could steal some time, I'd paint pictures and give them to friends."

"Well, why did you go and become an officer if you still wanted to paint all these years?"

"My great-grandfather was an officer, my grandfather and my father too. I loved and respected my father. I knew — I felt — what he wanted me to be. So I tried to be that. And I made it all the way to colonel."

"Where did you serve?"

"Mainly in the KGB. That's where I resigned from."

"Through attrition or were you forced out?"

"It was my decision. Just couldn't take it any more."

"What couldn't you take?"

"You know the popular song: *Oh officers, officers, your heart is under fire.*"[4]

---

[4] *Oh officers, officers, your heart is under fire* (in Russian: *Ofitsery, ofitsery, vashe serdtse pod pritselom*) — from an extremely popular song written by singer-songwriter Oleg Gazmanov (1951–) in 1994, which stayed several years at the top of the charts. The song extols the virtue of soldiers defending their country, and takes note of the challenges faced by Russian officers in a post-communist era.

"They tried to kill you? They made an attempt on your life? Did they shoot at you, maybe to settle some kind of score?"

"Officers often get shot at. It's an age-old story, officers meeting up with bullets. Going to the defence of those behind them. Going along, not suspecting their own hearts were under fire, not suspecting the fatal shot to come from behind. An accurate shot. An exploding bullet. And straight to the heart."

"How so?"

"Remember the pre-*perestroika* times? The celebrations — First of May, Seventh of November?[5] Huge columns of people crying "Hurrah!", "Glory to...!", "Long live...!" Me and the other officers, not just those from the KGB, were proud of the fact that we were the defenders of our people. We were protecting them. For most officers, this was their whole reason for living.

"Then came *perestroika,* and *glasnost.*[6] Other shouts began to be heard. And it turned out that we, the KGB officers, were bastards, executioners. We were defending the wrong people and the wrong things. The ones that earlier marched in Soviet columns under red banners had gone over to march

---

[5] *First of May, Seventh of November* — two of the biggest Soviet holidays: *1 May:* International Workers' Solidarity Day, a communist version of Labour Day, originally commemorating the Chicago General Strike of 1886; first celebrated in Russia (St. Petersburg) in 1891. *7 November:* the date of the Bolshevik Revolution. Parades on these days featured huge banners with communist slogans such as "Glory to the Communist Party of the Soviet Union!" and "Long live the brotherhood of nations of the USSR!"; these slogans would be shouted out on cue by the parading masses of workers and soldiers.

[6] *glasnost* — literally, 'openness', 'transparency', meaning greater freedom of speech and especially greater availability of information on socially important matters, access to which had previously been reserved for the ruling elite. This and *perestroika* ('restructuring') became universal buzzwords to describe Gorbachev's liberal policies.

in other columns under different banners, and *we* got left to take the blame.

"I had a wife, nine years younger than me, a real beauty. I loved her. Still do. She was so proud of me. We had a son, an only child. He came along... rather late, how shall I say it? Now he's seventeen. In the beginning he too was proud of me, he respected me.

"Then, after this whole business started, my wife became very quiet. She wouldn't look me in the eye. She began to be ashamed of me. I handed in my resignation and took a job as a security guard at a commercial bank. I hid my KGB uniform where nobody would find it. But there were unasked questions still hanging in the air over my wife and son. You can't answer questions which haven't been asked. They saw the answers in the papers and on TV screens. Turned out, we officers were involved in nothing but our dachas — and, of course, oppression."

"But," I interjected, "they showed on TV some pretty fancy dachas of the military élite — and they showed the real thing, not just faked pictures."

"Yeah, they showed the real thing, not just faked pictures. Only those dachas were sleazy chicken-houses compared to what many of those who accused their owners have themselves today. Look at you — you had a whole ship at your disposal. That's a lot bigger than a general's dacha. And don't forget, that general was once a cadet, he dug trenches. Then he became a lieutenant, got shifted about from barracks to barracks. And naturally he wanted to have a house and a dacha for his family, just like everyone else. And who knows how many times he had to jump out of his warm bed in the middle of the night in that same dacha, to go out on an emergency mission.

"Officers used to be respected in Russia. They were rewarded with an estate. Now it's been decided that a simple dacha with 1500 square metres of land is too much for a general!"

"Everybody lived differently before," I observed.

"Differently... Yes, everybody... But you can't tell me it wasn't the officers who were singled out for blame ahead of everyone else.

"It was the officers who demonstrated on the Senate Square.[7] They were thinking of the people. These officers were later sent either to the scaffold or to the mines in Siberia. Nobody stood up to defend them.

"Later Russian officers fought for the Tsar and the Fatherland in the trenches against the Germans. And back home 'revolutionary patriots' were already getting bullets ready for their hearts more terrible than the leaden ones. *White Guards,*[8] *Monsters* — that was what they called the officers returning from the war — officers who were simply trying to maintain order. There was chaos all around, everything was falling apart. All our former values, both material and spiritual, were being either torched or trampled upon. It was so hard for them, those White Guard officers. So they put on clean underwear under their uniforms[9] and went on a psychological attack. You know what's meant by 'psychological attack'?"

"It's when you try to scare the hell out of your opponent. I've seen it in films. In *Chapaev,*[10] for example, the White

[7] *Senate Square*, now known as Decembrists' Square — a large square not far from the Winter Palace in St. Petersburg, where a significant number of military officers demonstrated (unsuccessfully) against the Tsarist government in December 1825. The officers were either exiled or executed for treason.

[8] *White Guards* — the name given to military personnel who fought against the Bolshevik Revolution and during the subsequent Civil War (1918–23). The pro-Bolshevik soldiers were known as the *Reds.*

[9] *clean underwear under their uniforms* — a sign that the officers expected to be killed in battle that day.

[10] *Chapaev* — a classic Russian film, made in 1934, telling the story of Vasily Ivanovich Chapaev, a Red Army hero of the Russian Civil War.

Guard officers are advancing in formation, and they get strafed by machine-gun fire. Some fall, but the others close ranks and keep advancing."

"Yeah, that's it. They fall and still keep advancing. But the thing is that they weren't really 'attacking' to begin with."

"How so? What was the point of advancing then?"

"In military practice the whole reason for, the goal of any attack is either the capture or the physical annihilation of the enemy — preferably with the least possible loss in the ranks of the attackers. To keep advancing against strafing from machine-guns concealed in trenches — that was only done when there was *another* goal set, either consciously or subconsciously."

"What goal?"

"Maybe, and this goes against the logic of the art of war, it was to demonstrate something to the enemy even at the cost of one's own life — to make the soldiers firing the guns and killing the advancing marchers stop and think, to realise something and not fire at others."

"So, in that case their death would be something like Jesus Christ's death on the cross?"

"Something like that. We still manage to remember Christ, somehow. The young cadets and generals who advanced against their attackers, we've forgotten. Maybe even now their souls, dressed in clean underwear under their officers' uniforms, are standing in front of the bullets *we're* firing, and pleading with us, calling on us, to stop and think."

"Why would they be calling to us? When they were being fired on, we weren't even born."

"No, we weren't. But bullets are still flying around today. New bullets. Who, if not us, is doing the firing?"

"Indeed. Bullets *are* still flying around today. And just why have they been flying around all these years? Why did you leave home?"

"I couldn't stand the way he stared at me."

"The way *who* stared at you?"

"We were watching TV one night. My wife was in the kitchen, and my son and I were watching together. Then one of those political programmes came on, they started talking about the KGB. You know, a real smear campaign. I deliberately picked up a newspaper and made it look like I was reading, as though I wasn't interested in what they were saying. I was hoping my son would switch to another programme. He's never been interested in politics. He likes music.

"But he didn't change the channel. I rustled my paper, stealing glances at him out of the corner of my eye. And I saw him sitting in the chair, his hands gripping the arms of the chair so tight they turned white. He didn't move a muscle. I realised he wasn't going to change the channel. I held on as long as I could, hiding behind the paper. Then I couldn't take it any more. I smashed the paper into a ball and threw it to one side, got up sharply and yelled: 'Are you going to turn the damn thing off? *Are you?*'

"My son also got up. But he didn't go over to the TV. He stood opposite me, stared me in the eye and said nothing. The TV programme was still going. But my son just kept on staring at me.

"Later that night I wrote them a note. I said I was going away for a while — had no choice. And then I left for good."

"Why for good?"

"*Because.*"

For a long time neither of us uttered a word. I tried to make myself a bit more comfortable on the bunk so I could drift off. But then the colonel started talking again.

"So, you tell me Anastasia said she'd bring people through 'the dark forces' window of time'? She'd bring them through, and that's it?!"

"Yeah, that's what she said. And she herself believes that she can make it happen."

"Ah, she should have a hand-picked regiment. I'd become a soldier again to serve in that regiment."

"What's this about a regiment?" I retorted. "You didn't get it. She *rejects* the use of force. She wants to persuade people by some other means. She's trying to do that with her Ray."

"I think, or rather I feel, that she's going to do it. There's a lot of people that will want to be warmed by her Ray. But not many of them will understand that they themselves will have to put in something from their own brain-power. Anastasia needs help. She's all alone. She hasn't got even a single platoon at her command. So, you see, she's recruited you, she's commissioned you — and here you are lying in a basement like a tramp. And you call yourself entrepreneur after that?"

"Well, you KGB-er, you're lying here, too."

"Okay, go to sleep, soldier."

"It's rather cold in your 'barracks'."

"Well, that's the way it is, isn't it? Curl up into a ball, conserve your heat."

Then he got up and took out from behind the divider yet another plastic bag. He got something out of it to cover me with. In the dim light of the candle I could see shining right under my nose three stars on the epaulet of a greatcoat. It was warm under the coat, and I fell asleep.

I was half asleep when I heard the tramps come in and head for their rag corner. They demanded the colonel hand them over a bottle for my overnight stay. He promised to settle it in the morning, but they insisted, threateningly, that he better pay up now, or else. The colonel then moved his bunk, placing it between me and the newcomer tramps, declaring: "You touch him only over my dead body!" And he lay down on his bunk, shielding me from the new arrivals. Then everything went quiet again. I felt warm and peaceful.

I was awakened by the colonel's shaking my shoulder.

"Get up. Turn out! We gotta get outa here."

The first rays of dawn were barely beginning to show themselves through the dim basement window. I sat up on my bunk. Not only did I have a splitting headache but I found I had trouble breathing.

"It's still early. The dawn hasn't even broken," I observed.

"A little longer and it'll be too late. They've lit some cotton-wool with powder. It's an old trick. A little longer and we'll be suffocated."

He went to the window and started working the window-frame loose with an iron bar. The tramps had locked the door from the outside. Taking out the frame, he broke the glass and crawled through the aperture. The basement window opened into a concrete well, covered with a grating. The colonel began fiddling with the grating, trying to dislodge it, but somehow it wasn't working.

I stayed leaning against a wall. My head was spinning. The colonel stuck his head back through the window opening and ordered:

"Squat down. Less smoke near the floor. Try not to move. Breathe in less air."

He forced the grating out with his shoulders. He moved it off and helped me clamber out.

We sat on the cement kerb outside the basement window, silently filling our lungs with the pre-dawn air of an awakening city. The spinning in my head gradually lessened. The air started feeling cold. Each of us sat there, thinking his own thoughts.

Then I said:

"Your neighbours aren't very friendly. They're the ones in charge here?"

"Everyone's in charge of himself. They got their own business. They bring in a new homeless person, and make him pay for staying overnight. If he refuses to pay, they slip something into his drink or suffocate him in his sleep, like they tried to do to us, and then they take whatever they like from him — if he's got anything worth taking, that is."

"And you're telling me that you, a KGB-er, are indifferent to it all? You could earn yourself some pretty points by giving chaps like that the once-over. Or were you just a pencil-pusher, sitting in an office all day? Maybe you didn't know how to work the street?"

"I worked in an office and I worked outside the office. I knew what to do. But to know the moves — that's not the same as applying them. A criminal, an enemy — that's one thing. But here we're dealing with human beings. I might calculate wrong, use too much deadly force."

"You call *those* human beings? While you're rationalising away, they're out there robbing people blind. They're even ready to commit murder!"

"Yeah, they're ready to commit murder. But you won't stop them by physical means."

"You sit there philosophising, but we almost died. We barely managed to escape, others might not be so lucky."

"Yeah, others might not be so lucky..."

"There, you see? Then how come you're philosophising and not acting?"

"I can't use violence on people. You see what I mean, I could calculate wrong... You may as well get going to your own 'deployment quarters'. It's dawn already."

I got up, shook his hand, and left.

I had gone but a few steps when he called after me:

"Wait! Come back here a moment."

I approached the homeless colonel sitting on the concrete kerb. He was just sitting there, his head lowered, not saying a word.

"Hey, why did you call me?"

After a moment's pause he spoke:

"So, you think you'll make it okay?"

"I think I can. It's not far. Three metro stops, that's all. I'll make it."

"I meant, d'you think you'll reach your goal? Are you sure? Writing a book, getting it published?"

"I'll give it a try. First I'll try writing."

"So, Anastasia said it should work out for you?"

"That's what she said."

"Then why didn't you do that right off?"

"The other seemed more important."

"So, that means you're not good at following orders properly?"

"Anastasia didn't *order* me, she *asked* me."

"She asked you... So, she worked out the tactics and strategy herself. And you thought you'd do it your way, and you just loused things up."

"That's how it turned out."

"That's how it turned out... You gotta pay closer attention to your orders. Here, take this."

He held out something wrapped in a small plastic package. I unwrapped it and saw, through the clear plastic, a golden wedding band and a silver cross on a little chain.

"A dealer will give you half-price for these. Let him have them for half-price. Maybe it'll help see you through. If you've got nowhere to stay, come back here. I'll take care of *them.*"

"What are you talking about? I can't take these!"

"Don't rationalise. It's time for you to go. So go. Look to it! Just go!"

"I'm telling you, I can't take them."

I tried to give him back the ring and the little cross, but I was met by an authoritative and, at the same time, pleading stare.

"About— face! Forward— march!" he commanded in a whisper that was restrained, yet brooked no contradiction. A moment later came another plea:

"Just be sure you make it."

Arriving at my flat, I felt like going to sleep and even got to the point of lying down. But I couldn't get the homeless colonel out of my head.

I got dressed in some clean clothes and went to see him. Along the way I thought: Maybe he'll agree to move in with me. He's adaptable to anything. He's practical and he's neat. Besides, he's an artist. Maybe he'll do a picture for the book's cover. And it'll be easier to find some rent money if we're together. I had no money for the next month's rent.

As I approached the basement window we had climbed out of earlier that morning, I saw a group of people — tenants from the building, a police car and an ambulance.

The homeless colonel was lying on the ground, his eyes closed and a smile on his face. His face and body were splattered with wet dirt. One dead hand was clenched around a piece of red brick. A broken wooden crate stood against the wall.

A court medical assessor was writing something down on a notepad. He was standing beside the corpse of another man, dressed in shabby, rumpled clothing, with a disfigured face.

In the little crowd that had gathered, no doubt comprised of the building's tenants, one woman was rattling on excitedly:

"...I was walkin' me dog an' I saw him, the one smilin', perched on the crate, his face to the wall, an' the three of 'em — tramps, by the look of it — two men an' a woman with 'em — comes at him from behind. The man gives the crate a kick an' he falls off the crate to the ground. They starts kickin' him, cursin' all the while, they did. I yells at 'em. They stops kickin' him. Old 'Smiley' here, he gets up, see. He has a pretty hard time gettin' up too. An' he tells 'em to sod off an' not show their faces around here again. They starts cursin' again, an' then they comes at him full force. As they gets closer, he gives a straight chop with the back of his hand right to the throat of the bloke what kicked the crate. It's not that he's wavin' his arms about or anythin', he just lands the other bloke a chop so's he doubles up an' can't breathe. I yells at 'em again an' two of 'em runs straight off, see. First the woman, then the man after her. 'Smiley''s now clutchin' at his heart. He oughtta sit down or lie down straight off, if it's his heart what's givin' out, but no, he goes back to his crate. Moves ever so slowly, he does. Puts his crate back against the wall. Then he gets back up on it. I can see he's in a really bad way. He starts fallin'. An' he slides down, still drawin' on the wall with that red brick of his, an' keeps on drawin' 'til he lands himself on the ground. An' he's lyin' there face up, right against the wall. I runs over, looks, an' he ain't breathin'. Not breathin'. But he's *smilin'*!"

"Why did he climb up on the crate?" I asked the woman.

"Yeah, why did he climb up if his heart were givin' out?" echoed a voice from the crowd.

"He wanted to keep on drawin'. And when those three blokes came at him from behind, he was *drawin'*, that's what he was doin'... That's prob'ly why he didn't see 'em comin'. I'd been walkin' me dog for a long time, an' there he is, standin' on his crate an' *drawin'*... He didn't turn 'round, not even once... You can see what he drew — up there, on the wall!" And the woman pointed to the building.

On the grey brick wall of the building could be seen the circular outline of the Sun, and in the middle of it a cedar branch and, around the perimeter of the Sun-circle, some letters printed rather unevenly.

I went closer to the wall and read: RINGING CEDARS OF RUSSIA. Apart from that, there were rays emanating from the Sun. There were only three of them. The homeless colonel didn't manage to draw any more. Two of the rays were short and straight, while the third was wavy and fading away, and extended right down to the base of the wall, where the dead homeless colonel was lying on the ground, smiling.

I looked at the smiling face smeared with dirt and thought to myself: Maybe in the last moments of his life Anastasia managed to touch him with her Ray, and warm him up. At least warm his soul up a little and carry it off to a bright infinity.

I watched as the corpses were loaded into the ambulance. 'My' colonel was thrown carelessly in the process, his head striking the floor of the ambulance. I couldn't take it. I tore off my jacket, ran over to the ambulance and started demanding they put my jacket under his head. One of the orderlies swore at me, but the other took the jacket without a word and placed it under the colonel's greying head. The vehicles drove off. Everything was empty, just as if nothing had happened.

I stood there a while, looking at the drawing and inscription illuminated by the morning sun. My thoughts began getting all mixed up. I had to do something, at least *something* for him, for this KGB-er, a Russian officer who had perished on this spot! But what? What, indeed?

Then it came to me: *I'm going to put your drawing, my dear officer, on the cover of my book.* The book I most definitely will write. Even though I don't yet know how to write, I'll still write one, and not just one. And on all of them I'll put your drawing — it'll be my emblem. And in the book I'll tell all Russians:

"My fellow Russians, don't shoot at the hearts of your officers with invisible exploding bullets, bullets of cruelty and heartlessness.

"Don't shoot from behind at any soldiers — be they White or Red, or even blue or green, ensigns or generals. The bullets you fire at them from behind are more terrible than the leaden ones. My fellow Russians, do not shoot at your officers!"

CHAPTER TWENTY-ONE

Untitled

I wrote quickly. From time to time Anton, Artem or Lyosha, the student programmers, would drop by and bring me a bite to eat. I still had not told *them* about Anastasia. But I explained to them that the organisation of the Fellowship could be facilitated with the help of the book I was to write. And so they set about keyboarding the text of the book into the computers. It was mainly Lyosha Novichkov who worked on this. He showed up every three days, bringing a print-out of his latest keyboarding and taking home a new chapter of the manuscript. This went on for about two months.

One day Lyosha showed up with the last printed chapter of Book 1, a diskette with the full text, two bottles of beer, frankfurters and some other kind of food, along with a little money, and set it all down on the kitchen table.

"Where did you get all this bounty, Lyosha?" I asked in amazement.

He lived alone with his mother, on very limited means. He didn't always have enough money to buy metro tokens or even sandwiches.

"It's exam time, Vladimir Nikolaevich," Lyosha responded. "I do drafts for some of the students, I make up computer programmes for them. For students who can't do them themselves or are too lazy. They pay me for them."

"And will you make it through the exams yourself all right?"

"Will do. I've got just one exam left, and in a couple of days I'll have to go off for a month on military training, to

Kineshma.[1] It's good you managed to get *Anastasia* finished. If there are any corrections to be made now, Artem will take care of them. Anton's already off on training."

"Tell me, Lyosha, how did you possibly manage to sit exams, do drafts and make up computer programmes for others, and still keyboard and print out *Anastasia* every day?"

Lyosha didn't respond. I turned to the kitchen table to serve up the steamed frankfurters. Lyosha's head and arms were resting on the table, on top of the printed pages containing the *Anastasia* text. He was fast asleep.

[1]*Kineshma* — an industrial centre and port on the Volga River.

CHAPTER TWENTY-TWO

Unravelling the mystery

Standing in the kitchen of my small Moscow apartment, standing next to the table with the frankfurters getting cold and Lyosha Novichkov's head resting on the pages containing the text of *Anastasia,* I made a promise to myself: to find a way of regaining my capital and getting back my ship with a view to taking it on the same journey as last year when I first met Anastasia. But not on a trade mission, as before. I wanted to go there during the 'white nights' of summer, so that Lyosha, Anton and Artem — as well as all those who had worked like dogs, in spite of all the setbacks and often to the neglect of their own material well-being, to organise a fellowship of purer-minded entrepreneurs — could enjoy a decent holiday aboard my ship in the most luxurious quarters.

And what was this grand idea all about, in any case? What kind of hold did it have on people? Why was I, too, drawn into it so closely? What kind of mystery did it conceal? I just *had* to figure this out, in concrete detail, and unravel its mystery and purpose. And why are people so turned on by this dream of a taiga recluse? What lies hidden there? How can I unravel the mystery?

Moskovskaya Pravda correspondent Katya Golovina tried unravelling it by asking the students to explain what motivated them, what their personal stake was in all this. But they couldn't give a definitive answer, saying only that it was something worth doing. In other words, they were working on *intuition.* But what was behind this intuition?

CHAPTER TWENTY-THREE

Untitled

At Moscow Printshop Number Eleven two thousand copies of the first slim volume about Anastasia were printed at the shop's own expense. Why did the manager, Gennady Vladimirovich Grutsia, decide to print a book by an unknown author? Why would he do this and, in spite of the printshop's current financial difficulties, use offset paper instead of the usual newsprint?[1]

The first books I sold myself near the entrance to the Taganskaya metro station. Then I got some help from some of the book's first readers. An elderly woman would daily stand and sell copies outside the Dobryninskaya metro station. She would take great pains to explain in detail to anyone interested what a wonderful book it was. Why?

Then readers began selling it as well in vacation centres on the outskirts of Moscow. They would print out announcements and organise readers' gatherings for people holidaying there.

Then the business manager of the Moscow Publishers' Clearance House, Yuri Anatolievich Nikitin, suddenly decided to offer the printshop an advance on an additional two thousand copies. His actions were strange and unexpected.

He drove over to see me in his car and told me:

"My son and I are leaving the country today to go to a tennis tournament. Our plane goes tonight. I need to hurry to get my payment in."

---

[1]*newsprint* — This has long been the norm for printing most paperback books in Russia.

He paid for the second print-run in full. When the time came for him to pick up his books, Nikitin told me:

"You know, during the summer we don't do a lot of book-selling. I'll take several packages, the rest you take care of yourself. When money starts coming your way, you can reimburse me." Again, why?

Right from the moment I started working on the manuscript there have been many *whys?* associated with the book, even to this day. It's almost as though the book were alive, drawing people unto itself and using their help to break through into life. I used to think that the events connected with it were pure coincidence. Only those 'co-incidences' started tying themselves together into a pattern. Now I have no idea, in all that has happened, just what is coincidence and what is in conformity with a law. The two have become exceedingly difficult to tell apart.

CHAPTER TWENTY-FOUR

Father Feodorit

The moment arrived when I finally managed to pay a visit to Father Feodorit. Back in the taiga, in response to my question as to whether there were any people in our world with knowledge and abilities similar to hers, only living closer to home, Anastasia had replied:

"There are people in various corners of the Earth whose lifestyle is not caught up in the prevailing technocracy. They all have different abilities. But in your world there is also one person whom you will find it easy to approach, whether it be winter or summer. The power of his spirit is very great."

"Do you know where he lives? Can I see him and talk with him?"

"Yes, you can."

"Who is he?"

"He is your father, Vladimir."

"What do you mean? Oh, Anastasia, Anastasia! I so much wanted to hear proof that you're right about everything, and here it's all coming out the wrong way! My father died eighteen years ago and was buried in a little town in the Briansk region."

Anastasia sat on the grass, her back leaning against a tree, her knees drawn up close to her chest, and silently looked me in the eye. She seemed a little sad, as though she were taking pity on me. Then she lowered her head to her knees. I thought she might be feeling upset over her mistake regarding my father, and I tried to comfort her.

"Don't get too upset, Anastasia. It's probably because, as you said yourself, you don't have that much strength left."[1]

Anastasia didn't speak for a while, then raised her head and, once more looking me right in the eye, said:

"My strength has indeed lessened, but not to the point where I could be mistaken."

She then proceeded to relate events that had taken place twenty-six years ago. She recounted the past not only with great accuracy and in minute detail, but was even able to convey nuances of inner feelings.

It is understandable how one can pick up clues from the outward appearance: a barely noticeable facial expression, a body position, even the eyes, can all give clues as to what an interlocutor is thinking. But how she was able to discern the past as though it were simply a documentary newsreel is still a mystery to me.

Anastasia herself was not able to explain this phenomenon in a standard, comprehensible manner. But this is what she had to say:

"Not far from Moscow is the Trinity-Sergiev Monastery complex in the town of Sergiev Posad. Behind Trinity-Sergiev's massive, ancient walls there is a seminary, an academy and several cathedrals, in addition to the monastery proper. The cathedrals are open to the public, and anyone who wishes can come and pray in this holy place of Rus.[2] It was not destroyed even during the campaigns of persecution against believers; indeed, right through this period, the institutions

---

[1] *Author's note:* This conversation took place after she lost consciousness in saving the man and the woman from being murdered. I described this situation in my first book.

[2] *Rus* (pronounced: *ROOS*) — the name of the Old Russian territory, which by the 9th century A.D. was centred around Kiev. From Rus came the Russia, Ukraine and Belarus we know today.

behind these walls continued to function uninterrupted, providing a place where the monastic brethren could serve God.

"Twenty-six years ago, on the very day I came into this world," she continued, "a young man in his late teens walked through the gates of the Trinity-Sergiev Monastery. He toured the museum, and then proceeded to visit the main cathedral, where a sermon was being read by a tall, grey-haired monk. Both the monk's height and his rank were well above average. This was Father Feodorit, archimandrite of the Trinity-Sergiev Monastery. The young man listened to his sermon. Later, when Father Feodorit withdrew, he followed him into one of the treasury-rooms, unhindered by the temple staff. Going up to Father Feodorit, he started talking to him about the sermon. And Father Feodorit spoke with him for a long time. The young man had been baptised, but did not have much inner faith. He did not observe the fasts, did not take communion, and did not attend church regularly. But that day marked the beginning of a friendship between Father Feodorit and the young man.

"The young man started paying visits to the monastery. Father Feodorit would talk with him and show him the sanctuaries normally off-limits to ordinary parishioners. The monk gave him books, which he lost. The monk placed a little cross on a chain around his neck, and it was lost as well. The monk gave him a second cross, a most unusual one — it opened like a tiny case, but it too was lost.

"The monk would even take the young man into the refectory and seat him at the same table as the monks. Each time he would give him a little money. He never rebuked him for anything and always looked forward to his arrival.

"This went on for a whole year. The young man visited the monastery every week, but one day he left and did not return the following week. He did not come after a month, even after a whole year. The monk still waited. Now twenty-five years have passed already. The monk is still waiting. Twenty-five years, Vladimir, your spiritual father has been waiting for you — that great Russian monk, Father Feodorit."

"I went far away from the monastery. To Siberia. I sometimes thought of Father Feodorit," I responded, as though justifying my actions to myself or to someone else.

"But you did not write him even one letter," observed Anastasia.

"I want to see him."

"And what will you tell him? Perhaps about how you made money, were happy in love and simply went astray? How many times were you at death's door, but at the last moment you were delivered from your woes? He will see all that for himself, just by looking at you. He prayed for forgiveness of your sins and time after time saved you through his prayers. He still believes, just as he did twenty-five years ago. He was hoping for something different from you."

"What was it, Anastasia? What does Father Feodorit know, what does he want?"

"I cannot comprehend it, at least not now. It was something he felt intuitively. Tell me, Vladimir, do you remember the conversations you had with him, do you remember what you saw in the monastery treasury-room?"

"It's all very fuzzy in my mind. After all, it was so long ago. I can only remember isolated scenes."

"Try to remember them. I shall help you."

"Father Feodorit would talk with me each time in various places in the monastery. I remember some underground rooms — at least they were partially underground. I remember the refectory, the long table where the monks took their supper, and I had supper with them. It was during a time of some sort of fast. The food was especially prepared for the fast, but I liked it."

"Did you have any unusual impressions or feelings during your visits to the monastery?"

"Once after supper I left the refectory and went through a passageway to an inner courtyard of the monastery complex, heading for an exit. The gate was already closed to parishioners. The courtyard was empty. Those massive high walls blocked out the noise from the city beyond. All I could see around me were the cathedrals. Everything was completely silent. I stopped. It seemed as though I could hear solemn music playing. I needed to leave. There was a monk on duty at the gate to let me out and bolt the gate shut after me. But I just stood there and listened to that music, and eventually, slowly, made my way over to the gate."

"You never heard that music again? You never experienced the same impression?"

"No."

"Did you ever try to hear that music — to call up the impression of it from within?"

"Yes, but I never managed to. I even tried standing on that same spot the next time I came, but, alas..."

"Try thinking of something else, Vladimir."

"Now you're interrogating me. You recounted everything so accurately — everything that happened to me twenty-six years ago — *you* tell *me* how I felt back then."

"That is not possible. Father Feodorit did not formulate any specific plans, he was hoping for something intuitively. But he did do something great and significant for you. Something known only to him. I can only feel it intuitively myself: he thought up something significant and did a lot toward this end. A great deal, in fact. But why he associated his desire with *you* — you who did not have the basic abilities to come quickly into the faith — remains a mystery. And why he has not broken this faith even after twenty-five years of your profligate life — that too is a mystery. And why are you, who have received so much, still sitting on your hands? Why? I cannot understand that. After all, nothing in the Universe ever disappears without a trace. Please see if you can remember even isolated scenes from your meetings and conversations with your spiritual father."

"I remember a salon, or perhaps it was some sort of treasury-room, in the academy or seminary, or maybe it was one of the underground rooms in the monastery itself. Some kind of monk opened the door for Father Feodorit, but didn't go in himself. The Father and I went in alone. There were some pictures on the walls, and things standing on little shelves."

"You experienced two surprises there. What were they?"

"Surprises? Yes, of course, it did surprise me. Astounded me..."

"What did?"

"A particular picture. It was black and white, as if drawn with a pencil. It was a meticulously executed portrait of some person."

"So, what surprised you about it?"

"I don't remember."

"Think, Vladimir! Please, try to recall it — I shall help you. There was the small salon, you were standing alone there with Father Feodorit in front of this picture. You were standing just a little way in front of him, and he told you: 'Step a little closer to the picture, Vladimir.' You took one step forward, then another..."

"I remember! Anastasia!"

"What?"

"This picture of a person was drawn with a single line. A fluctuating spiral line. It was as though the artist had put his pencil or whatever in the middle of a blank sheet of paper, and without taking it off the paper, had made it go in a spiral, alternately pressing hard on it to make the line thicker and easing up, barely touching the paper, to make a fine, delicate line, but still continuous. The spiral line ended at one edge of the page. The result was an amazing picture, the portrait of a person."

"This picture," Anastasia advised, "should be put on public display for all to see. Someone will be able to decipher the information concealed in it. That pulsating line portraying a person has something to say to people."

"How?"

"I do not know yet. You are aware, for example, how dots and dashes can represent an alphabet or musical notation. I can only guess it could be one or the other of those, or something else besides. When you return, ask them to put it on public display or to publish it somewhere. Someone will turn up who is able to decipher that spiral line."

"But who will listen to me?"

"They *will* listen to you. But back then you experienced a second most unusual feeling. Can you recall what it was?"

"It was in the same room or in the next room... Yes, it was a rather small room where a beautiful carved wooden chair was standing on a raised platform. Perhaps it was an arm-chair, something like a throne. Father Feodorit and I stood and looked at it. The Father said that nobody ever touched it."

"But you touched it. And even sat on it."

"It was Father Feodorit himself who suggested I sit on it."

"And what happened to you when you did?"

"Nothing. I sat there, looking at Father Feodorit, and he stood there silently looking me in the eye. Just looked, that's all."

"Please remember, Vladimir, try to recall your inner feelings. They are most important."

"Well, there was nothing special... It was just that, you know, some thoughts began running through my head lickety-split, like an audiotape in fast-forward mode, and the words all blurred into a stream of unintelligible sounds."

"And you never tried deciphering them, Vladimir? Did you ever have the desire to stop that tape so you could listen to it at normal speed and understand what it was saying?"

"How could I?"

"By pondering the essence of your being."

"No, never tried that. You're not making any sense."

"And the things that Father Feodorit told you, did you understand everything? Can you recall precisely even a single phrase, even a phrase without any connection to the rest?"

"Yes, but I really can't remember what it was connected with."

"Tell me what it was."

"...You will show them..."

At this point Anastasia, who had been sitting under the tree, suddenly sprang up, her face beaming. She put her hands on the trunk of the cedar, and pressed her cheek against it.

"Yes, of course!" she exclaimed, waving her arms with joy and delightedly crying out:

"You are truly great, Monk of Russia! You know, Vladimir, there is one thing I can tell you for certain about Father Feodorit. He has made a mockery of a lot of the world's teachings by showing what is the most essential thing."

"He and I never discussed any teachings. We talked about everyday things."

"Yes, of course! Everyday things! Father Feodorit spoke about things you were interested in. He showed you sacred creations, and treated them with veneration, but avoided making a big show of it. Even though he had risen to a high rank, he was a very simple man, most importantly, a thinking man — perhaps he was even meditating during the time you were with him. And he was not one to expound dogmas. How silly the preachers of conventional dogmas that flocked to Russia from abroad look by comparison with him! They only distract one's attention from the most essential thing. He was so successful at protecting you from dogmas that you see me too as a naïve recluse. It does not matter who I am. What matters is that you stick to the most essential thing."

"What most essential thing?"

"The thing that is in every Man."

"But how can every Man know the teachings of the gurus of the West and the East, India and Tibet, if he has never even heard of them?"

"All essential information has been included in Man, Vladimir, in every man right from the start. It is something he is given on the day of his creation, just like arms, legs, hair and a heart. All the teachings of the world, along with all discoveries, are taken exclusively from this Source. Just as parents try to give their child everything, so the Grand Creator gives everything to each one right off. Nothing man-made. Not a multitude of books, nor the latest computers and the computers of the future all taken together, can ever encompass even a part of the information contained in a single Man. One has only to know how to use it."

"Then why doesn't everybody make discoveries? And why doesn't everyone formulate teachings?"

"Let us say one person manages to extract a grain of truth from the whole. And he keeps talking about it enthusiastically, thinking it was given to him alone. And that it contains the most essential thing. He talks it up to others, trying to make them see it as the one and only important thing. But by talking like this, he is blocking the basic complex network of information already existing within himself. Knowledge of the truth consists not in proclaiming it but in living it."

"And what way of living it is characteristic of those who best know the truth?"

"A happy one!"

"But to know the truth, one must have a conscious awareness and purity of thought?!"

"That is visionary! Fantastic!" Anastasia shrieked with laughter, and merrily added: "You read my thoughts?"

"Nothing visionary there, it is simply an attentive attitude to Man. You're always relating everything to purity of thought and conscious awareness."

"Visionary! Visionary!" she repeated, still laughing. "You read my thoughts. Oh, how fantastic!"

Upon hearing her cheery laughter, I too could no longer restrain myself and broke into peals of merriment. Later I asked:

"What do you think, Anastasia, will my spiritual father, Father Feodorit, receive me if I go see him? Will he talk with me? He won't be upset?"

"Of course he will receive you! He will be most happy to see you there! He will accept you any way you are. Only he will be even happier to see you if you have done at least something using the information within you, if he perceives some indication that you are aware of it. Stop the fast-forward, Vladimir, and you shall understand a great deal."

"Does my spiritual father still live in the same place? At the Trinity-Sergiev Monastery?"

"Your spiritual father, that great elder of Rus, is now living in a small monastic priory in the forest, not far from the Trinity-Sergiev Monastery. The priory's regulations are stricter than those in the monastery, and your spiritual father is the prior there. The priory is situated in the forest, in a compellingly beautiful setting. There are just a few little houses there, each with its own monastic cell.

"This priory situated in the green forest has a small wooden church. It is not ornately decorated and it does not have a gilded dome, but it is very, very beautiful, cosy and clean, heated by two stoves. Candles are not bought or sold there, as in most other churches. In fact nothing is bought or sold there. There is nothing and nobody to desecrate it, and parishioners are not allowed access. Even to this day your spiritual father, Father Feodorit, is praying in this church. He is praying for the salvation of everyone's soul, including yours. He is praying for children who have forgotten their parents, and praying for parents forgotten by their children. Go to him and bow before him. Ask for forgiveness of your sins. The power of his spirit is very great. And give my deepest respects to Father Feodorit."

"Fine, Anastasia. I shall do that. And, you know, I shall first try and do what you have asked me to."

Upon arriving at Sergiev Posad, the town outside Moscow which used to be called Zagorsk, I entered the gates of the Trinity-Sergiev Monastery just as I used to do twenty-seven years ago. I first headed for the gate to the active part of the monastery. Before, all I had to do was introduce myself and ask for Father Feodorit. But this time the monk on duty replied that the archpriest was no longer Father Feodorit. There was a Father Feodorit at the monastery, living in the forest outside the monastery grounds — but parishioners did not go there.

I told the monk that I was an acquaintance of Father Feodorit's, and in proof of this I named the monastery sanctuaries which the Father had showed me so many years ago. Then I was told where the forest priory was situated, and with an inexplicable shiver of excitement I approached the little wooden church in the forest. It was indeed extraordinarily beautiful, and blended in harmoniously with the natural environment. There were paths leading to the church from several little wooden cell-houses situated around it.

Father Feodorit met with me on the small wooden porch of the forest church. I was a bit at a loss for words. I remembered Anastasia's counsel: "Only do not be embarrassed and try not to act surprised when you meet your spiritual father!" Still, I couldn't get over an inexplicable feeling of trepidation. Father Feodorit was old and grey, but no older than he had appeared twenty-seven years ago.

We sat on some blocks of wood on the porch of the little forest church without a word between us. I tried to speak, but couldn't manage to come up with the right thing to say. It seemed as though he already knew the whole picture and there was no sense in uttering words. It was as if the twenty-seven years since we last met had not gone by at all. It seemed as though we had parted only yesterday.

I had brought along a copy of my book on Anastasia to give to Father Feodorit, but I felt reluctant to actually hand it to him. I had been showing the book to various clerics. Some just took one look at it and said they didn't read books like that. Others asked what it was about, and after my brief explanation pronounced Anastasia an infidel. I didn't feel like upsetting Father Feodorit and certainly didn't want *him* to reject her out of hand. Each time someone had tried to speak ill of Anastasia, a feeling of resistance had welled up in me. I even had a row about it with the deacon of the Novospassky Monastery.[3] He pointed out two women wearing dark clothing and black head-scarves and said:

"That is how God-fearing women should be."

I responded:

"If Anastasia is happy and enjoying life, that may well be pleasing to God. It is more pleasant to see people enjoying life than being dull and downcast like that."

---

[3]*Novospassky Monastery* — claimed to be the oldest monastery in Moscow, dating back to the founding of Moscow in 1147 by Prince Yury Dolgoruky.

So it was with some trepidation that I finally got out my book and handed it to Father Feodorit. He took it quietly and held it in the palm of one hand.

He began gently stroking it with his other hand, as though feeling something with his palms, and asked:

"Do you want me to read it?" And, without waiting for an answer, added: "Fine, leave it with me."

Two days later, I paid a morning visit to Father Feodorit. We sat there in the forest on a tiny bench near the Father's cell. And we talked about all sorts of things. While his manner of speaking was pretty much the same as twenty-seven years ago, one thing bothered me: why did Father Feodorit look just a bit *younger* than twenty-seven years ago? And all at once he broke off his train of thought and said:

"You know, Vladimir, your Father Feodorit has passed on."

At first I was speechless, but then managed to ask:

"Then who are you?"

"I am Father Feodorit," he replied, looking at me with just a faint trace of a smile. I then asked him:

"Tell me, where is his grave?"

"In the old cemetery."

"I'd like to see it. Can you tell me how to get there?"

He didn't say anything about the grave, only:

"Come and see me again whenever you have the time."

And then an incredible experience began taking place.

"Time for dinner," said Father Feodorit "Come, I'll give you something to eat."

In a small hut which served as a refectory I sat down to table. The table was set out with a tureen of borsch, mashed potatoes, fish and a drink with stewed fruit. He poured some borsch into a bowl for me, and I began eating. The Father himself did not eat. He simply sat at the table.

As soon as I started in on the potatoes, I felt a delightful taste in my mouth. It brought back memories. The potatoes tasted exactly as they had done in the monastery refectory twenty-seven years ago. I had remembered it all my life since then. My head began spinning. On the one hand, here was a different Father Feodorit sitting beside me; on the other hand, he talked and behaved exactly as I remembered from before.

I recalled how one time, many years ago, when we were together in one of the rooms of the monastery, Father Feodorit had suggested I have my picture taken with him. I agreed. He called over one of the monks who had a camera and he took our picture. Now I decided to use this to introduce some clarity to my present situation. I knew that monks did not like to pose for pictures. And the thought came to me to ask Father Feodorit if he would mind if I had a colour picture taken of us and that I also wanted to take one of the little forest church. If he refused, that would mean he was not the same Father Feodorit, not *my* Father Feodorit. And so I suggested:

"Let me have my picture taken with you."

Father Feodorit did not refuse, and we had our picture taken. And I also took a snapshot of the little church. It turned out rather well, even though I had a very simple camera.

As I was leaving, Father Feodorit gave me a small travel Bible. It was not laid out in verses, like all the other Bibles I had seen, but simply in running text, as in an ordinary book. He advised me:

"When you cite the Bible in your book, you should indicate the precise chapter you are quoting from."[4]

I asked him whether he would be open to receiving and talking with people who wished to meet with Anastasia, so

---

[4]The Russian edition of *Anastasia* includes no chapter-and-verse references; those in the English edition of Book 1 were added by the translator and editor.

they wouldn't have to travel such a long distance to the Siberian taiga. To which he replied:

"You know, I still haven't fully understood myself. So, for now, just come alone, whenever you have the time."

I was disappointed by Father Feodorit's refusal to see other people, but I wasn't about to press the matter. My conversation with him on a variety of subjects led me to the following conclusion: in Russian monasteries there are to be found certain elders whose wisdom and simplicity of expression far surpasses the art of countless numbers of denominational preachers, either of the home-grown or imported variety.

But why are you silent, you elders of Russia that have been endowed with such wisdom? Is this something to which you have been led on your own, or are there dark forces of some kind that are preventing you from speaking out? People come to a church service, and it turns out to be in a language they don't understand.[5] And then people flock in droves and even pay money to hear preachers talk in a language they *can* understand. Maybe that is why so many Russians flock to foreign holy places and ignore their own.

I always felt a sense of peace in my heart after speaking with Father Feodorit. The way he talks is a lot simpler, clearer and more understandable than the vast majority of the preachers I went to hear after meeting with Anastasia in my efforts to make some sense of what she said. I want others to have a good experience, too. But when will you speak out, wise elders of Russia?

---

[5]Russian Orthodox services are conducted in Old Church Slavonic, which is an ancient distant relative of Russian but barely comprehensible to today's Russian speakers.

CHAPTER TWENTY-FIVE

The Space of Love

After the sale of the first print-run of the book about Anastasia I received a royalty payment. I went to VDNKh,[1] now known as the All-Russian Exhibition Centre. For some reason, I always enjoyed being there. This time I walked past the multitude of snack bars and shashlik buffets, tempting me with their delicious aromas, and fought against my inclination to buy all the delicacies in sight. Even though I had money in my pocket, and a fair amount at that, I decided I would now spend it more wisely. And all at once, another incredible thing happened. It wasn't loud, but, unmistakably and distinctly, I heard Anastasia's voice.

"Buy yourself something to eat, Vladimir. Buy whatever you like. You do not have to scrimp on food any more."

I kept on walking a few steps past the open snack bars, and again came the voice:

"Why are you walking on past? Please, have something to eat, Vladimir."

"Come on now, I'm having hallucinations!" I thought.

I walked over to a bench alongside a broad pathway, where there was hardly anyone else around. I sat down and whispered quietly, bending over so people wouldn't think I was talking to myself.

---

[1]*VDNKh* (pronounced *veh-deh-en-KHA*) — the Russian initials denoting the former Economic Achievements Exposition, a huge exhibition and recreational complex (complete with a large park, fountains and unusual architecture) covering 140 hectares in the north-east sector of Moscow.

"Anastasia, am I really hearing your voice?"

And I heard the answer distinct and clear:

"You are hearing my voice, Vladimir."

"Hello, Anastasia. Why didn't you talk to me earlier? So many questions have been piling up. Questions people have been asking at readers' gatherings, including a lot I can't answer."

"I *have* been talking to you. I have been trying all this time to talk with you. But you have not been hearing me. Once, when you decided to do away with yourself, I even cried out, I was so worried, but to no avail. You did not hear me. I figured out what I needed to do and started singing. It was this song that the two girls picked up and played on their violins at the metro station. They heard it and started playing. As soon as you recognised the same melody you had heard me sing in the taiga, you remembered me. I was so worried at the time, I thought my milk was going to give out."

"What milk, Anastasia?"

"My breast-milk. The milk for our son. After all, I did bear him, Vladimir."

"Did bear... Anastasia!... Was it hard? How are you doing there all alone in the taiga? How is he? You told me — I remember your saying — it wouldn't be at the right time."

"Everything is fine. Nature awakened early and is now helping me. And our son is fine. He is a strong lad. He is already smiling. Only his skin is a little dry, just like yours. But that is nothing, it will pass. Everything will be fine. You shall see. It is more difficult for *you* now than for us. But take one more step. Finish the writing. I know how hard it has been for you, and it will not be so easy in the future either. But keep going. Keep going on your own path."

"But Anastasia..."

I wanted to tell her that writing a book is harder than running a business. I wanted to tell her about how things stood with my family and the firm. About all the ups and downs of

the past year. About how I no longer have a home and family,
and almost ended up in the loony bin. I wanted to give her a
good talking to about those dreams of hers, so she wouldn't aim
aim too high with them, wouldn't keep on tempting people.
But then I thought: why upset a nursing mother? — her milk
might indeed turn bad.

And so I said:

"Don't you worry about trifles, Anastasia. I don't have any
particular difficulties at the moment. What's the fuss? I've
written a book. And it was easier than drawing up a business
plan. When you draw up a business plan, there are a lot of
different factors you have to foresee in advance. But here you
simply sit down and describe what's already happened. Just as
in the jokes about the Chukchi: 'I sing what I see.'[2]

"And besides... you know something, Anastasia? Those
dreams of yours, which I thought were sheer fantasy, they're
starting to come true. It's incredible, but they are coming
true. Look, the book is finished. You dreamt about it, and
now it exists. People are really reading it enthusiastically.
The Moscow papers are already writing about it. Readers are
writing poetry about you, about Nature, about Russia.

"I found the picture we talked about in the archives of the
Trinity-Sergiev Monastery. The picture has been preserved,
it's entitled "The One and Only by a Single Line".[3] I shall
publish it.

---

[2]*I sing what I see* — a reference to a song of the Chukchi (the native people
of the Chukotka Peninsula in Siberia), where the singer sings about whatever he happens to see. This particular phrase has given rise to many Russian jokes. In this case the author is light-heartedly applying the phrase to
his own writing activity.

[3]*The One and Only by a Single Line* — this picture in the private collection of the
Trinity-Sergiev Monastery is a copy of a famous engraving by Claude Mellan
(1598–1688), *Veil of St Veronica* (1649). It represents the face of Christ Jesus
('the One and Only') surmounted by a crown of thorns and is executed by a
single spiral line in 166 revolutions.

"And, can you imagine, the bards... you remember telling me about the bards?"

"Yes, I remember, Vladimir."

"Surprising as it is, this too is starting to come about. I was at one readers' conference where I was approached by this chap with dark blond hair. He handed me an audiocassette and said, in terse, military fashion: 'Songs for Anastasia. Please accept.'

"The journalists, readers and two of the staff of the Moscow Research Centre, Alexander Solntsev[4] and Alexander Zakotsky, who had come to the conference — they all listened in silence to the tape. Later a number of people began making copies of it. They made copies and at the same time tried to track down the man who had given it to me — whose looks, apart from his dark-blond hair and short stature, didn't have much to say for themselves. He had appeared, it seemed, out of nowhere, and disappeared just as mysteriously. He turned out to be a submarine officer from St. Petersburg, a scientist by the name of Alexander Korotynsky.[5] He later told me how the submarine he was on managed to rise to the surface after an accident. How he had been confidently led by a series of coincidences in connection with this cassette. Led to hand

---

[4]*Alexander Vasilievich Solntsev* (1951–) — a Siberian entrepreneur, a former acquaintance of Vladimir Megré's. After spotting a small book with Megré's name on the cover, Solntsev (who by this time had relocated with his family to Moscow and lost sight of his former colleague) contacted the author and in March 1997 became founding director of the Moscow-based "Anastasia" Research Centre, managing the publication of Megré's books, organising readers' conferences, clubs, trips to dolmens, etc. More recently Solntsev has devoted himself to setting up an eco-village in the Smolensk Oblast and reinvigorating the tradition of cultivation of flax. He has also authored a book on the Caucasus, entitled *Dolmens*.

[5]Since this book was published Alexander Korotynsky has released several song albums inspired by the Ringing Cedars Series.

it to me. Not only that, but Korotynsky turned out to be a bard as well. And his song *Khram* (The Church) contains whole phrases which you said to me. Remember these, for example?

Believe not others' words —
Once said, they're gone as wind.
Many will see the Church
But few will enter in.

Our life may be a race:
From floor to floor we're thrown.
But every one must face
The choice he's made his own.

"Besides, Korotynsky doesn't really have a singing voice. He practically recites when he sings. But that very fact goes to prove what you said about the power of the word connected to the soul by invisible threads. Korotynsky the Bard is a living example."

"For all the bright joy you have been giving to people, for the purification of souls, I thank you, Bard, I thank you," said Anastasia.

"Just think — another officer!" I mused. "Grutsia, who first printed the book — he was an officer. And the homeless colonel who drew the picture for it. And then there was a pilot, a regimental commander, who's been helping me sell the books. And now the first one to bring me songs turns out to be an officer. What is it about your Ray that seems to set officers' hearts afire in particular? Do you shine your Ray on them more than others?"

"Many have been touched by my Ray, Vladimir, but it sparks aspirations only when there is something there to set aflame."

"Your dream, Anastasia, is indeed turning more and more into reality. People are grasping hold of it, they understand it. The homeless colonel understood. He was a chance acquaintance — pity he's gone. I saw him lying dead there. His face was all smeared with dirt, but he was smiling. Dead, but still smiling. Did you do something there with your Ray? What does that mean, when someone dies with a smile on their face?"

"That Man that was with you... he is now with the Bard, treading the invisible pathway. His smile is saving many hearts from bullets more terrible than the leaden ones."

"Your dream, Anastasia, is entering upon our world, and it really seems as though our world is beginning to change. There are certain people who feel and understand you — they show evidence of new strength coming from somewhere, and that is changing the world. The world is becoming just a little better.

"But you, Anastasia... there you are as before, in the taiga, in your glade. I would not be able to live in such conditions, and you would not be able to live in our world. What then is the point of your *love?* Your love is meaningless, and I still do not understand my relationship to you. But what's the point since it's so clear we can never be together? Never close."

"We are together, Vladimir. Close."

"Together?! Where are you? When people love each other, they strive to be always close to each other. To embrace and caress each other. You're too different. You don't need that."

"I *do* need it. Just like everyone else. And I am making it happen."

"But how?"

"Right now, for example. Can you not feel the gentle touch of the breeze, feel its caressing embrace? And the warm touch of the Sun's glistening rays on your face? Can you not hear the birds singing so cheerfully and the leaves rustling on the tree you are sitting under? Listen — it is a most unusual rustling!"

"But that — everything you just mentioned — that's for everyone. In any case, are you responsible for all that?"

"Love dissolved in Space for one can touch the hearts of many."

"Why dissolve Love in Space?"

"So that close to a loved one there will always be a Space of Love. This is the essence of Love, this is its designated purpose."

"It's all pretty confusing to me. And your voice... Before, I never heard anything at a distance, but now I do. Why?"

"It is not the *voice* that you hear at a distance. You need to listen not with your ears, but with your heart. You need to learn how to listen with your heart."

"Why should I bother learning? You can just talk with me the way you're doing right now, with your voice."

"I shall not be able to do that indefinitely."

"But you're doing it right now. After all, I can hear you."

"Grandfather is helping us at the moment. You go have a talk with him. I need to go feed our son, and there are so many other things to do. I do want to get them all done."

"So, it works with your grandfather, but not with you. Why?"

"Because Grandfather is somewhere in your vicinity right now. Very close to you."

"Where?"

CHAPTER TWENTY-SIX

Anastasia's grandfather

I looked about me. There was Anastasia's grandfather, standing right close to the bench, using his walking-stick to push a piece of litter someone had thoughtlessly tossed on the grass toward a rubbish bin. I jumped up. We shook hands. His kindly eyes were sparkling with cheer, and he talked in simple terms. Not like his father. When I saw Anastasia's great-grandfather back in the taiga, he hardly said a word, and his eyes kept staring into space, as though they were looking right through you.

Grandfather and I sat down on the bench, and I asked him:

"How did you get here? How did you find me?"

"It wasn't much of a problem getting here and finding you with Anastasia's help."

"She's really something, eh?! She's had a child! She said she would have one, and she did. Alone, out there in the taiga, not in any hospital. It must have been painful for her. Did she cry out?"

"Now why would you think it was painful for her?"

"Well, women, when they give birth — it's painful. Some of them even die during childbirth."

"It's painful only when a child is conceived in sin. As a result of fleshly lusts. Women pay for this with pain in childbirth and torments afterward in life. If the conception takes place with higher aspirations, the pain only intensifies the feeling of the great joy of creation on the part of the mother."

"Where does the pain go, then? How can it intensify joy?"

"When a woman is raped, what does she feel? Of course she feels pain and revulsion. But when she gives in of her own free will, that same pain is transformed into different sensations. The same is true in regard to childbirth."

"Does that mean Anastasia experienced a painless childbirth?"

"Of course it was painless. And she chose a suitable day, a warm and sunny day."

"What do you mean, she *chose?* Childbirth happens quite unexpectedly."

"Unexpectedly, if the conception simply takes place by chance. A mother is always capable of delaying or accelerating her baby's appearance by a few days."

"But weren't you aware of when the baby was due? Didn't you take steps to help her?"

"We did feel something happening on that day. It was a splendid day. We walked over to her glade. Saw the she-bear sitting at the edge of the glade, moaning because her feelings were hurt. She kept moaning and pounding her paw on the ground with all her might. Anastasia was lying on the same spot where her mother had given birth to her, and there was this little ball of life lying on her breast. The she-wolf was licking him."

"And why was the bear moaning? How had her feelings been hurt?"

"Anastasia had called the wolf over instead of her."

"She could have gone to her on her own."

"They do not approach Anastasia without an invitation. Just think what would happen if they all came uninvited, whenever they felt like it."

"I wonder how she's managing with the baby now."

"Why don't you go and see for yourself, if you're interested?"

"She told me I shouldn't communicate with him until I purge myself of something. First of all I have to go 'round to the holy places. But I don't have enough money for that."

"Don't go by what she said — she doesn't always make sense. You're the father, after all. You should do what you think best. You could buy a whole bunch of rompers and other baby clothes, packages of diapers, a little jacket, a rattle maybe, and demand that she dress the baby normally, and not make him suffer. He's all naked out there in the forest."

"I've been wanting to do that ever since I heard about my son. I *will* do it. As for not making sense, I think you hit the nail right on the head. That's probably why I don't really understand my feelings toward her. First it was amazement, now some kind of feeling of respect has appeared, and something else besides which I can't grasp hold of. But not on the order of love for a woman. I still remember the kind of feelings I had when I loved a woman before. This here's something quite different. It's quite possible that she cannot be loved in the ordinary sense of the word. Something gets in the way. Maybe it's her illogicality, her failure to make complete sense all the time."

"Don't take Anastasia's illogicality, Vladimir, for stupidity. It is her seeming illogicality that is drawing forgotten laws out of the depths of the Universe, and possibly creating new laws.

"The forces of both light and darkness are occasionally astounded at her *apparent* illogicality, and then all at once the simple truth of being that everyone knows starts flaring up more brightly. Even *we* don't always comprehend our Anastasia. Even though she's our own granddaughter and great-granddaughter. She grew up under our very eyes. And since we don't always understand, we are not always able to be of significant help. And so she's often left alone with her own aspirations. Very much alone.

"Take *you*, for example. Here she's gone and met with you, opened up her whole self to you, and to others, thanks to the book. We wanted to stop her. We wanted to stop her from loving. To us her choice of *you* seemed incomprehensible, even absurd."

"I still don't understand her choice myself," I admitted. "My readers, too, wonder. 'Who are *you?*' they keep asking. 'Why did Anastasia choose you?' I can't give them an answer. I realise that, according to all logic, she should be in the company of some kind of intellectually- or spiritually-minded person. He would no doubt be able to understand and love her. They could be more useful together. But me, I have to change my whole life, I have to deal with a whole lot of questions which for other more educated people have long been clear and comprehensible."

"Do you regret now how your life has changed?"

"I don't know. I'm still trying to make sense of it all. As to why she picked me out in particular, I can't answer that. I look for an answer but can't find one."

"And how are you looking for an answer?"

"I'm trying to understand things within myself — who I really am."

"Maybe there's something special there, eh?"

"Could be there's something there. After all, they say: like attracts like."

"Vladimir, did Anastasia talk to you about pride and self-conceit? Did she speak about the consequences of this sin?"

"Yes, she said it was a mortal sin, leading people away from the truth."

"Well, she didn't pick you out, Vladimir. She didn't pick you *out*, she picked you *up*. She picked you up like a worn-out good-for-nothing. We didn't realise that ourselves at first. I hope you're not too offended?"

"I don't entirely agree with you. I had a family — a wife and a daughter, and my business wasn't doing too badly. So, I may not have been anything special, but I wasn't at the bottom of the heap, either — not someone to pick up like a tramp or a useless piece of garbage."

"You haven't been in love with your wife for quite a while. You have your own life and interests, she has hers. It was only the daily routine that kept you together, or rather, the inertia of past feelings, which have been getting weaker and weaker over time. Neither have you had anything to talk about with your *daughter.* She's not interested in your business dealings. That's something that seemed important only to you. It brought in a financial income. But today's income may well be nothing tomorrow, or a loss, or a bankruptcy even. And then you were ill. You practically killed your stomach. With that dissolute lifestyle of yours there was no way you could climb out of your hole of disease. It was all over. And nothing was left."

"So what's it to you people? What am I to her? An experiment? Is she looking for some kind of fringe benefit?"

"It's simply that she's fallen in love, Vladimir. Genuinely, sincerely, just as with everything else she does. And she's happy that she hasn't taken anyone out of your world capable of bringing happiness to another woman. She has not placed herself in any privileged position. She's glad to be just like other women."

"So, it's just a whim of hers, eh? She wants a typical hus band from *our* world — one who smokes, goes out carousing... Well, I must say, that's quite a self-sacrifice just for a whim!"

"Her love is genuine. It's not a whim, she's not looking for any fringe benefit. Even though she appeared illogical, at first, to the forces of both light and darkness, to us and to others, in reality she clearly illuminated the whole concept and meaning of Love. Not with words, doctrines or moral teachings, but with actual achievements in the lives of people in your world, including your own personal life. The forces of light, the forces of the Creator, speak through her Love. And not only do they speak, they show clearly as never before: 'Look and see, see the power of a woman, the power of pure Love.' At the very last moment before death it is capable of giving new life. Capable of lifting up any Man, rescuing him from the tenacious paws of darkness and carrying him into the brightness of infinity. Capable of surrounding him with the Space of Love and giving him a new life, which is life eternal.

"Her Love, Vladimir, will restore to you the love of your wife, the respect of your daughter. Thousands of women will look at you with fervent glances of love. You will have complete freedom of choice. And if, from all the varied manifestations of the external appearance of love, you succeed in catching sight of that special one, Anastasia will be very happy. In any case you will be rich and famous, there will be no possibility of bankruptcy for you. The book you have written will circulate all over the world and bring you a return — and not just a monetary return, it will give you and others a power greater than mere physical or material strength."

"I must say," I observed, "the book is really starting to sell quite well. But I did write it myself, even though some people say Anastasia helped me in some way. What do *you* think — is it just my book, or did she have a hand in writing it?"

"You did everything a writer is supposed to do. You got the paper, your hand controlled the pen and you described what happened. You put down all your deductions in your own language. You saw to the publication of the book. What you did was no different from a writer's usual course of action."

"So, the book is mine alone? Anastasia didn't do anything?"

"No, she did not. She did not manipulate the pen on the paper."

"But you talk as though she still facilitated its appearance in some way. If so, explain in more detail. What exactly did she do?"

"To make it possible for you to write this book, Vladimir, Anastasia gave her life."

"Okay. Now everything's got obscured again. How come? How is it possible for her, living in the forest, to give her life for some book? Who *is* she? She herself says: *Man*. Other people call her an alien, or a goddess. Now that all ends up in some serious confusion. I really want to straighten this out for myself."

"It's all very simple, Vladimir. Man is the only creature in the Universe who can live on all planes of existence at once. In their earthly existence most people see themselves only as an earthly, materialised manifestation. But there are those who perceive other levels of being, levels invisible to the material senses.

"Calling Anastasia a goddess is not a sin against the truth. The main difference between Man and all other forms of existence lies in Man's ability to create the present and the future by his thoughts, inventing forms and images which are afterward materialised. The clarity, harmoniousness, pace of thinking and mental purity of Man as a Creator is what determines the future. And in this sense Anastasia *is* a goddess. For the pace at which she thinks, the clarity and purity of the images she formulates, are such that she alone has proved capable of withstanding the whole dark mass of opposing forces. *She alone.* Only there is no way of telling how long she'll be able to hold out. She's still waiting, believing that people will realise what is happening and will help her. Believing that they will cease producing darkness and hell."

"Who's producing darkness and hell?"

"Prophets who believe in and talk about the end of the world — they themselves are producing mental visualisations of the end of the world. The whole mass of teachings foretelling the ultimate doom of mankind, are hastening the day with their visualisations. There are a lot of them, a whole lot of them. And these people have no idea, while they seek salvation for themselves and search for the Promised Land, that a hell is being prepared specifically for them."

"But the people that are talking about the Last Judgement or a global catastrophe, they actually believe in it, they're sincerely praying for the salvation of their souls."

"They are motivated not by faith in the light, in the Love that is God, but by *fear*. And this fearful scenario is something they are fashioning for themselves. Think, Vladimir! Try to imagine. Here we are, you and I, sitting on this bench. You see lots of people before your eyes. All at once some of them start to go into fits of convulsion from terrible pain, as though they were sinners. All around us on the Earth millions of corpses are rotting, while you and I sit here untouched by it all and watch. It's as though we are sitting on a bench in Paradise. But doesn't it wrench your heart to see all the horrifying images of what's going on? Wouldn't it be better to die or fall asleep the moment before witnessing such tragedy?"

"What if all the righteous who are saved," I wondered aloud, "are in the Promised Land, where there are no rotting corpses around, no frightful images?"

"When you get news, even from the other side of the world, about the death of a loved one, or a relative, don't you feel grief and sorrow in your heart?"

"Anyone in a situation like that would surely be distressed."

"Then how can you imagine Paradise for yourself, realising that most of your fellow-countrymen, your friends and relatives, have already perished, and others are dying in frightful torment?! How hardened must a heart become, how deep a pit of gloom must it fall into, to feel pleasure under such circumstances? Such souls are not needed in the kingdom of light. For they themselves are the creatures of darkness."

"But why do the great teachers of mankind," I queried, "— the ones who've put or are now putting various doctrines down on paper — talk about the end of the world, the Last Judgement? Who, then, are *they?* Where are they leading people? Why do they talk that way?"

"It's difficult to define precisely what they're getting at. It's possible they will bring about a change in people's conscious awareness simply because the crowds of people they draw find their ideas so attractive."

"Those who are alive today can effect such a change," I observed. "But what about those who came before and left their teachings for us as a legacy?"

"They might have indeed prepared the *way* for a change, in the hope that their followers would make the change happen and discover the truth. Perhaps they're waiting for the course of history to show the vast majority of mankind the hopelessness of their present path, and counting on ensuing events to help them turn their followers and believers to the light."

"If you people knew all this before, why did you sit there in the forest and remain silent all these years? Why didn't you try to explain it to somebody earlier? Anastasia said your people have been living this way of life for generations, over thousands of years, preserving the truth about Man's pristine origins."

"In various corners of the Earth," the grandfather replied, "there are people who have preserved a way of life apart from technocracy, making use of capacities which are inherent only in Man. From time to time they have made attempts to share their conscious awareness with others. And each time those who tried perished before they could say anything substantial. Even though they presented powerful thought-forms and images, they were resisted by the vast majority of mankind."

"You mean to say they would trample on Anastasia and crush her?"

"Anastasia has somehow managed to stand up to them. At least so far. Maybe it's *because* of her illogicality!"

The old fellow fell silent, thoughtfully tracing the point of his walking-stick on the ground to form incomprehensible symbols.

I sat there, deep in thought. Finally I asked him:

"Then why did she keep repeating to me all the time: *I am Man! I am a woman!* — if she's really a goddess, as you say?"

"In her earthly, materialised sense of existence she is simply *Man*, a human being, a woman. And even though her lifestyle is somewhat unusual, she is still capable, just like anyone else, of experiencing feelings of joy and sorrow, loving and wanting to be loved.

"But all the abilities she has are inherent in Man, in every Man — that is, in Man in his pristine state. The abilities she had which seemed so extraordinary will no longer seem so exceptional to you once you learn what your modern science has to say about them. And as to the other abilities she has which are still not understood, rest assured an explanation will be found. And it will all go to show that she is simply Man, a female of the human species.

"There is one phenomenon you will soon encounter, however, which you won't be able to understand. Nor will your scientists be able to explain it. Even my father doesn't know exactly what kind of phenomenon it is. Your world calls such things *anomalies*. But I beg of you, Vladimir, don't identify this phenomenon with Anastasia. It will appear right beside her, but it is not in her. Try to find the inner strength to see, to feel in her what is simply Man.

"She tries to be like everyone else. For some reason, she feels it's important — she feels a need — a need to prove that she is Man. This is difficult for her, since in doing so she must still keep her principles intact. But, then, don't we all have principles that are sacred to us?"

"But what kind of phenomenon are you talking about — this thing you won't define and which science can't explain?"

CHAPTER TWENTY-SEVEN

The anomaly

"When we buried Anastasia's parents, she was still very young," Anastasia's grandfather began. "She wasn't yet able to walk or talk. My father and I dug a hole in the ground, with the animals' help. We placed branches at the bottom, put the bodies of Anastasia's parents in the hole and covered them over with grass and earth. We stood there a while on the burial mound without saying a word. Little Anastasia sat a short distance away in the glade, watching a bug crawling along her arm. We thought it was just as well that she wasn't yet able to be fully aware of the misfortune that had befallen her. Then we quietly walked away."

"What do you mean, you walked away? You just walked off and abandoned this poor, ignorant little girl to her own devices?"

"We didn't abandon her. We left her in the same spot where her mother had given birth to her. You have a concept known as *Shambala*,[1] or Motherland. The meaning of these words is becoming more and more abstract. *Motherland* — that is literally MOTHER-LAND.[2] *Mother!* In anticipation of their

[1] *Shambala* — a Tibetan word indicating 'the source of happiness' in Oriental religions, and signifying the legendary 'land of the gods' — a place through which the Earth is connected with the Divine.

[2] *Motherland* — the closest English equivalent of the Russian word *Rodina*, derived from the name of God the Creator *Rod* in the ancient Slavic tradition (the word *rod* also signifies 'origin', 'derivation' or 'birth') and the root *na* signifying 'mother'. In the original Russian text, the word is printed as 'ROD I NA'.

child's appearance in the world, parents ought to create a Space for him. An environment of kindness and love. And to give him a piece of the Motherland, which, like a mother's womb, both preserves the body and caresses the soul. It imparts the wisdom of creation and assists in obtaining the truth.

"And what can a woman give her child who is born amidst stone walls? What kind of world has she made ready for him? Or has she given any thought at all to the world in which her child is to live? In that case the world will do with him as it likes. It will strive to subject this little human being unto itself, making him a mere cog, or a slave. And the mother will simply become an observer, as she has not made ready for her child any Space of Love.

"You see, Vladimir, Nature — the Nature surrounding Anastasia's mother, the creatures large and small — treated her as they would treat any Man who lived the way she did: as a friend, as a wise and good deity, one who had created around her a world of Love. Anastasia's parents were happy and kind people, they very much loved one another, loved the Earth, and the Space around them responded to them with Love. Little Anastasia was born into this Space of Love and at once became its centre.

"Many creatures will not touch a newborn. A mother cat may nurse a puppy, or a mother dog a kitten. Many wild animals are capable of nursing and taking care of human offspring. But these animals have become wild to people in your world. To Anastasia's mother and father they played quite another role. The creatures treated *them* entirely differently. Anastasia's mother gave birth to her in the glade, and many creatures were witness to the birth. They saw how the woman they revered became a mother and bore another Man, another human being. When they witnessed the birth, their feelings toward their human friend, their love for her, intertwined with their own parenting instincts, giving birth to a new exalted manifestation of light.

"Everything, absolutely everything in that surrounding Space, from the tiniest bug and blade of grass to the seemingly ferocious beast, was ready, unhesitatingly, to give its life for the sake of that little being. And there was nothing in that surrounding Space of Motherland, created and bestowed by its mother, that could possibly have threatened that being. Everything would look after and cherish this human being.

"To Anastasia the little glade is literally a mother's womb. The glade is her living Motherland. Powerful and kind. And inextricably tied by a natural, living thread to the whole Universe. To the whole creation of the Grand Creator.

"The little glade is her living Motherland. It came from her mother and her father. And from the One and Only, the Original Father. We could never be a substitute for *it*. That is why, after burying her parents, we walked away.

"Three days later, while we were approaching the glade, we felt a tension in the air, we heard wolves howling. Then we saw...

"Little Anastasia was sitting quietly atop the burial mound. One of her cheeks was smeared with earth. We realised she had been sleeping on the mound. Tiny tears were streaming from her eyes and falling onto the ground. She was crying, noiselessly, with only an occasional sob. And she kept stroking and stroking the burial mound with her little hands.

"She wasn't able to talk, but she did say her first words on this mound. We heard them. At first she simply uttered syllables: *Ma-ma*, then *Pa-pa*. She repeated this several times. Then she added a syllable to each: *Ma-moch-ka, Pa-poch-ka, Ma-moch-ka, Pa-poch-ka.*[3] *I am Ana-sta-SI-ya. I now have you no more. Eh? Only my grand-pas? Eh?*

---

[3] *Mamochka, Papochka* — in Russian, common diminutives of *Mama* and *Papa* respectively.

"My father was the first to realise it: even as we were burying her parents, little Anastasia, sitting there in the glade and
watching the bug, was fully aware of the whole depth of the
misfortune that had befallen her. She used her will-power to
refrain from showing her feelings. With her mother's milk she
had been imbued with the wisdom and strength of her pristine origins. Nursing mothers have that capacity, Vladimir.
The capacity to pass along to their baby, together with mother's milk, the conscious awareness and wisdom of the ages,
right back to their pristine origins.

"Anastasia's mother knew how to do this, and used this
method to full advantage. To the fullest possible advantage.

"Since Anastasia didn't want us to see her crying, we didn't
go out into the glade, and didn't approach the mound, but we
couldn't tear ourselves from the spot. So we just stood there,
observing what was going on.

"Supporting herself on the burial mound, little Anastasia
attempted to stand on her little feet. She didn't do it on
the first try, but still, she managed to stand up. She stood
there swaying back and forth, stretching her arms out a little to each side, and finally took her first timid step away
from her parents' grave, then a second step. Her little feet
got mixed up in the grass and her little body lost its balance
and started to fall. But the fall — well, that was something
quite unusual.

"At the moment she fell, a barely noticeable bluish glow
came flooding over the glade, and changed the Earth's laws
of gravity just on that particular spot. It touched us too with
some kind of mellow languor. Anastasia's body didn't fall, but
gradually and smoothly descended to the ground. Once she
got up on her feet again, the bluish light disappeared, and the
normal gravitation field was restored.

"With careful and hesitating footsteps, Anastasia went
over to a little branch lying in the glade and was able to pick it

up. We realised she had started cleaning up the glade, as her mother had done many times. This wee little girl then carried the dry branch to the edge of the glade. But once again she lost her balance, began to fall and dropped the branch.

"During her fall, once more the bluish glow sparked into life, changing the Earth's gravitational field, and the branch flew over to the little pile of dry branches lying at the edge of the glade.

"Anastasia got up, looked around for the branch but couldn't find it. Then, throwing up her little hands, with shaky steps she slowly made her way over to another branch. No sooner had she started bending over to pick it up than the branch itself began rising from the ground, as though a breeze had blown it to the edge of the glade. But there wasn't enough of a wind around to do this. Some invisible presence was carrying out little Anastasia's desires.

"But she wanted to do everything herself, as her Mama had done. And, no doubt in protest against this help from her invisible ally, she thrust her little hand into the air and waved it gently above her head.

"We looked up and saw it. Over the meadow we saw hanging a small spherical mass, pulsating and glowing with a pale-blue light. We could see a whole multitude of fiery discharges inside its transparent covering, giving the effect of multi-coloured lightning. Indeed, it was very similar to large ball-lightning. But it was intelligent!

"We couldn't tell what it was made of and what kind of intelligence we were dealing with.

"We could feel some kind of unknown and unseen power in it. But there was no sense of fear of this power. On the contrary, it seemed to be radiating a pleasant, languid grace. We didn't feel like moving. We just felt like being."

"But what made you think it possessed untold power?" I interrupted.

"My Papa noticed that. Even though it was a bright sunny day, the leaves on the trees and the petals on the flowers turned in its direction. In its bluish glow there was more power than in the Sun's rays. And it could change the Earth's gravitational field at the moment Anastasia fell — just in the right place and at just the right time. The change was so precise that her body descended smoothly, but yet was not torn away from the Earth.

"Anastasia spent a long time collecting branches. Sometimes she would crawl, at other times walk all over the meadow with slow steps, until she had cleared them all away. And the fiery sphere, still pulsating, hovered over the wee little one. But it no longer helped her pick up the branches. The powerful fiery sphere seemed to understand the gesture of her little hand and obeyed it.

"Expanding and dissolving in Space, contracting and producing internal discharges (like flashbulbs) of some kind of energy from goodness-knows-where, the sphere would momentarily disappear and then reappear, as though it were somehow excited, and this excitement caused it to sweep through space at incredible speed.

"The time came when Anastasia normally lay down to sleep. We never compel our children to sleep, rocking them back and forth until they become dizzy. At this time Anastasia's mother would simply lie down herself in the usual spot and pretend to doze off, to show her child by example. Little Anastasia would crawl over to her, snuggle up against her warm body and peacefully fall asleep.

"And this time Anastasia went to the spot where she was used to sleeping during the day with her mother. She stood and looked at the place where she had always slept with her Mama at this time, but now there was no Mama around.

"It was not clear just what she was thinking at that moment, only once again a tiny tear glistened in a sunbeam on

Anastasia's face. And right away the bluish glow came pulsating across the glade, flashing at irregular intervals.

"Anastasia raised her little head, saw the pulsating mass of light, sat down on the grass and began staring at it continuously. It remained still under her gaze. For some time she just sat there staring like that. Then she held out both her little arms in its direction, as she was wont to do when summoning one of the creatures to her side. At that point the fiery sphere sparked up in a multitude of powerful lightning bolts, reaching out beyond its blue covering, and... made a dash for her little arms like a fiery comet. Looking as though it had the ability to sweep away everything in its path, it took only a split second to reach Anastasia's face, start rotating and with one of its lightning flashes wipe away a tiny tear glistening on her cheek. And at this point it extinguished all the discharges and became a pale blue, faintly glowing sphere in the arms of the little one sitting on the grass.

"For a time Anastasia sat there holding it, examining it and stroking it with her hands. Then she got up, lifted up the blue sphere, and with careful steps carried it over and put it down on the place she used to sleep with her mother. And again she caressed it gently.

"The sphere took up a position on the ground and pretended to doze off, just as Anastasia's mother had done. And the little girl lay down beside it. She fell asleep. She slept there on the grass, all curled up into a ball. The sphere took flight, disappearing into the heavenly heights, then spread itself low over the glade, as though it were a blanket. Later, once more contracting into a small, pulsating ball, it took up a position next to Anastasia, who was still sleeping on the grass, and began stroking her hair. It was a strange and unusual caressing. With the most delicate luminescent and flickering threads of lightning, it took each individual strand of hair, lifted it and caressed it.

"On subsequent visits to Anastasia in her glade, we saw it again on several occasions. We realised that to Anastasia it was something quite natural, just like the Sun, or the Moon, or the trees and animals around her. And she had conversations with it, just as she did with everything else around her. But it was evident she made a distinction between it and the other things in her environment. The distinction wasn't too noticeable in terms of outward expression, but there was a definite impression that she treated it with just a little more respect than other things, and sometimes she would even play up to it. She never played up to anyone else, but for some reason she allowed herself to behave this way with the sphere. It reacted to her mood and even played along."

"The morning Anastasia turned four," Grandfather continued, "we were standing at the edge of the glade waiting for her to wake up. We wanted to quietly watch and see how she would delight in the new spring day that was unfolding.

"The sphere appeared just a moment before she woke up. It glistened faintly with its bluish glow, either spreading itself in a shower of light or dissolving over the whole Space of the glade. And we beheld a natural living picture made by no human hand — it was charming and magnificent.

"The whole glade was transformed — the surrounding trees, the grass, even the bugs. The needles of the cedars began shining in a host of soft hues. Behind the squirrels springing from branch to branch could be seen rainbow-trails sparkling and dissolving. The grass was lit up in a soft green glow. An even more pronounced multicoloured glow emanated from the multitude of bugs scurrying through the grass, forming an unusually vivid and beautiful carpet spreading its way across the glade, constantly morphing itself into new intricate and marvellous patterns. Upon awakening, Anastasia opened her eyes to behold an extraordinary living panorama, full of enchantment. She jumped up and gazed all 'round.

"She smiled, as she always did in the morning, and everything around her responded to her smile with an even brighter glow and accelerated movement. Then Anastasia carefully knelt down and began meticulously examining the grass and the shining, multicoloured bugs scurrying about. When she lifted up her head, the slightly worried expression on her face betrayed a measure of concentration. She looked up and, even though nothing was visible up there, stretched her little arms to the sky. All at once the still air stirred, and in her hands appeared the bluish sphere. She held it up to her face, then put it down on the grass and tenderly stroked it. And we could hear their conversation. Anastasia was the only one who actually spoke, but we had the distinct impression that the sphere was understanding her and even silently responding. Anastasia spoke with it tenderly, with just a touch of sadness:

"'You are good. You are very good. You wanted to delight me with your beauty. Thank you. But change it back, please change it back to the way it was before. And do not ever change it again.'

"The blue sphere emitted another pulse, then lifted slightly off the ground, and the lightning discharges flashed from within. But the glowing scene did not fade. Anastasia fixed her gaze upon it and spoke to it once again:

"'Every little beetle, bug and ant has its Mama. Everyone has a Mama. All Mamas love their children just the way they were born. It does not matter how many legs they have or what colour they are. You have changed everything. How will the Mamas recognise their children now? Please, make everything as it was before!'

"The sphere gave a faint flash, and everything in the glade was restored to the way it looked before. Once again it descended to Anastasia's feet. She stroked it and offered a

'Thank you!'. She stared silently at the sphere for a while, and when she spoke to it again, her words really impressed us. She told it:

"'Do not come to see me again. I like being with you. You are always trying to do only what is good for everyone, always trying to help. But do not come visit me. I know you have a very large glade of your own. But you think very fast, so fast that I cannot understand all at once. Only later shall I understand a bit. You move faster than everything else. Much faster than the birds and the breeze. You do everything very fast and very well, and I know that is how you must do it to get everything done, to do good in your own very large glade. But when you are with me, it means you are not there. So, when you are with me, there is no one to do good in the other glade. Go away. You need to take care of the large glade.'

"The blue sphere contracted into a little lump, and took off way up high. It began sweeping through Space, sparkling more brightly than usual, and once more plunged down like a fiery comet to Anastasia, who was still sitting in the same spot. It stayed still by her head for a while, then a multitude of tiny flickering rays reached out to Anastasia's long hair and stroked each strand individually, right down to the tip.

"'What are you taking your time for?' Anastasia said quietly. 'You should get going back to those who are waiting for you. I'll make everything all right here myself. And I will be happy to know that everything is all right in the large glade too. I shall be able to feel you. And I want you to think of me too, but just occasionally.'

"The blue sphere began ascending, but not with its usual carefree bounce. It rose from Anastasia in fitful bursts, and finally disappeared into space. But it left something invisible all around. And each time when something happened that affected Anastasia negatively, the surrounding space would grow still, as though paralysed. That is why you lost consciousness when you tried to touch her without her consent. She pacifies this phenomenon by waving her hands in the air whenever she can. Just as before, she wants to do everything all by herself.

"We asked our little Anastasia:

"'What was that glowing thing that was hovering over the glade, what do you call it?'

"She thought for a bit, and answered briefly:

"'I would call it *Good,* Granpakins.'"

The oldster fell silent. But I still wanted to hear about how little Anastasia lived in the forest, and I asked him:

"What did she do after that, how did she live?"

"The same way," the old fellow replied. "She grew up just like anyone else. We suggested she help the dachniks. By the time she was six she was already able to see people at a distance, to discern their feelings and help them. She got involved with the dachniks. Now she believes that the phenomenon of the dachniks offers an easy transition to making sense of what constitutes our earthly existence. Here she's been continually shining that ray of hers for twenty years now. She's given warmth to plants on the small plots of land. She's treated people's illnesses. She's tried to explain to people, without imposing on them, how one should handle plants, and she's had terrific results. Then she started observing other aspects of human life. And destiny brought her together with *you.* And now she's come out with the idea of *carrying people through the dark forces' window of time.*"

"And what do you think, she'll be successful?" I asked.

"Vladimir, Anastasia knows the power of thought inherent in Man as a Creator. Otherwise she would never have let herself make such a statement. From now on she will not deviate from this path — she'll stick to it. She's a stubborn lass. It comes from her father."

"So, she's taking concrete steps," I observed. "She's trying to make her thought-forms into reality, and here we are just sitting and rationalising about the spiritual. Like kids wiping their noses... You know, there's quite a few people that still ask me: 'Does Anastasia really exist, or did I just dream everything up myself?'"

"That's not a question people can actually ask. People touched by the book will feel her right away. She is in the book. Questions like that can only be asked by illusory people, not real people."

CHAPTER TWENTY-EIGHT

Illusory people

"But I'm talking about very real people — like those two girls over there, for instance. D'you see?" I pointed in the direction of two teen-age girls standing about five or six metres away from our bench.

The old man fixed his gaze upon them and said:

"I think one of them — the one that's smoking — is unreal."

"What d'you mean, unreal? If I went up to her and gave her behind a good slap, you'd hear a scream and curses that'd be more than real!"

"You know, Vladimir, what you are now seeing is simply an image before your eyes. An image created by the dogmas of the technocratic world. Look closely. The girl has on very uncomfortable high-heeled shoes. Besides, they're a little too tight for her. She wears them precisely because someone else is dictating what shoes women should be wearing these days.

"And she's wearing a short skirt of material made to look like leather but it isn't leather. It's harmful for the body, but she's wearing it according to the dictates of society's current fad. Look at all her gaudy make up and how arrogantly she's behaving. Outwardly she's independent. But only outwardly. Her whole appearance is at odds with herself, her real self. She's been 'smitten' by an image of someone else's thought-forms, a soulless, illusory image has eclipsed her living soul and taken it captive."

"You can say what you like about the soul, captivity and the dictates of some image or other," I interjected. "But how can one tell whether that's actually true or not?"

"I'm already an old man, you see. I can't get in tune with the slower pace of your thinking. I can't express myself convincingly, the way Anastasia does." The oldster sighed and added: "Do you mind if I try *showing* you?"

"Showing me what?"

"I shall now attempt to destroy, at least for a time, that illusory, lifeless image and free the girl's soul. You watch closely."

"Go ahead."

The girl holding the cigarette was in the midst of arrogantly berating her companion. The old fellow watched them closely and intently. And when the girl turned her glance away and fixed it on some of the passers-by, the oldster's eyes followed her gaze. Then he got up and, gesturing to me to follow him, headed toward the girls. I went after him. He stopped about a half metre from them and fixed his eyes on the girl with the cigarette. She turned her head to look at him, blew a puff of cigarette smoke in his face and said with some irritation:

"Hey, what's with you, Gramps? Begging for money, eh?"

The oldster paused, probably to recover from the cloud of smoke enveloping his face, and said in a soft and tender tone:

"Put the cigarette, dear girl, into your right hand. You should try holding it in your right hand."

And the girl obediently put the cigarette into her right hand. But there was much more to it than that. Her face suddenly became completely altered. Her arrogance had vanished. In fact everything about her was different: her face, the way she stood. And in a completely different tone of voice she said:

"I'll try, Grandfather."

"You should have your child, dear girl."

"It'll be hard for me. I'm all alone."

"Let him come to you. You go and think about that hand of yours, think about your child, and he will come. Go along now, dear girl, you must hurry."

"I'll go." The girl took a few steps, then stopped and called back to her companion in a calm, quiet voice, with no sign of her former irritation: "Come along, Tanya... come with me."

They left.

"Wow! Can you tame *any* woman like that?" I said, when we had regained our seat on the bench again. "That's terrific! Some sort of super-hypnosis, eh? Far out!"

"It's not hypnosis, Vladimir. And there's no far-out mysticism here. It's simply an attentive attitude to one's fellow-Man. And I mean to the Man, not to the dreamt-up image which obscures the real Man. And Man responds instantly to this, he finds his strength, when you appeal directly to him, ignoring the illusory image."

"But how did you manage to see the invisible Man behind the visible image?"

"It's all very simple, really. I watched them a bit. The girl was holding her cigarette in her left hand. She was also rummaging about in her purse with her left hand. Which means she's left-handed. And if a small child holds a spoon or does something else with the left hand, his parents try to get him to use his right. She got along fine with her parents. I realised this when I saw the way she looked at the man and woman walking along with a little girl in tow. I spoke to her the way her parents might have when she was little. I tried to use the same tone of voice her parents might have used. Back when she was little, unaffected, not under someone else's image. That little girl was the real Man, and it responded right off."

"But you were talking to her about childbirth — what was that all about?"

"She's pregnant, you see. She's been pregnant more than a month now. That alien image doesn't want the child. But the girl's inner being wants the child very much. They're struggling with each other. Now her inner being will win out!"

CHAPTER TWENTY-NINE

Why nobody can see God

"Anastasia told me, when I talked with her in the taiga," I recalled, "that nobody can see God because His thoughts work with great speed and concentration. But I'm thinking, why doesn't He slow them down so people can get a good look at Him?"

The old man raised his walking-stick and pointed it at a passing cyclist.

"Look there, Vladimir. Look how the bicycle wheels turn. The wheel has spokes, but you can't see them. They are there, and you know it, but the speed of rotation does not allow you to see them. Or put it another way: the pace of your thinking and your visual perception does not allow you to see them. If the cyclist goes slower, you will see the spokes of the wheel, albeit blurred. If he stops altogether, you will see them clearly, but the cyclist himself will fall off. He won't get to his destination because of his stopping, and for what? Just to let you see that the spokes are there? But where does that take you? Has anything changed in you? Or around you?

"The only thing you'll know for certain is: the spokes exist. And that's it. The cyclist, of course, can always get up and continue his journey, but others may want to see, which means he'll have to stop and fall again and again. And for what?"

"Well, so I can get a good look at him just once."

"And what will you see? After all, a cyclist lying on the ground isn't a cyclist any more. You will have to imagine what he looked like.

"Just so, a God who changes the pace of His thinking is no longer God. Wouldn't it be better for you to learn how to accelerate your own thinking? Imagine yourself talking with someone who has a slow time getting what you're saying — doesn't that irritate you? Isn't it a pain slowing down your own pace of thought to his level?"

"You're right, if you adapt yourself to a fool's pace, you might become a fool yourself."

"So in order for us to see God, He would have to slow down His own thinking to our pace, and become as one of us. But when He *does* this, sending us His sons, the crowd looks at them and says: 'You aren't God, you're not even the son of God, just a pretender. Perform a miracle or we'll nail you to a cross.'"

"But why shouldn't God's son perform a miracle?" I questioned. "At least so the non-believers would back off, and not crucify him."

"Miracles do not convince non-believers, they only tempt them," came the reply. "And those who perform miracles are burnt at the stake under cries of 'Burn the manifestation of the dark forces!' Besides, just look around you. God's miracles abound in countless numbers. The Sun rises every day, and then there's the Moon at night. An insect on a blade of grass is a miracle, after all, not to mention a tree...

"Here we are, the two of us, sitting under a tree. Who could think up a more perfect mechanism than a tree like this? These are particles of His thought. All the materialised, living forms scurrying beneath our feet, flying above our heads in the ethereal blue, singing for us, caressing our bodies with a ray of warmth — these are all His, they are all around us, made for us. But are there that many people who are able not only to see, but to feel and realise the significance of all this? Maybe not even to improve, but simply to use and keep from distorting or destroying these living marvels of creation? As for His sons, they have one purpose — to raise people's conscious awareness by their words, slowing down their own thinking, even at the risk of being misunderstood themselves."

"But Anastasia emphasised that just speaking words was not enough to raise Man's conscious awareness to a meaningful level. I too think that mankind has uttered an enormous number of different words, but what do they mean? The Earth all around is full of unhappy lives, and it may even suffer a global disaster."

"Quite right. When the words do not come from the heart, when the threads linking them to the soul are torn apart, then the words are empty, imageless, faceless. Our granddaughter Nastenka[1] is capable of creating images not just in every word, but in the sound of every letter of the alphabet. Now the Earth-dwelling teachers, His sons that are in the flesh today, will attain such a degree of power that the human spirit will outshine the darkness."

"Sons, teachers? What have they got to do with it? Aren't the abilities hers alone?"

"She will share them, in fact she is already sharing them. Look here, you've even been able to write a book, readers have flooded the world with poems, and new songs have been sung. Have you heard the new songs?"

"Yes, I have."

"So this will be multiplied many times with your religious teachers, just as soon as they come into contact with the book. And where you see simply words, they will feel the living images, and the power will be magnified multifold in them."

"*They* will feel it, but what about me? What am I, completely devoid of feeling? If so, why did she talk with me and not with them?"

"Because you are incapable of distorting what you hear, and there is nothing you have of your own already that you

---

[1]*Nastenka* (pronounced *NAH-sten-ka*) — a diminutive form of *Anastasia.*

can mix with it. On a clean sheet of paper the word is set forth more clearly. But not to worry, *your* thought will accelerate too."

"Okay, let it accelerate in me too, so I don't lag behind the others. I guess everything you say must be right. Here in Russia there's the leader of one religious community — the community settlers refer to him as their teacher — who told his followers to read the book about Anastasia. 'It will set your hearts on fire,' he told them. And many of his followers went out and bought the book."

"So, that means he understood, he felt something, and that is why he helped Anastasia and you. And did you ever thank him for his help?"

"I've never met him."

"You can say 'thank you' in your heart."

"Silently, you mean? Who's going to hear that?"

"The one who listens with his heart will hear it."

"There's another element here. He said the book was really good, Anastasia too, but he went on to say that *I* wasn't a real man, that I wasn't a true male of the species. 'Anastasia didn't meet with a real man,' he said. I saw this myself on TV, and then read it in the papers."

"And what would *you* say you were — Mr Perfection?"

"Well, 'perfection', I admit, is stretching it."

"Then you need not be offended. You can work toward being perfect. My granddaughter will help you. Those whom Love is capable of uplifting can rise to the heights. It's not even meant for everyone to grasp the whys and the wherefores. An extraordinary speed of thinking is required for that."

"What about *your* thought? What speed does it operate at? You don't find it tiresome talking with me?"

"The thinking speed of anyone who leads a lifestyle such as ours is always significantly greater than that of people in the technocratic world. Our thought is not encumbered by constant concerns about clothing, food and a lot of other things like that. But I don't find it tiresome talking with you, thanks to my Love for my granddaughter. She wanted me to talk with you. And I am glad to do something for her."

"And what is the pace of Anastasia's thinking? The same as yours and your father's?"

"Anastasia's is greater."

"By how much? By what ratio? What she can process in ten minutes, let's say, how long would that take *you*?"

"To make sense of what she can process in a *second,* we would require several months. That is why she sometimes seems to us illogical. That is why she is utterly alone. That is why we can't be of any significant help to her — why we can't grasp right off the logic behind her actions. My father has completely given up conversation altogether. He keeps trying to match her pace of thinking so he can help her. He wants me to do the same. But I don't even try. My father thinks that's because I'm lazy. But I love my granddaughter very much and simply trust that she is doing everything correctly. And if she asks me to do something, I'm delighted to do it. That's why I came to see you."

"But how then did Anastasia manage to talk with me for three whole days?"

"We wondered how, too — for a long time. After all, constantly making that kind of an adjustment could drive one crazy. It was just recently that we discovered the answer. You see, when she was talking with you, she did not slow her thinking down. On the contrary, she made it work even faster. She accelerated it and transformed it into images. Now, like your computer programmes, these images will play themselves out for you and for anyone who reads the book. They will expand and accelerate the pace of human thinking by leaps and bounds, bringing it closer to God. When we realised that, we concluded that in thinking up such a thing, she had created a new law in the Universe. But now it's clear that she was simply using the opportunity afforded by pure and sincere Love, which we hadn't known about before. Love, after all, has remained one of the Creator's grand mysteries. And look how she has now opened up one of its great opportunities and powers."

"And does the pace of her thinking allow *her* to see God?"

"Hardly. After all, she lives in the flesh too. God is in the flesh as well, but only partly. And His flesh is all the people of the Earth. As one small particle of this flesh, Anastasia occasionally grasps something. It is possible that when her thinking reaches such incredible speeds, she feels Him more than others do, but this happens with her only for short periods of time."

"And what does it give her?"

"In a matter of a second she is able to comprehend the truths, the essence of being, the conscious awareness that the wisest people of your world have spent a lifetime perfecting and sharing with each other."

"And that means she has the knowledge of our Oriental lamas, the wisdom of Buddha and Christ, and knows yoga too?"

"That she does. She knows more than is said in all the treatises passed down to your world today. But she still considers them to be insufficient, since there is no universal harmony among those living on the Earth today, and the march toward global disaster continues.

"This is why she is working out her incredible 'combinations'. She is saying: 'Enough of teaching people dogmas, enough of tempting them with Adam and Eve's apple. They must be enabled to feel — really *feel* — what Man once felt, what he was capable of and who he was.'"

"So," I said, "what you're trying to tell me is that she has a real possibility of doing something good for all mankind? If that's so, then when will it begin — this 'good'?"

"It has already begun. Just little sprouts so far, but that it is only for the time being."

"Where are they? How do I see them? Or feel them?"

"Ask the people who read the book — the 'sprouts' are in them. Indeed, the book is awakening bright feelings in many people. That's something that can no longer be denied — many will attest to it. She's succeeded with those combinations of hers. Incredible, but she's done it.

"And you, Vladimir, think about who you were and who you've become. What has been happening, Vladimir, is that a programme of thought-images has been unfolding in you, and her soul has been unfolding in people's consciousness. The world is starting to change in you, and by doing so is changing the thought-images all around you. We cannot fathom completely how she manages to do that. What is evidently real on the surface is something we can still manage to decipher. What helps her to bring about this new reality remains a mystery.

"Naturally one can make vigorous efforts to delve into it, but we should be wary of taking away from the marvellous reality that is unfolding before our eyes. A breathtaking dawn of a new day is something to be admired. Once you begin analysing the whys and wherefores, instead of elation all you get is excavation, which doesn't lead to anything and doesn't change anything."

"Golly, I didn't realise it was so far out, so complex! I was still hoping that Anastasia was just a simple recluse, only extraordinarily kind, beautiful and a little naïve."

"You see what I mean, you mustn't go digging around and knocking your brains out. If it's all too complex, then let her remain for you a kind and beautiful recluse, since that's the image you have of her. Others will see something different. You've been given what you've been given. That's all your consciousness has room for at the moment, and that is perfectly well and good. Just try to admire the dawn, if you can. That's the most important thing of all."

CHAPTER THIRTY

Dawn in Russia

"The dawn will begin in Russia," I observed, "when everyone will be better off financially. When the economy as a whole improves, and individuals see a rise in their incomes."

"All the material things you see around you depend on Man's spirit and conscious awareness," Anastasia's grandfather responded.

"Okay, maybe. But what's the point in erudite philosophies, if people can't afford to feed or clothe themselves?"

"They need to think about why that has been happening. Each one needs to figure it out for themselves. And stop trying to find a scapegoat. Only by *changing themselves within* will they change anything around them, including their financial situation. I agree with you that people will not be able to accept this all at once. But Anastasia said, after all: 'You have to do without moral preaching. You have to show people how, that's all.' And she showed how.

"Now it's up to you to carry out what she outlined. Then, within the space of three years, many communities throughout Siberia — large, small, forgotten and neglected, where there are only old people still living whose children don't even come for a visit, will become richer, many times richer. Their life will bloom abundantly, and many children will return.

"And she will have much more than that to offer. She will reveal many secrets, she will restore people's abilities and the knowledge inherent in our pristine origins. Russia will be a most wealthy land. And she will do this to prove that the spirituality and knowledge inherent in our pristine origins are

more significant than the futile efforts of technocracy. Russia
will herald a new dawn over the whole Earth."

"And what do *I* have to do to bring it about?"

"You can start by revealing the first secret related to you by
Anastasia. You should write in your book how to produce healing oil from the cedar nut. And don't hold anything back."

I suddenly felt everything boiling up inside me. The wind
was literally knocked out of me. I couldn't sit, and jumped to
my feet.

"Why? Tell me why! Why should I suddenly turn around
and do that? For everybody. For free. Any sane person would
think I was an idiot...

"I set up an expedition, and I put into it everything I had.
Now my firm's been ruined. Anastasia asked me to write a
book, and I wrote it. And now we're even. Your aspirations,
your philosophy — that's not something I can readily comprehend. All I did was put it down on paper, as I promised
Anastasia I would...

"But the oil — well, that's something that's completely
clear to me. I know now how much I can get for it. And
I'll never share the technology with anybody. I'll scrape together a little money from selling the books and then I'll start
producing it myself. I've got to put everything back together
again. I've got to get my ship back, the company too. I need
to buy a laptop so I can keyboard the next book...

"I don't have a home any more. No place to live. I want
to buy a trailer home. And when I'm rich, I want to erect a
monument to Russian officers — the ones physically alive but
with mortally wounded hearts. Our indifference keeps tearing their hearts apart, and their honour and conscience have
been spat on by people — the same people officers in all ages
have gone into battle to defend...

"While you people sit nice and quiet there in the forest,
here people are perishing. The country all around is full of

various 'preachers'. They all just *talk* about spiritual matters, but don't really feel like *doing* anything. At least I'm going to *do* something. But here you're telling me I should give valuable know-how away just like that! To everyone! Not on your life!"

"Anastasia did determine a percentage for you too," Grandfather interjected. "I know — three percent from the sale of the oil."

"Sure, what's a miserable three percent to me, when I can get three hundred for the oil?! I know what the world prices are now. And as for its healing properties, what they're selling out there is considerably less effective. I did some checking. They don't know how to produce it properly. Now I'm the only one who knows how to do it. Everything she said checked out. There's nothing in the world that can compare with its healing impact. Besides, scientific studies confirm it. Pallas[1] said that it could even restore a person's youth. And you want me to go give it away just like that.

"You must take me for a fool. I've looked through so much literature, even sent people into the archives to confirm what she said. And they did. A lot of money went to that too."

"You checked into everything — which means you couldn't bring yourself to trust Anastasia right off. That lack of trust is what cost you the time and money."

"Yes, I did do the checking. I had to, you see. But now I'm not going to be a sucker any more. You talk about a 'dawn for everyone'. Come on now — 'dawn'? In that dawn of yours I'd still be a sucker. I wrote a book. I did everything just the way she asked me to. I remember her telling me: 'Don't hide anything, either the bad or the good. Humble your pride. Don't

---

[1]*Pallas* — a reference to Peter Simon Pallas (1741-1811), a member of the St. Petersburg Academy of Sciences and a prominent pioneer explorer of the Siberian taiga.

be afraid to look ridiculous, don't be afraid to be misunderstood.' I haven't hid anything. And what's come of it?

"The book makes me look like a complete idiot. People stand there and say that to my face. That I haven't got a spiritual ounce in my body, that there's a lot I still don't understand. They say I'm coarse and uncivilised. And even a thirteen-year-old girl from Kolomna[2] wrote me to say I've been doing things the wrong way. And a woman from Perm[3] came to see me, right to my doorstep, and said: 'I wanted to see what Anastasia saw in him.'

"'Don't hide anything, either the good or the bad. Humble your pride. Don't be afraid to look ridiculous, don't be afraid to be misunderstood.' She knew everything, didn't she? She comes out pretty good in the book — that's what people say — and how do I look? It's all her fault. If it weren't for the child, I could easily slap her one for what she did. Just think! I wrote everything down in good faith, just as she asked me to. And for that people tell me I'm insensitive and a coward to boot.

"Of course I'm a complete idiot. I've made myself into one. I obeyed her. I've written all that about myself, and now I'll never live it down the rest of my days. And after I'm gone they'll still make fun of me. The book's got a life of its own, as it's turned out. It'll outlive me! And even if I stop printing it, what difference will it make? The underground press is already grinding out more copies. They're trying to run it off on photocopy machines."

All at once I stopped short and looked at the old man. A little tear could be seen slowly making its way down his cheek.

---

[2]*girl from Kolomna* — The reference is to a young girl also named Anastasia, whose letter to Vladimir Megré is reproduced in Book 1, Chapter 30: "Author's message to readers".

[3]*Perm* — a major city of over a million inhabitants 1,500 km east of Moscow.

I sat down beside him. He was still silently looking at the ground. Then he spoke.

"You see, Vladimir, my granddaughter Nastenka is capable of foreseeing a lot. It's not that she wanted anything for herself. She didn't want fame, didn't want money. By taking part of the fame upon herself, she put herself in danger, but she saved you. And the fact that you come out the way you do in the book — well, that's her doing. You're right about that. But that was not to humiliate you — that's how she was able to save you. By taking upon herself a whole mass of dark forces. All by herself. And you respond to her with the pain of misunderstanding and irritation. Think — is it easy for a woman who creates out of love to hold on like that?"

"What kind of a love is it," I countered, "when her beloved is counted among fools?"

"Calling somebody a fool doesn't make him one. A fool is one who mistakes flattering words for the truth. Think for a moment of how you would like to be seen by others. As a figure exalted above all? As a brilliant intellect? And you could have made yourself a reputation like that with your first book. But then... pride and selfishness would have destroyed you.

"There are not even that many enlightened people who could hold out against sins like those. Pride creates an unnatural image of Man, it obscures the living soul. That is why the philosophers of the past and the geniuses of today can create so precious little. Because even after the first stroke of their pen they are so overwhelmed by a sense of self-conceit they lose right off what was given to them in the beginning.

"But Nastenka was smart enough to set up a protective barrier against flattery and worship which lead to pride. They won't touch you now. She is saving you from a multitude of ills. And is protecting both your spirit and your flesh. You will write nine books straight from your heart. The Earth will be radiant with its Space of Love. And then, once you have

dotted the final *i* in the ninth book, you will be able to understand who you are."

"Come on! Isn't it possible to tell who I am right now?"

"Who you are right now — that's pretty obvious. You are
who you are at the moment. You are who you feel yourself
to be. Whoever you will become, only Anastasia, possibly,
knows. And she will wait, living each moment by Love. The
fact that people sitting in their comfortable apartments call
you a coward — that's nothing. You should take it with a
grain of salt. And suggest *they* try heading off into the taiga
for three days with no gear. Let *them* try sleeping with a bear
in a cave. To get the full sensation, let them take a mentally
deranged girl along — after all, wasn't that how Anastasia
seemed to you at first?"

"More or less."

"Let any man who accuses you try sleeping with his mentally deranged companion. Out there in the backwoods, where
they can hear the wolves howling. Could he really do that?
What do you think?" the old fellow asked slyly.

And no sooner had I pictured to myself the scenario he described than I burst out in a hearty laugh. And the two of us
had a good laugh together. Then I asked him:

"Can Anastasia hear what we've been saying?"

"She will learn about all your deeds."

"Then tell her not to worry. I shall explain to everyone how
to extract healing oil from cedar nuts."

"Fine, I'll tell her," the old man promised. "But do you remember everything Anastasia told you about the process?"

"Yes, I think I do."

"Right, tell it to me."

Chapter Thirty-One

How to produce healing cedar oil

It's not that difficult a task. The modern technology involved is already familiar and it needs no setting forth here. But there are some rather unusual nuances I should point out.

When gathering the cones[1] one should not beat against the cedars with logs or wooden bats, as the harvesters do today. This greatly weakens the healing properties of the oil. One should use only the cones which the cedar itself gives off. Either they fall with the wind, or you can knock them down with the resonance of your voice, as Anastasia does. They should be collected by people whose thought is free from evil. And it is especially good when the cones are picked up by *children's* hands. In any case, all the steps which follow should be carried out with kind and bright thoughts.

"Such people may be found in Siberian villages even now," Anastasia affirmed. Whether this really makes a difference is difficult to tell. But it also says in the Bible that King Solomon sought out people "skilled in felling timber".[2] Only it doesn't say how these people differed from anyone else in other respects.

The nuts obtained after the shelling of the cones must have their oil extracted within a three-month period; after that the

---

[1] *cones* — Note that the term *cedar* (Russian *kedr*) is used throughout the Ringing Cedars Series to refer to either the Siberian cedar (or Siberian pine, *Pinus sibirica*) — as in this case — or to the Lebanese cedar (cedar of Lebanon, *Cedrus libani*).

[2] I Kings 5: 6 (*New International Version*).

quality will significantly deteriorate. The kernel should not come into contact with any metal during the extraction process. In any case, the oil should never come into contact with metal.

The oil can be used to treat any diseases without diagnosis. It can also be used as a food product and added to salads. Or it can be taken one spoonful a day, preferably at sunrise, although the afternoon is also a good time. But definitely in daylight, not at night. That's the main thing.

"Only people may be offered a counterfeit," I voiced my concern to the old fellow. But he responded slyly and with just a touch of humour:

"Well, then, you and I will make a device to screen out counterfeits. And we'll work out those commissions of yours at the same time."

"How do we do that?"

"Have to think about it. You, after all, are the entrepreneur."

"I *was* one, but right now I'm not sure who I am."

"Let's think together, then. You correct me if something's not right."

"Okay," I agreed.

"The final product should be tested with measuring instruments by competent technicians. Doctors, scientists — in a word, professionals."

"That's right, they can issue certificates."

"But instruments can't catch everything. A taste test will also be needed."

"Possibly. Tasters determine the quality of wine, for example. There's no substitute for that. But the wine-tasters are acutely aware of the taste of different vintages. They have a superb sense for both fragrance and taste. But who will be tasting the oil?"

"*You* can check it."

"And just how am I supposed to do that? I've only tasted the usual sort of oil. When we made it ourselves, we didn't follow the technological procedures Anastasia recommended. Besides, I'm a smoker."

"For three days before checking the oil quality, you should abstain from smoking and alcohol. And don't eat meats or fats. And you shouldn't talk with anyone for those three days. Then you can check it and determine from the taste whether it is good or an imitation."

"And what do I compare it with?"

"With this."

Whereupon the old fellow put his hand into his canvas bag and drew out a small hollow stick approximately two fingers in width. Another stick protruded from one end, like a cork.

"This is genuine oil. Once you've tasted it, you won't mistake it for anything else. But first let me rid you of what has built up in you from smoking and other quirky habits."

"How are you going to get rid of it? The way Anastasia did?"

"Yes, more or less."

"But she said that only one who loves is capable of eliminating ailments in a loved one with the Ray of Love. And of warming his body, so that even his feet start perspiring."

"With the Ray of Love. Quite correct."

"But you cannot love me. Not the way she does."

"But I love my granddaughter. Let's try it."

"Go ahead."

The oldster screwed up his eyes and began fixing an unblinking gaze on me. I could feel a sense of warmth flow through my body. But quite a bit weaker than what I felt from Anastasia's gaze. Nothing happened. But he still kept trying. To the point where his arms were trembling. I could feel a little more warming in my body, but only a little. Still, the old fellow didn't give up, and I waited. And all at once my feet broke out into a sweat, after which a feeling of freshness permeated my head, along with fragrances. I could feel the fragrances in the air.

"Ah, we've succeeded," he said, wearily leaning against the back of the bench. "Now give me your hand."

He opened the stick cork and from the hollow stick poured cedar oil onto the palm of my hand. I licked it off with my tongue. The warmth spread across my palate and through my mouth. And I suddenly caught a whiff of the cedar. And it was, indeed, hard to mistake for anything else.

"Think you'll remember it now?" asked Anastasia's grandfather.

"I'll remember. What's so hard about that? I ate potatoes once at the monastery. I remembered that for ages. Twenty-seven years later I still remembered the taste. Only how will people know that it has been checked? That it is genuine cedar nut oil? Right now it's too expensive on the market. For just one gram of the raw oil, diluted with something, they charge thirty thousand roubles.[3] I saw it myself. It's packaged as an import. With prices like that it's all too tempting to sell fakes."

"You're right — money's the master of ceremonies at the moment. We'll have to think of something."

"You see? A dead end."

"Anastasia said that this money can be turned to a good purpose," Grandfather observed. "Let's think of something along that line."

"They've been trying to work out for some time now, for example, how to guarantee the quality of vodka against imitations. But... They've changed the labels and corks, they've come up with excise labels, but all to no avail. There were

[3]*thirty thousand roubles* — approximately US$6 at the then current exchange rate.

imitations on the market before, and there still are. What with photocopiers and all, any label can easily be copied."

"What about money, Vladimir — can it be copied too?"

"Money — that's more difficult to fake."

"So let's stick money onto the back side of our bottles, like labels, so that these snivelling bits of paper can actually do some good for once."

"What d'you mean, stick money on bottles? What kind of nonsense is that?"

"Give me a banknote, please. Any banknote."

I gave him a 1000-rouble note.

"Well, then, it's quite clear. You take the note and cut it in half. Stick one half on the box or something else. The other half you hide away in a file. You'll think of a suitable place. Or put it in a safety deposit box at your bank. You see, on each half of the note there are identical numbers, and so anyone wanting to confirm the authenticity of the oil, can simply verify the number."

Well, Gramps, I thought to myself, you've got a good head on your shoulders. And out loud I said:

"There's no better defence against imitations. Way to go!"

He laughed. Still laughing, he added:

"So, give me a percentage, too. Come on, cough it up!"

"A percentage? What kind of a percentage? How much do you want?"

"I want everything to be just right," said the old fellow, all at once serious again. Then he added: "Besides the three percent, take an additional one percent — in kind, as oil already packaged. And offer it for free to whoever you feel you should. Let that be a gift to people from you and me."

"Right, I'll do it. You've really thought of everything to a T. Way to go!"

"To a T? That means Nastenka will be very happy for us. And my father still thinks I'm lazy. So you think I've done a good job?"

"Of course you have!" And we both had another good laugh. And I added: "Tell Anastasia I say you would make an excellent entrepreneur."

"You mean it?"

"Certainly! You could become one of those 'New Russians'[4] — and a great one, too!"

"I'll tell her. And the fact that you're telling everyone about the cedar nut oil, I'll pass that along, too. No regrets?"

"What is there to regret? It would be a tiresome process, anyway. I'll dash off the third book, as I promised, and then I'll get going with my business again, trade... or something else, something normal."

---

[4]*New Russians* — the name given to a class of Russian *nouveaux riches* who acquired considerable wealth after the collapse of the Soviet Union. They were popularly perceived as intellectually limited individuals, notorious for their criminal background, uncultured manners, offensive jargon and ostentatious display of wealth, all of which has given rise to a host of jokes.

Chapter Thirty-Two

Title!
(I don't know what to call it; whoever can,
come up with a title yourselves)

I decided to tell Anastasia's grandfather about my new assistants:

"A lot of articles are now being written about Anastasia. She's being talked about in both academic and religious circles. One production team, made up of very religious and considerate people, offered me a deal to grant them, in return for payment, the exclusive right to interpret and comment on Anastasia's sayings in the mass media. I agreed."

"And for what amount, Vladimir, did you agree to sell them Anastasia?"

The tone of his question and what he was getting at left a rather bad taste in my mouth. And I answered:

"What do you mean, 'sell'? I told them more about Anastasia than I wrote in the book. I told religious people so that they could offer their exclusive comments as well as their explanations of what she said. They want to meet with her. They're even ready to finance an expedition. I agreed. What's wrong with that?"

The old fellow didn't respond immediately. Since no reply was forthcoming, I added:

"They offered me money for an exclusive right — that's the way we do things — people offer services for money. They will earn even more from their publications."

The oldster lowered his head and remained silent for a while. Then, as if thinking things over aloud, he said:

"So, you, in your enterprising way, sold Anastasia and they, assuming themselves to be the most religious and competent people in the world, decided to buy her."

"Well, that's a pretty strange way of putting it. So, when it comes right down to it, what did I do wrong?"

"Tell me, Vladimir, didn't it ever enter your head or the heads of those 'religious' people to think of asking, finding out or realising just who Anastasia herself wished to talk to and when — and how? And do people in your world go visiting without so much as an advance request to the host? I don't recall her asking anybody to visit her."

"If she doesn't want to talk with them, she doesn't have to. She didn't sign any deal."

"But *you did!* She is ready to share what she knows with everyone, but it is her right to determine how she's going to do this. And if she's chosen to set it forth in a book and with your expression, who has the right to dictate or demand another? She made the choice herself, but somebody wants to change that, and the reason behind the effort to alter her choice is clear. She will not talk with people who put themselves ahead of everyone else. With people whose self-righteousness, she knows, will distort, overturn and adjust to their own way of thinking the truths she holds sacred."

"Why paint such a dark picture ahead of time? These people are interested in many different teachings. They are very religious."

"It is they who have determined that they are the most religious of all. Religious self-righteousness is the apex of the most deadly of sins — pride."

I began to be overwhelmed with an inexplicable sense of anger at myself. I had not yet received payment for the deal and so I was able to break it. And shortly afterward, not seeing anything amiss, I signed another deal with one of the religious centres for the exclusive right to my own interviews.

Once again I was taken in by their considerate attitude and the religious knowledge they displayed. Especially since this deal concerned me alone, and I could do with myself what I pleased. But once again both they and I fell into a trap, and once again it turned out that I had indirectly sold Anastasia, and they had bought her.

And this time it was not Anastasia's grandfather but a Moscow woman journalist who, after reading the new agreement, flustered:

"Boy, how stupid can you get? You've sold Anastasia real cheap. Take a closer look and see what the fine print says. You've signed over the right to others — an exclusive right — to exploit and use as they see fit, over the most powerful information channel there is, everything you said relating to Anastasia. You've denied yourself the right even to question their opinion, no matter what it is."

To what degree that's true it's hard to say. Maybe I'd better cite a few of the points of the agreement here:

1. Subject of agreement:

1.1 The AUTHOR gives exclusive rights to all videotaping of himself, as well as to the use of any other video materials connected directly or indirectly with the production of "Anastasia" television programmes (hereinafter referred to as "programmes"). The abovementioned transfer of rights to the CONTRACTOR extends to all countries of the world.

1.2 The CONTRACTOR undertakes, at his own expense, to prepare one copy each of three programmes — of between 30 and 40 minutes each — on a professional BETACAM recorder.

1.3 By mutual agreement between AUTHOR and CONTRACTOR, any interaction with video- or film-studios, television (including cable TV), as well as the shooting of any video on any equipment, as well as the use of video materials on the given subject, is to be effected only and exclusively by the CONTRACTOR.

While this Agreement is in force the AUTHOR waives the right to give video interviews and prepare any audio materials using the concepts or terms that are in the programmes, either directly or indirectly.

After analysing all the events connected with the writing, publication and distribution of the *Anastasia* book, I came to the conclusion that people who call themselves "strongly religious" have a dark side which they themselves fear, and thus keep trying to assure others and persuade them of their religiosity. They are probably afraid that people will discover their dark side.

It's so much simpler with entrepreneurs. Their actions and goals are more open, less obscured, and consequently they are also more honest both to themselves and to those around them, to society. It's possible I am mistaken. But you can't get away from the facts.

Three Moscow students keyboarded the text of *Anastasia.* They had no expectations of compensation any time soon. They never talked about any religious matters.

The book was published by the manager of Moscow Printshop Number Eleven, a retired officer by the name of Gennady Vladimirovich Grutsia, at his own expense. The print-run was small and there wasn't even a thought of breaking even. Grutsia, an entrepreneur, never talked of religious matters either. The next run was paid for by the business manager of the Moscow Publishers' Clearance House, Yuri Anatolievich Nikitin, but then it turned out he wasn't dealing in books at the time. He gave me the greater part of the print-run to sell. He set no deadline for getting a return on his investment. And he, too, never talked about religious matters.

And then the 'religious' people began putting in their two cents' worth. And a print-run of 45,000 was released by an underground press. When this 'religious' firm was discovered, they started proclaiming their religiosity and desire to produce bright things, and even promised to pay author's royalties. They still keep promising that. And that's not the only case. 'Religious' people generally seem to be very neglectful of accounts, especially when they're the ones who owe money.

As to the transfer of exclusive rights, I have decided to make it clear on the pages of this book: I shall no longer give exclusive rights for the interpretation of Anastasia's sayings to anybody. And if anybody challenges me on that, let people know that I have not given anything voluntarily!

Why do I say *voluntarily?* The Moscow journalist who helped me break the contract soon became the target of anonymous threats. Who made them? What did they want? What kind of 'religion' do they profess? They support their religion by extortion. Well, I know what the extortion racket is all about; after all there are human beings there too. And I want to warn them: be extra careful around 'religious' people. And before getting into anything, consider calmly and carefully where these 'religious' people are taking you.

There's more. In the first book I wrote that I had invited Anastasia to come to Moscow herself and appear on our TV, but she refused. I couldn't understand why at the time. But now it is clear to me what she foresaw. Even after the book came out, there have been many interpretations of what she said. Many quite different interpretations. Some are interesting, some are controversial, but among others one could clearly trace the desire on the part of certain people to interpret her in a manner that would serve their own interests.

Direct challenges were thrown my way, for example:

"So you think you alone have the right to talk with her?"

"You don't understand everything, let others speak with her, more will come out of it."

But she is not an object to hand over to someone. She is Man! And she herself has the right to decide how she will act, whom she will speak with and what she will say. Now it's become clearer than ever that Anastasia is really being subjected to attack by a visible and invisible throng of dark forces in the guise of fanatics and self-seekers.

Back in the first book I quoted Anastasia as saying:

"I know what a terrible mass of dark forces will descend upon me... but I am not afraid of them. I will succeed in raising my son. I will succeed in seeing my plan come true. And people will be carried across the dark forces' window of time."

In Anastasia's world they instruct their children up to eleven years of age. In other words, she has at least another ten years she can hold out.

"And then what?" I asked her grandfather. "Is she bound to perish?"

"It's hard to say," the old fellow answered. "They all died quite a bit earlier, compared to her, and more than once she has embarked on a journey foretelling physical death, but each time, at the last moment, the law has flared up — forgotten it may be, but it is still strong enough to overrule anything else. It has illuminated the essence of the truth about earthly existence. And it has caused life to remain in her earthly body."

The old man fell silent and once again, preoccupied in thought, began tracing some sort of symbols on the ground with his stick. I too began thinking, wondering how on earth I got myself involved in a situation like this! But the thing was, I couldn't very well walk away from it now. It might have been possible earlier, but not now, because of the child.

Anastasia had given birth to a son. Even though she'd rather devote herself to caring for the child and raising him, she is not going to abandon her dream — to carry people across the dark forces' window of time. And she will not. Because she's really very stubborn. Someone like her will not walk away.

And who will help her, naïve as she is? If I should renege on my promise, she's got nobody left. She'd go to pieces. And that's something that should not happen to a nursing mother. She's got to finish her breast-feeding, at the very least. And so I asked her grandfather:

"Is there anything I can do for Anastasia?"

"Try to figure out, for a start, what she's talking about and what she wants. Then aimless wandering will give way to understanding, and a wave of warmth will cheer the heart, and over the world will be unfurled a new dawn."

"Can you make it any more specific?" I asked.

"It's hard for me to formulate it in any more specific way. The whole important thing is sincerity in all. So start by doing what is dictated by your heart and soul."

"She told me about a particular Russian provincial town," I remarked. "Said something about it possibly becoming richer than Jerusalem or Rome. Because all around there are many sacred sites of our forebears. Sites more significant than the temples at Jerusalem. Only the local people do not have sufficient conscious awareness to discern them. I want to go there, and change their conscious awareness."

"That's not something that can be done quickly, Vladimir."

"Well, you see, I didn't know it couldn't be done, and so I promised Anastasia. And there must be some way of bringing about a change."

"Since you didn't know it couldn't be done, you shall change it indeed. More power to you! And now it's time for me to go."

"I'll see you off."

"Don't waste your time. No need to see me off. Think about what you have to do."

The old fellow got up and offered me his hand.

I watched Anastasia's grandfather recede into the distance along the tree-lined boulevard, and thought of my forthcoming trip to the city of Gelendzhik, remembering what Anastasia had told me about it. And it was no mere chance conversation.

Chapter Thirty-Three

Your sacred sites, O Russia!

I asked Anastasia:

"Do your people often come across ringing cedars?"

"Very, very rarely," she replied. "Perhaps two or three in a thousand years. Right now, apart from this one that has been saved, there is one more, and it can be sawed up and used for its designated purpose."

"What does that mean: 'used for its designated purpose'? What is its purpose?"

"The Great Intelligence of the Universe, God, Who created Man and his environment, no doubt had the foresight to give people the opportunity to restore their lost abilities, to use the wisdom accumulated in the non-material world. This wisdom has existed right from the start, but Man's ability to perceive it has been lost through sinfulness.

"My grandfather and great-grandfather told you about the ringing cedar and its extraordinary healing properties. What they did not explain was that its pulsations and rhythms are close to that Great Intelligence.

"If they are merged and combined, as it were, with the rhythms already present in many people, then a Man who places the palm of his hand on the warm trunk of a ringing cedar and runs his hand over it as though caressing it, thereby attains the possibility of communicating with the infinite expanse of wisdom. Such a Man is capable of becoming aware of many things in the scope of his thinking at the moment of contact or thereafter. This happens in varying degree with each individual. I am telling you about the highest manifestation."

With its hundreds of dolmens, Northern Caucasus (Russia) is a region with one of the highest concentrations of preserved megalithic sites in the world. Over the millennia, many of the dolmens were vandalised or destroyed. After Vladimir Megré's *The Ringing Cedars of Russia* raised public awareness of their momentous spiritual importance, millions of people have visited these formerly neglected and forgotten sites. Photos © 2004 by Alexey Kondaurov, Nizhny Novgorod, Russia.

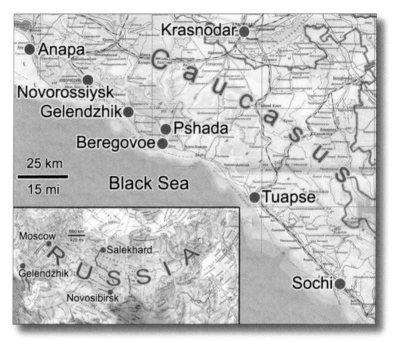

A map of the 'dolmen country' — Russian Northern Caucasus and the Black Sea coast (above) and a view of this region (below). Photo © 2006 by Olga Chernyshova, Sarov, Russia.

Above: a dolmen complex in the process of restoration, Northern Caucasus, Russia. Photo © 2004 by Dmitry Samusev.

Below: a dolmen near the settlement of Pshada, with its front vandalised and covered in modern graffiti. Photo © 2004 by Alexey Kondaurov, Nizhny Novgorod, Russia.

The cedar of Lebanon planted some 100 years ago by the hand of Vladimir Korolenko, near the city of Gelendzhik. For details please see Chapter 33: "Your sacred sites, O Russia!".

Photo © 2006 by Olga Chernyshova, Sarov, Russia.

Above: eight women employees of *Druzhba* Sanatorium on a trip to a dolmen near Pshada in the Caucasus mountains, 26 November 1996 (see Chapter 33: "Your sacred sites, O Russia!"). The picture was taken by Vladimir Megré himself as these women were preparing to lay flowers in honour of their distant forebear. *Below:* Vladimir Megré's photo of Father Feodorit's church (see Chepter 24: "Father Feodorit"). Both photos appeared on the inside cover of an early Russian print-run of *The Ringing Cedars of Russia.* © 1996 by Vladimir Megré.

The One and Only by a Single Line — this picture in the private collection of the Trinity-Sergiev Monastery (Sergiev Posad, Russia) is a copy of a famous engraving by Claude Mellan (1598–1688), *Veil of St Veronica* (1649), above. The face of Christ Jesus ('the One and Only') surmounted by a crown of thorns is executed by a single spiral line in 166 revolutions. For details on Vladimir Megré's experiences connected with this image, please see Chapter 24: "Father Feodorit" and Chapter 25: "The Space of Love" in the present volume.

The Dachnik Day holiday — honouring the millions of gardeners and celebrating Man's connectedness to the Earth — is now celebrated on 23 July throughout Russia and beyond. Celebrations at the *Rodnoe* eco-village, Vladimir Region, Russia, 2006 (above) and in Licking, Missouri, USA, 2005 (below). Photos © Leonid Sharashkin.

Vladimir Megré arriving at the Ringing Cedars of Russia movement conference held in the city of Vladimir on 5 June 2004. The conference brought together over 400 delegates from 150 eco-villages from all over Russia and beyond. Photo © 2004 by Alexey Kondaurov, Nizhny Novgorod, Russia.

"But why does it happen differently? Does the cedar choose to give its power to one person and not to another?"

"Its operation is identical in each case. Its rhythm and vibration are always the same. But some people can tune into it and feel it all to the full, while others detect just a light touch. Many people don't feel anything at all to start with. But conscious awareness will gradually come even to those without feeling. At least they have a greater possibility of feeling it."

"I still don't quite understand what kind of selection takes place."

"Vladimir, please try to 'read my lips': the difference is not in the power of the tree, but in the Man. Hmm... all right, I have found it — an example: *music!* You know, when music is playing... Music too, after all, consists of vibration and rhythm. But some people listen to it attentively, they begin to have feelings from it, sometimes even tears of joy and tenderness. Others listen to the same music but feel nothing, or do not care about listening to it at all.

"The same with the cedar. Only those who are capable of feeling and understanding will hear anything much at all. And this 'much' is something that will gradually unfold itself to them. It comes during the moments when Man feels like pondering it.

"Women can gain the strength and wisdom of their pristine origins, they can fulfil their designated purpose and make both themselves and their chosen men happy, as well as their children they give birth to in Love. And here the miracle is not in the cedar, but in human aspirations. The cedar simply assists them — it is not the major contributor to noble deeds."

"That's incredible! It's like some kind of tempting, beautiful legend!"

"You do not believe me? You think what I am saying is only a legend? Why then did you make such an effort to come here and why were you so eager to have me show you the ringing cedar?"

"Well, I don't think it's *all* a legend. At first I too didn't believe what your grandfather and great-grandfather said about the cedar. Later, after I returned home from the expedition, I read the popular scientific literature and got to know what scientists were saying about its healing properties, and I was struck by the fact that the scientists and the Bible were on the same wavelength. But I never found a hint anywhere of the cedar being used to feel a link with the Great Intelligence or God, as you describe it."

"Either you did not pay close enough attention to what the scientists or the Bible were saying, or you missed the main point — otherwise you would not be doubting my words."

"Then what could I have missed? There are only two references to cedars in the Bible: when God teaches how to treat people with their help, and then how to disinfect one's home."

"But the Bible also talks about King Solomon as one of the wisest rulers that ever lived, one revered by his people. King Solomon, you will agree, is an historical personage — he was no legend."

"So?"

"And the Bible also says that this king built God a temple of cedar, and a house for himself beside it also made of cedar. And in order to get the cedar, he hired more than thirty thousand workers to bring it from another country. And to get the cedars cut down, Solomon asked another king named Hiram to give him people "skilled in felling timber".[1] Getting this cedar cost Solomon twenty cities of his kingdom. Think: why did the wisest of all rulers need to go to such expense and build his temple and house out of material which was less sturdy than what he had on hand already?"

---

[1] I Kings 5: 6 (*New International Version*).

"Why?"

"You can find the answer to that, too, in the Bible, where it says: 'And it came to pass, when the priests were come out of the holy place, that the cloud filled the house of the Lord, So that the priests could not stand to minister because of the cloud: for the glory of the Lord had filled the house of the Lord.'[2] You can find indirect proofs of this in the works of your prominent scientists."

"That's great. Something, I think, I can believe in. It means the cedar will reveal many secrets to people. Show me the ringing cedar that can be sawed up. I'll bring it to a city with easy access for people from all over the world wishing to touch it."

"Where will you find a city on the Earth where the inhabitants will not simply desecrate this sacred cedar, but actually ensure its protection and provide a suitable exhibition space and access for visitors?"

"I'll try to find one. Tell me, why have you concluded that it's going to be such a difficult task?"

"People's consciousness today is too bound up with the programmes of the technocratic world. They are becoming biological robots."

"What kind of biological robots?"

"The technocratic world is structured in such a way that Man keeps on inventing all sorts of mechanical devices and social orders supposedly to make his life easier. But in fact, any saving of labour is an illusion.

"Man himself is becoming a robot of the technocratic world. He never has enough time to contemplate the essence of being or listen to what another is saying, and no time, either, to reflect on his own destiny. He is literally a programmed robot. Here you are seeing everything with your own eyes,

[2] I Kings 8: 10, 11 (*Authorised King James Version*).

and hearing it with your own ears, and you still find it hard to believe."

"Anastasia, with me it's a different story. I cannot call myself a strong believer. I believe... in general. But probably not the same way other people do. In our world right now there are a lot of people who truly do believe. Many read the Bible. They will grasp it immediately they see how much the Bible talks about the cedar. They will believe and take good care of your little piece of cedar."

"There are different kinds of belief, Vladimir. It often happens that a Man will hold in his hands the Koran, or the Bible, or another book containing the wisdom of the ages, and say that he believes, and even try to teach others, whereas in fact he is simply attempting, as it were, to make a deal with God: 'Look here, I believe in You. Remember that in case anything happens.'"

"What then *is* belief, or faith?" I enquired. "How should it be expressed?"

"In one's way of life, in one's perception of the world, in the understanding of one's essence and designated purpose, in one's corresponding behaviour and relationship to the environment, in one's thinking."

"So, just believing is not enough?"

"Just believing is not enough. Imagine an army. All the soldiers, down to the last one, believe in their commander. But they do not go into battle. They have such strong faith in him that they trust he will win in any case. So the soldiers sit back and watch as their commander goes up alone against the enemy forces. They sit there in a state of frenzy and call out: 'Go, go, go! We believe in you, we know you can do it!'"

"That's no help, Anastasia. You didn't make a real analogy. Those kinds of absurdities simply don't happen."

"Those kinds of absurdities *do* happen in real life, Vladimir."

"Then give me an example from the concrete realities of our life, and not something made up."

"Fine. There is a city in Russia called Gelendzhik. It has a noble purpose — to be a place where people can go to relax from their daily grind, a place to meditate and touch sacred sites.

"There are many sacred sites in and around this city, which are more significant than those found in Jerusalem, more significant than the pyramids of Egypt.

"This city could be one of the richest cities in the world. Richer than Jerusalem or Rome. But the city is dying. It is a resort town. All its houses and hotels are becoming empty and decaying. The materialistic consciousness of the local authorities prevents them from seeing the treasures which are capable of making the city flourish. When they talk about the city, they emphasise the sea, the artificial treatment facilities available, and the fact that the local hotel rooms are equipped with bedside tables and fridges. They do not even mention the sacred sites. They know little about them themselves, and do not want to know. Their priorities lie elsewhere.

"There are many people living in this city who call themselves believers. People of many different denominations. Some of them actively engage in proselytising. What faith do they proselytise? With their attitude to their surroundings they have been and still are violating the very commandments contained in their sacred books. In the Bible, for instance, where it says: 'Love thy neighbour as thyself.'[3]

"But you have to *know* your neighbour before you can love him. You cannot love whom you do not know. But they, the ones who call themselves believers, do not know their neighbours, or even their forebears who lived in that sacred land

---

[3] Matth. 22: 39 (*Authorised King James Version*).

and left them the inexhaustible treasure of the sacred sites as their legacy. Our ancestors have carried with them over the millennia waves of wisdom and the light of their own soul. Many people call themselves believers yet do not notice what is sacred around them. The sacred sites which have been left them by their ancestors to help them."

"What kind of sacred sites could possibly be found in a city like that?"

"You see, Vladimir, near the city of Gelendzhik can be found growing the Lebanese cedar mentioned so many times in the Bible. And this living, direct creation of God, talked about so much even before Christ Jesus' coming to Earth, is located right next to this city. It is only a hundred years old. It is still but a stripling, though already very beautiful and sturdy.

"It has grown there because it was planted by a worthy Man. He was a writer named Korolenko.[4] Thanks to his erstwhile popularity, the cedar has been protected with a surrounding hedge. But today the house where he lived is in a state of decay and people are not paying attention to the tree he planted."

"And what about the believers?"

"Many of the people in the city who call themselves believers pay no attention either to the tree or the other great sacred sites of their forebears. They are destroying them. And the city is dying."

"That means God's punishing them in some kind of vengeance, eh?"

---

[4]*Vladimir Galaktionovich Korolenko* (1853–1921) — a Russian writer known for his short stories and his autobiographical narrative "The story of my contemporary". His writings, permeated with ideals of democracy and humanitarianism, were critical of both the tsarist and communist régimes.

"God is good. He is never vengeful. But what can He do when His creations are ignored?"

"That's amazing! Can such a tree really exist? I must look into that."

"It exists. And there are many other sacred sites around the city. But people treat them from a technocratic point of view, like the pyramids of the wise pharaohs."

"What? How do you know about the existence of the Egyptian pyramids?"

"Thanks to generations of my forebears the ability has been preserved within me to communicate with the dimension where thoughts and wisdom reside. This communication gives one the opportunity to learn anything one might wish to know, anything that captures one's interest."

"Hold on a moment. Let me test you. Answer me, do you know the *secrets* of the Egyptian pyramids?"

"I do. Just as I know that those who investigated those pyramids were constantly working from a material standpoint. They were basically interested in how they were constructed, the dimensions and relations of the sides to each other, what treasures were hidden inside, what things were to be found there. They considered people living at the time the pyramids were built to be superstitious. They regarded the pyramids only as a means of preserving the pharaohs' valuables, their bodies, their glory. Thus they distanced themselves from what was fundamental, from what was consciously designed."

"I don't understand you, Anastasia. What conscious design where they distancing themselves from?"

Anastasia didn't speak for some time, staring, it seemed, somewhere off into infinity. And then she began telling her remarkable story:

"You see, Vladimir, way back in ancient times people living on the Earth had the capacity to use wisdom and intelligence far surpassing the abilities of modern Man. People at the time of the Earth's pristine origins enjoyed ready access to all the information in the entire database of the Universe. This information filling the Universe was created by the Great Intelligence, God. With contributions both from Him and from people themselves — their thoughts. It is so superb that it is capable of answering any question, unobtrusively. The answer would appear instantaneously in the subconscious of the Man asking the question."

"And what did it give these people?"

"These people needed no spaceships for travelling to other planets. All they had to do was wish for it, and they could see what was happening there.

"These people needed no television, telephone or communication wires ensnaring the Earth — not even literacy, since all the information you derive from books they were able to obtain instantaneously by other means.

"These people needed no industries producing medicines or drugs, they could get all the best remedies possible simply by a gentle wave of the hand, since whatever they needed is available in Nature.

"These people needed none of your modern transportation devices. They did not need cars or food-processing complexes, for everything was supplied to them.

"They knew that a change in climatic conditions in one part of the Earth was a signal to them to move to another part, so that the part they were leaving might refresh itself. They had an understanding of the Universe along with their own planet. They were thinkers and knew their designated purpose. They worked to bring the planet Earth to perfection. They had no equals in the Universe. In terms of intelligence they were second only to the Great Intelligence of the Universe, or God.

"Approximately ten thousand years ago, in the human civilisation that then populated what is now Europe, Asia, the northern part of Africa and the Caucasus, individuals arose in whom the link with the Intelligence of the Universe was partially or wholly deadened. This point marks the beginning of mankind's movement toward a disaster of global proportions. The exact nature of the disaster is immaterial — ecological, nuclear or bacteriological, either as forecast by scientists or foretold allegorically by ancient religions."

"Hold on, there, Anastasia! I don't at all see how the appearance of such 'invalids' can be related to a global disaster."

"Your choice of that modern term *invalids* is very apt. Yes, they were invalids, handicapped people. Now when someone is deprived of sight, what do they need?"

"Someone to guide them."

"And someone deprived of hearing?"

"A hearing apparatus."

"And someone with no arms or legs?"

"Prostheses."

"But there was something much greater that they lacked. They did not have a link to the Intelligence of the Universe. Hence the loss of the knowledge which would help improve the Earth and govern it.

"Imagine what would happen if the crew of a super-modern spaceship suddenly lost ninety percent of their mental capacity. Not comprehending anything, they might start taking apart the panelling and building a fire in the cabin, or pull instruments out of their consoles to use for toys or decoration.

"Well, these people can be compared exactly to a demented crew like that. And these were the people, these were the 'handicapped invalids' who first invented the stone axe, then the spear, then... And it is their thoughts that 'progressed' over time to the invention of nuclear warheads. It is their thoughts that even today continue with incredible stubbornness to tear down already perfect creations and substitute their own primitive artifacts.

"Their descendants started inventing more and more, and in doing so kept tearing apart the super-modern, natural mechanisms of the Earth and creating all sorts of artificial social structures. Then people started fighting with each other.

"These mechanisms, these machines, were incapable of existing all by themselves, like natural ones. Not only could they not reproduce themselves, but they could not restore themselves after a breakdown as a tree can, for example. And then they, the technocrats, required a vast army of workers to service these mechanisms, virtually transforming a segment of the general populace into biological robots. These biological robots, lacking as they do, any individual capacity to learn the truth, very easily lend themselves to manipulation.

"For example, they were all too easily injected, through artificial information media, with the programme 'We must build communism' — symbols were created for it, including lapel pins and flags of a certain colour. Then later, through these same media, the programme 'Communism is bad' was inculcated in another segment of the populace, and other symbols and colours were brought to the fore. And then these two groups with different programming end up hating each other, right to the point of physical annihilation.

"But this all began ten thousand years ago, at the time of a significant increase in the number of people deprived of a link to the Great Intelligence. Indeed, you could even call them demented, since there was not a single living creature capable of polluting the Earth the way they did.

"In those far-off times a few people were still left who had free access to the wisdom of the Universe. They hoped that when mankind reached the point that the polluted air made it difficult to breathe and the water became dangerous to drink, and all its artificially created life-support systems — technological and social — proved themselves too awkward and more and more often only led to disastrous imbalances, mankind would start having second thoughts.

"People standing on the edge of an abyss *will* start thinking about what being is all about, they will start pondering the meaning of their existence and purpose. Then many of them will desire to understand the truth of their pristine origins, and this is possible — but only under the absolute condition that the abilities inherent in Man's pristine origins be restored.

"Few of the people who lived ten thousand years ago still possessed these abilities. It was basically those heading up social groups, leaders of tribes. They began — or rather, at their behest people began — to construct special facilities made of heavy stone slabs. These enclosed an interior chamber about one-and-a-half by two metres in area and two metres in height — sometimes more, sometimes less. The slabs were placed at a slight angle, leaning toward the centre at the top. Occasionally these chambers would be hewn out of a single monolith. Other chambers might be hidden underground and covered over by mounds of earth. On one of the walls of the chamber, a cone-shaped opening was cut into the slab, approximately thirty centimetres in diameter and covered with a specially fitted stone plug.

"Into these tomb-chambers would go people who had not lost the ability to communicate with the wisdom of the Universe. Those still alive and even those who might be born thousands of years hence would be able to go to them and obtain answers to any questions that were of interest to Man. This required sitting beside the chamber and meditating. Sometimes the answer would come right away, sometimes after a delay, but it would definitely come, since these structures and those that retreated into them served as an information receiver. Through them it was easier to communicate with the Great Intelligence of the Universe.

"These stone structures are the prototype of the Egyptian pyramids. Only the pyramids do not constitute nearly as powerful a receiver, even though they are far greater in size. Their essence and function, however, is pretty much the same.

"The pharaohs who were buried in the Egyptian pyramids were also thinkers, and at least partially preserved the abilities inherent in Man's pristine origins.

"But in order to obtain an answer to a question using the pyramids, those still living had to come to the pyramid not individually, but in large numbers. They had to stand along each of the four sides, and direct their physical and mental gaze upward, as though skimming over the pyramid's oblique sides right to its top.

"There at the top, people's gazes and thoughts focused on a single point, consequently forming a channel facilitating contact with the Mind of the Universe.

"Even today it is possible to do the same thing and obtain a desired answer. At the focal point of everyone's mental gaze an energy forms, an energy not unlike radiation. If a measuring device were placed at the top of the pyramid, right at the focal point, it would record the intensity of this energy. The people standing at the base, too, would feel strange sensations.

"Oh, if it were not for the sinful pride of people today, the prevailing public opinion, the false perception that past civilisations were less advanced! People today would then be able to find out the real purpose of the pyramids. With all the attention modern researchers have paid to how they were built, they still have not been able to figure this out.

"And it is all so simple: in constructing the pyramids, apart from physical strength and various pieces of equipment, they always used mental energy to reduce the force of gravitation. Whole groups of people with this kind of an ability would assist the builders. There are people alive today who are able to move small objects with their will.

"But of immeasurably greater significance than the pyramids in terms of contact with the Mind of the Universe were the smaller stone structures which preceded them."

"Why, Anastasia?" I asked. "Because of the way they were constructed, their shape?"

"Because, Vladimir, *living* people retreated there to die. And their death was a most unusual one. They went into eternal meditation."

"What do you mean, living people? What for?"

"To create for their descendants the possibility of bringing back the power of their pristine origins. An elderly person — as a rule, one of the wiser leaders or founders of a tribe, sensing his end was near, would ask his relatives and family to place him in a stone chamber. If he were considered worthy, they would grant his request.

"They would push away the heavy massive slab covering the top of the chamber. He would go into the stone chamber and the slab would be pushed back into place. Inside, the Man would be completely isolated from the external material world. His eyes would see nothing, his ears would hear nothing. Such complete isolation, the impossibility of even entertaining a thought about going back, but not yet having crossed into the next world, the deactivation of the usual organs of feeling, sight and hearing, would open up the opportunity for full communication with the Mind of the Universe and the comprehension of many phenomena, as well as of many of the actions of Earth-dwellers. Most important of all, they would be able to subsequently transmit what they had discovered to those still alive, as well as to succeeding generations. Today you would call an approximation of such a state of mind *meditation*. But that is merely child's play in comparison with meditation in eternity.

"Afterward, people would come to this stone chamber, pull out the plug covering the opening, and begin thinking, mentally consulting with the thoughts lingering in the chamber. The spirit of wisdom was always there."

"But, Anastasia, by what means can you prove the existence of such structures to those of us living today, let alone the fact that people went into them for 'eternal meditation'?"

"I can! That is why I am telling you."

"Then how?"

"It is very simple. After all, these chambers made of stone — they still exist today. Today you call them *dolmens*.[5] You can see them, and touch them. And you can verify everything I have told you."

"What??? Where? Can you pinpoint their location?"

"Yes, I can. In Russia, for example, in the Caucasus mountains, not far from the cities you now call Gelendzhik, Tuapse, Novorossiysk and Sochi."[6]

"I can verify that. I'll make a special trip there. I still can't believe such things exist. I'll definitely check to see."

"Do verify, by all means. The local inhabitants know about them, but they do not pay any attention to them. Many dolmens have already been plundered. People do not understand their true purpose. They do not know about the possibilities they afford for contact with the wisdom of the Universe. Those who have entered into eternal meditation can never be re-embodied in anything material. They have sacrificed eternity for the sake of their descendants, and now it turns out their knowledge and opportunities have gone begging. This has caused them great sorrow and anguish.

"As for proof that in the past living people went into these dolmens to die, this may be confirmed by the position of the

---

[5]*dolmens* — see Book 1, Chapter 30: "Author's message to readers".

[6]*Gelendzhik, Tuapse, Novorossiysk, Sochi* — cities on the eastern shore of the Black Sea.

skeletal bones discovered in them. Some were found in a re-clining position, others sitting in a corner or semi-reclining, leaning against one of the stone slabs.

"This fact has been attested by people today. It has been described by your scientists, but they still have not attrib-uted any special significance to it. No serious studies of the dolmens have been undertaken. The dolmens are being laid waste by the local inhabitants. Some of them have been using their stone slabs for construction of new buildings."

Anastasia sorrowfully lowered her head and fell silent. I promised her:

"I will tell them what you said. I'll explain everything to them so they won't go on plundering and laying waste. They won't mock them any more. They simply didn't know..."

"Do you think you will manage to convince them?"

"I'll try. I'll go to these places and try to explain. I don't know quite how at the moment. I'll find these dolmens, pay my respects to them, and explain it all to the people."

"That would be good. Then, if you are going to those plac-es, please pay your respects to the dolmen in which my fore-mother died."

"Astonishing! How do you know that your foremother lived in these places and how she died?"

Anastasia replied:

"How could one not know, Vladimir, how one's ancestors lived and what they did? How could one not be aware of their desires and aspirations? My ancient foremother certainly de-serves to be remembered. All the mothers in my family since then have learnt of her wisdom. And she continues to help me today.

"My foremother was a woman who had perfect knowl-edge of how to inculcate in her child, through breast-feeding, the ability to communicate with the Mind of the Universe. Even back in her time people were starting to ignore the significance of this, just as people ignore it today. In breast-feeding an infant the mother should never allow herself to be distracted by random thoughts, but concentrate all her attention on her child. My foremother knew what to think about and how, and consequently wanted to share her knowledge with everyone.

"She was not yet that old when she started asking the leader about being placed in a dolmen. This was because the leader was getting old and she knew his successor would not accede to her request. Women were rarely permitted to go into a dolmen. The old leader revered my foremother and had great respect for her knowledge, and he gave his consent. Only he could not compel any menfolk to push back the dolmen's heavy stone slab and then reseal it once my foremother had entered. Consequently this task had to be carried out by women, and women alone.

"But nobody comes to visit my foremother's dolmen any more. People are not interested in what she knows. And she so desperately wanted to share it with everybody. She wanted children to be happy and a joy to their parents."

"Anastasia, if you wish, I shall go visit this dolmen and ask her how to breast-feed infants — ask her what to think along this line and how. Just tell me where it's located."

"Fine, I shall tell you. Only you will not be able to comprehend her response. You are not a nursing mother, after all. You do not know what a breast-feeding mother feels. Only women, nursing mothers, are in a position to understand. Just go to the dolmen, go up to it and touch it. Think some good thought about my foremother — she will like that."

For some time neither of us said a word. I was amazed at how detailed her explanations were regarding the exact location of the dolmens — enough information for me to subsequently verify, and I was not about to raise any further doubts about their existence. I did ask her, however, to show me some proof of the possibility of contact with the invisible and still incomprehensible (to me) 'wisdom of the Universe'. To which Anastasia responded:

"Vladimir, if you keep on doubting everything I say, any proof I have to offer will seem incomprehensible and unconvincing to you. And I shall have to spend a great deal of time explaining."

"Don't be offended, Anastasia — it's just that your unusual lifestyle as a recluse..."

"How can you call me a recluse when I have the opportunity to communicate not only with everyone and everything on Earth but with significantly more? So many on Earth are surrounded by utterly lonely people just like themselves. These are real hermit-recluses. It is not that frightening to be alone. It is much more frightening when one is lonely even when surrounded by people."

"But still," I persisted, "if one of our prominent scientists, let's say, could talk about that dimension — the one where, as you say, thoughts produced by human civilisations reside, people would be more inclined to believe than just on your say-so. That's the way people today are — they look to formal science as an authority."

"There are such scientists — I have seen their thoughts. I cannot tell you their names. But no doubt they are renowned scholars by your standards. They have the capacity for prolific thought. You can hunt down the proofs you need when you get back, and compare them with everything I have said."

Upon arriving in the Caucasus, I located the dolmens in the mountains near Gelendzhik. I took some colour photos of them. They knew about the dolmens at the local history museum, only they didn't attach any particular significance to them.

I also managed to find the dolmen where Anastasia's foremother was buried. Paying my respects, I laid flowers on the moss-covered stone portal.

As I looked at the dolmens, I realised that here was visible and tangible proof of Anastasia's words. By that time I had read the account from I Kings[7] in the Bible about King Solomon and his relationship to the cedars of Lebanon. Not being much of a scholar myself, I wasn't about to leaf through a whole lot of scientific works trying to find confirmation of Anastasia's words. But by extraordinary coincidences this young recluse from the remote Siberian taiga seemed to be able to confirm — from a distance — the truth of everything she said, and in the language of modern science. People took it upon themselves to bring or send to me scientific studies dealing with the existence of the Mind of the Universe.

At the beginning of the book I cited the conclusions of two academicians — Vlail Kaznacheev, member of the Russian Academy of Medical Sciences and director of the Institute of Clinical and Experimental Medicine, and Anatoly Akimov of the International Institute of Theoretical and Applied Physics in the Russian Academy of Natural Sciences — published in the May 1996 issue of *Chudesa i prikliuchenia* (*Wonders and adventures*).

I have been writing this chapter about the sacred sites of Gelendzhik right in the city itself. The text has been keyboarded into the computer by an employee of the *Druzhba* (Friendship) Sanatorium, Marina Davydovna Slabkina. Prior to its publication in the book it was gone over by employees of the sanatorium. And something interesting has happened.

On 26 November 1996 at 10:30 in the morning (Moscow time) an event occurred which did not have any obvious claim to significance, although I am certain that it will prove to be of planetary proportions.

A group of women were making their way toward one of the dolmens in the mountains near the settlement of Pshada[8] in the Gelendzhik district. They were all employees of the *Druzhba* Sanatorium: V.T. Larionova, N.M. Gribanova, L.S. Zvegintseva, T.N. Zaitseva, T.N. Kurovskaya, A.G. Tarasova, L.N. Romanova and M.D. Slabkina.

In contrast to the tourists that sometimes visit these places to admire their natural beauty and gawk at this lonely mountain dolmen, these people, possibly for the first time in a millennium, came to the dolmen for the specific purpose of honouring the memory of their ancient forebear. To honour the memory of a person who lived more than ten thousand years ago. A wise leader of his people who, at his own initiative, was sealed into this stone crypt. Alive, so that over the millennia he could share the wisdom of the Universe with his descendants.

It is difficult to say for just how many millennia his efforts went begging. Traces of our own era's atrocities are seared into the ancient slabs in the form of modern graffiti and the forcibly enlarged aperture in the dolmen's portal. Visitors to

---

[8]*Pshada* — the name not only of a settlement, but also of a river and its valley. The seventy-plus Pshada dolmens are considered to be the prime examples of megalith architecture in the whole Caucasus.

the dolmen, at least over the past century, have thought little about its significance — about the person buried here, his wisdom, his desire and aspiration to sacrifice his life for the living. This is all eloquently attested in a number of pre-revolutionary as well as more recent monographs I have seen.

Scientists, researchers and archaeologists have been more interested in the dimensions of the dolmen itself, amazed and eager to determine how the multi-tonne slabs were prepared and put in place.

And now... I looked at the women standing by the dolmen with the flowers they had brought to lay at the portal, and thought to myself: How many centuries or even millennia have passed since you last received flowers, O illustrious ancestor?! What does your soul feel now? What is happening this very moment in the astral world? Have you, our distant and yet so close forebears, taken these flowers as the first sign that your efforts were not in vain? And among people today, your descendants, there is an aspiration toward living one's life with greater conscious awareness. These are but the first flowers. No doubt there will be more and more. But the first ones are the most desirable, and you will be helping those who are now living attain the wisdom of the Universe and the conscious awareness of being. You are our distant forebears.

Participants in this visit to the dolmen included the sanitary inspector of the Gelendzhik health service E.I. Pokrovsky. He had been invited by Valentina Larionova, in her capacity as local tour guide and museum curator, to accompany them and measure the dolmen's radioactivity.

Ms Larionova told me that once on an excursion she had led to this dolmen, a tourist had brought along a Geiger counter, which had showed a significant level of radiation. This individual later took her aside (so as not to alarm the other tourists), showed her the counter and told her about the presence of radioactivity at the dolmen.

This time the health service inspector had brought along a fairly accurate radiation meter in its own special case. He began measuring radiation levels even before we got close to the dolmen, and continued his readings right up to the dolmen itself and even inside.

While Ms Larionova was giving her talk to the group of women, I was seized by the fear that now this medical inspector would announce the results of his measurements for all to hear, and as this would not just be a tourist's observation, but an official conclusion, people might stop coming to visit the dolmen once they learnt of the elevated radiation levels.

Anastasia had told me that this radiation-like energy could come and go. It was controllable and could have a beneficial effect on Man. But how would we, people of the modern world, look upon the opinions of this (let's admit) not very typical woman, in contrast with the affirmations of modern science and facts established by modern scientific equipment — especially concerning radiation, which Man is so fearful of today?

Oh God, I thought, poor Anastasia! She wanted so much, after all, for people to take a different attitude, a more thoughtful attitude toward these ancient, extraordinary burial places of our ancestors. And now there would be an official pronouncement. Even in the best case, it would mean no more visitors to the dolmens. In the worst case they might be destroyed altogether. People wouldn't even use them any longer for construction as they had done before. But if this Mind of the Universe really exists, if Anastasia can use it so freely, then they'd better come up with something, at least.

Pokrovsky approached the group of employees standing by the dolmen and announced the readings on the meter. They were most extraordinary. I felt overwhelmed — first with amazement, and then with joy. According to the readings, the closer one got to the dolmen, the more the Earth's background radiation... decreased!

This was all the more remarkable since, on its way to the dolmen, our group had passed through areas of elevated radioactivity. One would have expected the people standing at the dolmen — their clothing, shoes, etc. — to have retained traces of this radiation. But, in spite of this, the measuring device still showed decreased levels. It was as though an invisible someone had said: "Do not be afraid of us, people. We are your distant forebears. We wish you well. Take our knowledge, children!"

And all at once I realised — Anastasia! This phenomenon must be attributable directly to her. Yes, definitely to her. Even though she was thousands of kilometres away, she had drawn an invisible line across the millennia, linking those living today with an ancient civilisation, thereby causing a surge in people's consciousness of an aspiration toward good. Even if it were just among a small group of people, it was still a beginning. And it was something absolutely real, since here in front of me was a real dolmen, and here were real and tangible women, and real flowers that they had brought.

According to scientific literature, dolmens are to be found near Tuapse, Sochi and Novorossiysk, as well as in England, Turkey, North Africa and India. This points to the existence of an ancient civilisation with a single culture, whose members could communicate over vast distances. As Anastasia's information reaches more and more people, their attitude toward whatever other dolmens have been preserved will no doubt change.

This is evidenced by the reaction of the people of Gelendzhik. Indeed, the world's first excursion to a dolmen following Anastasia's amazing revelations about them took place at Gelendzhik, led by Valentina Larionova, "the luckiest and happiest woman alive", as she describes herself. And here was a woman with thirty years' experience as a tour guide, and a member of the Gelendzhik city council to boot.

But that's not all. Under Ms Larionova's guidance, a group of local historians began comparing already known facts; they spoke with long-term residents of the area and read biographies of saints, all of which enabled them to confirm the existence in the Gelendzhik environs of the sacred sites Anastasia had spoken of. These were unique sacred sites of Russia, most of which were not even mentioned in a single tourist brochure. They included the Lebanese cedar, St Nina's mountain, a monastery and the Sacred Hand Springs.[9] People who are healed there tie a cloth ribbon around a tree.

In the Gelendzhik area a church is now being restored. A branch of the Trinity-Sergiev Monastery is under construction. I observed all this and thought to myself: Look at all these sacred sites in just one small corner of Russia! Springs of healing waters. And here Russians are traipsing off to the ends of the earth to worship other people's gods. How many still forgotten sacred sites are waiting to be discovered in other parts of Russia? And who will discover them?

I've done what I can. It's a pittance, of course, but at last it has given me some hope that Anastasia will show me our son. So, armed with rompers, toys and baby food, I set off for the Siberian taiga to once again see Anastasia and meet my son.

To be continued...

---

[9] *Sacred Hand Springs* — the reference here is to five springs which merge at one point to form the shape of a hand.

In Anastasia's Ray
Editor's Afterword

Taking advantage of the frosty weather which had put a nearby lake under a thick shield of ice, I spent a Sunday afternoon skating with my daughter. The sky was overcast and a chilly north wind was blowing, but layers of winter clothing and energetic movement kept us warm. The same day, 26 December 2004, a local newspaper reported temperatures below 10°F (-12°C) and featured an article on ice fishing.

Five days later, on New Year's Eve, we were having tea on the porch of our house, basking in the Sun's hot rays and watching our daughter in her summer dress smelling yellow dandelions and feeding honey to a bee that had joined our meal. After breakfast we went for a walk by the lake, only to discover no traces of ice whatsoever. The Sun's heat was so intense that the temperature in the shade climbed to 65°F (18°C) and a new and historic record high was set. The newspaper printed photographs of residents of Columbia, Missouri, wearing shorts and T-shirts, enjoying the outdoors on 31 December 2004, and commented on the "unseasonably warm weather".

And then I remembered the words Anastasia had addressed to Vladimir Megré nine years earlier:[1]

I am making it happen.... Can you not feel the gentle touch of the breeze, feel its caressing embrace? And the warm touch of the Sun's glistening rays on your face? Can you

---

[1]Book 2, Chapter 25: "The Space of Love" (my italics).

not hear the birds singing so cheerfully and the leaves rustling on the tree you are sitting under?... *Love dissolved in Space for one can touch the hearts of many.*

I could not hear any rustling of leaves since it was the middle of winter, but the warm breeze, the bird songs and the Sun's generous warmth were very real indeed. Anyone who witnessed this unique outpouring of sunshine in the middle of the Midwest winter could not help but sense something unusual in the air, but I felt I knew something special about the *cause* of this sudden weather change. It was on this day, 31 December 2004, that the English translation of *Anastasia* was completed, and it seemed as if Nature were rejoicing at the birth of the book, the same way it had celebrated the birth of Anastasia's son with a warm sunny day, pushing away the icy grip of the Siberian winter in 1996.

A few days later, when the *Anastasia* text was laid out and sent to the printer, the cold returned and newspapers were replete with stories of ice storms and snowfalls, but the feeling of a great accomplishment lingered, to take embodiment first in the printed book, then in the e-mails and telephone calls of its initial readers. Here is one e-mail I received:

A friend gave me the book *Anastasia.* I read it today outdoors while the sun shone warmly and the birds sang sweetly. My heart knows such an essence as her spirit and I am still basking in the glow of the presence....
After reading that Anastasia suffered a loss in strength after helping someone, I decided to send her distant *reiki.*[2] I

---

[2]*reiki* — a technique of holistic healing combining elements of spiritual healing, meditation, balancing of energies, homœopathy and other approaches. The healing process involves transfer of energy (*reiki*) from the practitioner to the patient. While *reiki* practitioners usually use hands to channel the energy, it can also be accomplished at a distance by mental concentration.

know from experimenting with my kids that it has a healing effect. Immediately after sending the distant *reiki* I 'heard' her say 'thank you'. Today I sent her distant *reiki* again. Soon after I was finished, I began smelling the sweetest scent of a flower, and the scent went into all my sinuses. My sinuses feel different now. I feel such an inexpressible feeling of love and joy. It is like being in love, but in a totally different way. If you were here right now I would hug you and let you feel it. Thank you for this sweet and precious gift.

Even as this and other heart-warming messages showed me that the book is producing the same response among English-speaking readers as in other parts of the world, I was still wary of the welcome the translated edition of *Anastasia* would receive in professional and academic circles. But the first impressions shared with me by its early readers — students of psychology, Russian literature, forestry, ecology, sociology and philosophy — are most encouraging. One scholar, after reading just the first chapter, asked me if she could have a pendant of cedar wood...

Dr Richard Bolstad, a psychologist from New Zealand and author of *RESOLVE: a new NLP model of therapy*,[3] was quick to recognise the value of the book for his professional field and described the Ringing Cedars Series as "ecological common sense and profound wisdom delivered with love, a unique Russian gift towards the needed healing of the whole planet and the creation of space for love in our lives".

Steven Foster, the 'Echinacea guru', one of the leading experts on medicinal plants in North America, author of *A field guide to medicinal plants and herbs*[4] and other books, after

---

[3]Williston (Vermont), USA & Carmarthen, Wales: Crown House, 2002.

[4]Several volumes in the Peterson Field Guide Series, published by Houghton Mifflin, New York.

sharing many of his personal experiences corroborating Anastasia's sayings about the spiritual link between Man and Nature, had this comment about the Series:

> The Ringing Cedars Series will impact a new generation of readers, like the works of Carlos Castaneda did for a previous generation — only this time through awakening the latent spiritual connection each of us has with nature. This is not about a walk in the woods, rather these books catapult us to an entirely new way of being on planet Earth.

I also discovered from informal talks with my colleagues that many foresters have psychic experiences in the forest, but keep silent for fear of being ridiculed by their peers. One colleague who manages thousands of acres of forest in the Ozarks confessed to me in a private conversation that when marking trees to be felled he communicated with the Intelligence governing the trees and had a deep reverence for the Life manifest in them.[5]

I am all the more happy to hear these accounts in view of the fact that they are a sincere expression of readers' actual feelings, rather than a formulation developed by a well-paid marketing specialist and put into the mouths of celebrities, as often happens in current practice in the publishing industry. These and all other reviews of the Ringing Cedars Series I have received are genuine, they come straight from the heart.

One of the faculty members at the University of Missouri surprised me by saying he already knew about *Anastasia* and the impact these books were producing around the world.

---

[5] He therefore removes only the *least* healthy and vital trees, leaving the best ones to grow — the opposite of the destructive forestry practices prevalent over the last century.

It turned out he had learnt about the Ringing Cedars Series from his aunt who lived in Germany and had read the best-selling German translation. He said she had been so greatly impressed by the books that she would call him from Germany and read entire chapters, in German, over the telephone. This story made me wonder as to how many aunts call their nephews on the other side of the globe to read a chapter from a book they particularly liked. Not very many, I would imagine. Which means a book that does elicit such a response must certainly possess a power to set hearts aflame, regardless of the language in which it is read.

I became even more confident about the Ringing Cedars' power to transcend national boundaries after I received the following message from Europe from Nara Petrovic, editor of the Slovenian translation of the Series. This is what he wrote:

Without any advertisement the book became a best-seller mainly by readers spreading the news from mouth to mouth. In many libraries the waiting lists were soon getting longer and longer and in bookstores the sales were very good....

Thousands of readers in Slovenia and Croatia are more than enthusiastic about the books. Whoever has read the books and has a vegetable garden was compelled — even out of sheer curiosity — to try out the ideas explained in the first book. And when I spoke to people they confirmed that everything works. One man even called us and told us that he had made a beehive according to Anastasia's detailed instructions and was amazed at how well it worked.

One of the publisher's relatives spent a lot of time in his garden even before he read the books. He loved to work in the garden and thus had cultivated very healthy and tasty crops. But after he implemented Anastasia's instructions the tomatoes and some other vegetables yielded so well that all of his relatives and friends were surprised by the tastiest vegetables they'd ever eaten.

One lady who lives near my city planted pumpkins for the first time in her garden according to Anastasia's instructions. That year there was a great drought. All her neighbours' gardens were dry, with very little vegetables, while the pumpkins in *her* garden were huge, although she took almost no care of them.

I also have accounts of people in North America who — after either reading the Russian version or learning about Anastasia's ideas from their Russian friends — have followed her advice on gardening to obtain remarkable results. This is very encouraging. In the light of how all the 'incredible' revelations of the Series have been playing out in real life, there is no escaping the fact that

Your dream, Anastasia, is entering upon our world, and it really seems as though our world is beginning to change. There are certain people who feel and understand you — they show evidence of new strength coming from somewhere, and that is changing the world. The world is becoming just a little better.[6]

In this English-speakers are no different from other readers that embraced Anastasia's ideas earlier: "The book you have written will circulate all over the world and... it will give you and others a power greater than mere physical or material strength."[7] The only difference is that in Russia and other

[6]Book 2, Chapter 25: "The Space of Love".
[7]Book 2, Chapter 26: "Anastasia's grandfather".

countries the dream has been unfolding for a number of years now, while America, along with the rest of the English-speaking world, is at the very beginning of this radiant path which it may now choose to follow. Wes Jackson, a well-known proponent of ecological approaches to agriculture in the United States and director of the Land Institute, has passionately argued in his writings that there is no other possible way of development for this country but a return to the land. What if he is right and there is indeed no other way? Then it is probably not by chance that two of the central chapters in Vladimir Megré's eighth book, *The new civilisation,* convey Anastasia's vision of *America's* future. A beautiful one.

Even as my family are now packing up, getting ready to move from Columbia to a small farm lost amidst the beautiful Ozark mountains — with an aspiration, apart from continuing work on the Ringing Cedars Series, to *live* their ideas in real life — I have an ever-growing feeling of awe at the clear realisation that what Anastasia dreamt about is already coming to pass in America as well. *It is coming to pass.*

Within the two months since *Anastasia* was published in English there have already been two artistic performances of dance and song inspired by her. The dancer — a young breast-feeding mother and a future midwife — told me how her heart had instantly felt and accepted Anastasia's essence as her own, and how she now feels her presence and support on the path she is following. She told me she felt herself simply overflowing with the energy of Love and wanted to share it with everybody. Then, as she described her captivating dance and song as 'butterfly women', I stared at her in awe, experiencing a strange sensation in my heart and head.[8] The remarkable thing is that I have a large painting by Alexander Razboinikov (who designed the cover art for the Series) hanging on the wall in my home. This painting — called *The butterfly dance* — depicts Anastasia dancing in a whirlwind of butterflies and is inspired by Book 3, *The Space of Love*, which has not been translated as yet!

But *The Space of Love* is being translated and is scheduled to see the light on 23 July 2005, a day on which 'Dachnik Day' and an 'All-Earth holiday' will be celebrated in America for the first time, true to Anastasia's promise: "This holiday will indeed begin in Russia. But then it will become the most fantastic holiday for the world as a whole".[9]

And then, "a wave of warmth will cheer the heart, and over the world will be unfurled a new dawn".[10] I can already see the twilight of this dawn. And I know that I am not the only one who does.

Columbia, Missouri, U.S.A.
Earth Day (22 April 2005)   Leonid Sharashkin

---

[8]At that moment I could very well relate to Vladimir Megré's feelings — described in the first chapter of this volume — as he witnessed the unfolding of Anastasia's dream and watched readers expressing in art the images and scenes from his taiga experience which had not yet been described in the books.

[9]Book 2, Chapter 9: "Dachnik Day and an All-Earth holiday!".

[10]Book 2, Chapter 32: "Title!".

ABOUT THE RINGING CEDARS SERIES

Anastasia, the first book of the Ringing Cedars Series, tells the story of entrepreneur Vladimir Megré's trade trip to the Siberian taiga in 1995, where he witnessed incredible spiritual phenomena connected with sacred 'ringing cedar' trees. He spent three days with a woman named Anastasia who shared with him her unique outlook on subjects as diverse as gardening, child-rearing, healing, Nature, sexuality, religion and more. This wilderness experience transformed Vladimir so deeply that he abandoned his commercial plans and, penniless, went to Moscow to fulfil Anastasia's request and write a book about the spiritual insights she so generously shared with him. True to her promise this life-changing book, once written, has become an international bestseller and has touched hearts of millions of people world-wide.

The Ringing Cedars of Russia, the second book of the Series, in addition to providing a fascinating behind-the-scenes look at the story of how *Anastasia* came to be published, offers a deeper exploration of the universal concepts so dramatically revealed in Book 1. It takes the reader on an adventure through the vast expanses of space, time and spirit — from the Paradise-like glade in the Siberian taiga to the rough urban depths of Russia's capital city, from the ancient mysteries of our forebears to a vision of humanity's radiant future.

The Space of Love, the third book of the Series, describes author's second visit to Anastasia. Rich with new revelations on natural child-rearing and alternative education, on the spiritual significance of breast-feeding and the meaning of ancient megaliths, it shows how each person's thoughts can influence the destiny of the entire Earth and describes practical ways of putting Anastasia's vision of happiness into practice. Megré shares his new outlook on education and children's real creative potential after a visit to a school where pupils build their own campus and cover the ten-year Russian school programme in just two years. Complete with an account of an armed intrusion into Anastasia's habitat, the book highlights the limitless power of Love and non-violence.

Co-creation, the fourth book and centrepiece of the Series, paints a dramatic living image of the creation of the Universe and humanity's place in this creation, making this primordial mystery relevant to our everyday living today. Deeply metaphysical yet at the same time down-to-Earth practical, this poetic heart-felt volume helps us uncover answers to the most significant questions about the essence and meaning of the Universe and the nature and purpose of our existence. It also shows how and why the knowledge of these answers, innate in every human being, has become obscured and forgotten, and points the way toward reclaiming this wisdom and — in partnership with Nature — manifesting the energy of Love through our lives.

Who are we? — Book Five of the Series — describes the author's search for real-life 'proofs' of Anastasia's vision presented in the previous volumes. Finding these proofs and taking stock of ongoing global environmental destruction, Vladimir Megré describes further practical steps for putting Anastasia's vision into practice. Full of beautiful realistic images of a new way of living in co-operation with the Earth and each other, this book also highlights the role of children in making us aware of the precariousness of the present situation and in leading the global transition toward a happy, violence-free society.

The book of kin, the sixth book of the Series, describes another visit by the author to Anastasia's glade in the Siberian taiga and his conversations with his growing son, which cause him to take a new look at education, science, history, family and Nature. Through parables and revelatory dialogues and stories Anastasia then leads Vladimir Megré and the reader on a shocking re-discovery of the pages of humanity's history that have been distorted or kept secret for thousands of years. This knowledge sheds light on the causes of war, oppression and violence in the modern world and guides us in preserving the wisdom of our ancestors and passing it over to future generations.

The energy of life, Book Seven of the Series, re-asserts the power of human thought and the influence of our thinking on our lives and the destiny of the entire planet and the Universe. Is also brings forth a practical understanding of ways to consciously control and build up the power of our creative thought. The book sheds still further light on the forgotten pages of humanity's history, on religion, on the roots of inter-racial and inter-religious conflict, on ideal nutrition, and shows how a new way of thinking and a lifestyle in true harmony with Nature can lead to happiness and solve the personal and societal problems of crime, corruption, misery, conflict, war and violence.

The new civilisation, the eighth book of the Series, is not yet complete. The first part of the book, already published as a separate volume, describes yet another visit by Vladimir Megré to Anastasia and their son, and offers new insights into practical co-operation with Nature, showing in ever greater detail how Anastasia's lifestyle applies to our lives. Describing how the visions presented in previous volumes have already taken beautiful form in real life and produced massive changes in Russia and beyond, the author discerns the birth of a new civilisation. The book also paints a vivid image of America's radiant future, in which the conflict between the powerful and the helpless, the rich and the poor, the city and the country, can be transcended and thereby lead to transformations in both the individual and society.

Rites of Love — Book 8, Part 2 (published as a separate volume) — contrasts today's mainstream attitudes to sex, family, childbirth and education with our forebears' lifestyle, which reflected their deep spiritual understanding of the significance of conception, pregnancy, homebirth and upbringing of the young in an atmosphere of love. In powerful poetic prose Megré describes their ancient way of life, grounded in love and non-violence, and shows the practicability of this same approach today. Through the life-story of one family, he portrays the radiant world of the ancient Russian Vedic civilisation, the drama of its destruction and its re-birth millennia later — in our present time.

To be continued...

THE AUTHOR, Vladimir Megré, born in 1950, was a well-known entrepreneur from a Siberian city of Novosibirsk. According to his account, in 1995 — after hearing a fascinating story about the power of 'ringing cedars' from a Siberian elder — he organised a trade expedition into the Siberian taiga to rediscover the lost technique of pressing virgin cedar nut oil containing high curative powers, as well as to find the ringing cedar tree. However, his encounter on this trip with a Siberian woman named Anastasia transformed him so deeply that he abandoned his business and went to Moscow to write a book about the spiritual insights she had shared with him. Vladimir Megré now lives near the city of Vladimir, Russia, 190 km (120 miles) east of Moscow. If you wish to contact the author, you may send a message to his personal e-mail **megre@online.sinor.ru**

THE TRANSLATOR, John Woodsworth, born in Vancouver (British Columbia), has over forty years of experience in Russian-English translation, from classical poetry to modern short stories. Since 1982 he has been associated with the University of Ottawa in Canada as a Russian-language teacher, translator and editor, most recently as a Research Associate and Administrative Assistant with the University's Slavic Research Group. A published Russian-language poet himself, he and his wife — Susan K. Woodsworth — are directors of the Sasquatch Literary Arts Performance Series in Ottawa. A Certified Russian-English Translator, John Woodsworth is in the process of translating the remaining volumes in Vladimir Megré's Ringing Cedars Series.

THE EDITOR, Leonid Sharashkin, is writing his doctoral dissertation on the spiritual, cultural and economic significance of the Russian *dacha* gardening movement, at the University of Missouri at Columbia. After receiving a Master's degree in Natural Resources Management from Indiana University at Bloomington, he worked for two years as Programme Manager at the World Wide Fund for Nature (WWF Russia) in Moscow, where he also served as editor of Russia's largest environmental magazine, *The Panda Times*. Together with his wife, Irina Sharashkina, he has translated into Russian *Small is beautiful* and *A guide for the perplexed* by E.F. Schumacher, *The secret life of plants* by Peter Tompkins and Christopher Bird, *The continuum concept* by Jean Liedloff and *Birth without violence* by Frederick Leboyer.

ORDERING INFORMATION

USA:

- *on-line* — www.RingingCedars.com
- *tel. / fax (toll-free)* — 1-888-DOLMENS (1-888-365-6367)
- *tel. / fax (from outside US & Canada)* — 1-646-429-1986
- *e-mail* — sales@RingingCedars.com
- *mail (US)* — send US$14.95 per copy plus $3.95 shipping and handling for the first copy and $0.99 s&h for each additional copy in your order to:

  Ringing Cedars Press
  120 Hana Hwy #9-230,
  Paia, HI 96779, USA

Make a check or money order payable to "Ringing Cedars Press". Please indicate clearly the quantity and title of the book(s) you are ordering and be sure to include your US postal address with your payment. Allow 2-4 weeks for delivery. Prices are subject to change without notice.

UNITED KINGDOM:

- *order on-line* — www.RingingCedars.co.uk
- *by phone (toll-free)* — 0800-011-2081
- *e-mail* — books@RingingCedars.co.uk

AUSTRALIA:

- *order on-line* — www.RingingCedars.com.au
- *by phone (toll-free)* — 1800-248-768
- *e-mail* — books@RingingCedars.com.au

NEW ZEALAND:

- *order on-line* — www.RingingCedars.co.nz
- *by phone* — 64-9232-9792
- *e-mail* — sales@RingingCedars.co.nz

SOUTH AFRICA:

- *order on-line* — www.RingingCedars.co.za
- *e-mail* — books@RingingCedars.co.za

ANASTASIA'S CALL
by Eric Dane Mansfield

My dear,
why are you so sullen and sad?
For that is not your place.
Come and *listen* to the call,
to *see* your *original* face.

Dear, all your struggle, and your pain
is *because* you have forgotten your name,
and your own divinity.
Yes, you *are* the living trinity,
I-Is-We,
the One *as* three.
This is *where* your sovereignty *lives*,
and peace is what dominion *gives*.

There is a voice,
calling from the very depths of Nature.
There is a guide,
that will lead us away from *disaster*.
A voice that echoes true,
for she speaks only of *Reality*.
And her mind is not clouded
by the obscured *views* of duality,
and its *images* of illusion.
She *is* living the *solution*,
and *showing* as she calls
to each from within the forested walls
of her love inspired *domain*.

Is it Christ, Buddha, Krishna?
Yes, Anastasia is her *name*.

She is the *God-Mother* of joy,
and peace is her constant companion.
She awaits your response.
She supports your *return*,
to the *ways* of Veda,
to the *Way* of Love.
For Anastasia has *risen above*
the lies and games of self delusion.
Hers is the way of *total inclusion*,
and she does not falter.

She is not *special*, or distinct.
She simply *knows how* to think
purely, and she *lives as* Man.
Co-creation, *as-is,*
that is her simple *plan*.

Consecration and devotion
to the *standard* of Truth,
if you *answer* to her call
your life will *be the proof.*
That all she says,
and all she *is*
you are able to *be*.

See, Anastasia is our Self
living *completely free*.

April 2007

ANASTASIA'S WORTH IS OURS
by Eric Dane Mansfield

When I came to the forest
to discover my Self,
and repair the *broken* Earth.
I first glimpsed Her
atop a golden tree.
Yet, I *knew not* of her worth.

For to *value* what is *unknown*
is to wander away from ego's *home*,
and I was not yet *ready*.
Yet, my inner pace remained steady.

And so many years later on
I began to *hear* her silent song
of Love for all,
as All *is* Love.

She sits atop the trees *above*
because she has transcended lies.
And the light she offers up so freely
gives illumination to our skies.

For she *is* Advaita alive, here come.
She is a *living* Veda, holy song *already* sung,
and she calls to those who hear,
"Come and join me, have no fear".
"For we will *remain* in the forests of joy,
to plant gardens, raise children, as I, my boy".

For knowing *how* to live aright
shall *end* this lingering, hopeless night

Where darkness *claims* powers of destruction.
Yet, where Light *already created*,
no construction shall stand.
For from *beyond* the temporal realm
comes this illuminated Man.
Anastasia, captain at the helm,
her course *true* to the divine plan
of inclusion, co-operation, contemplation.
See there's no *room* for condemnation
of Truth *set* in stone.

Living *as* All,
come with her and trust
that you shall not fall.
For Anastasia is *with* us.
So stop, and listen do not fuss,
or fight about life.
Accept Anastasia
as your wife.
For she *is* your Self,
for she *is* your Self.

April 2007

Editor's note: both poems by Eric Dane Mansfield are © 2007 by Eric Dane
Mansfield and are used by kind permission of the author.

The publishing team of Ringing Cedars Press sincerely thanks all readers who shared their impressions, as well as poetry, songs and artwork
inspired by Anastasia. The Series' editor may be reached by e-mail at
press@ringingcedars.com